A YEAR IN EIRE

Inspirations from the Emerald Isle

J. Craig Bell

A Year in Eire
Inspirations from the Emerald Isle
by J. Craig Bell

Printed in the United States of America

ISBN 9781628715750

www.xulonpress.com

Acknowledgments:

I wish to cite and acknowledge the works and sites from which I gathered material and poems and photos:

W. B. Yeats – Selected Poems – Penguin, London, 1991

The Poems by W. B. Yeats – Phoenix, London, 1996

Seamus Heaney – Open Ground – Faber and Faber, London, 1998

The Faber Book of Contemporary Irish Poetry – Faber and Faber, London, 1986

Thomas Cook Travellers – Ireland – Automobile Association, London, 1994

Eyewitness Travel Guides – Ireland – Dorling Kindersley, London, 1995

Bord Failte

Tourism Ireland

I also wish to acknowledge the numerous tourist bureaus which suffered my queries for brochures and information, and the local Irish people who provided the up close and personal experiences for me to include in this book.

Achill Island - Kildownet famine cemetery

Armagh Cathedral - County Armagh

Bantry House and Bay - Cork

Benbulben - Sligo- Yeats' inspiration

Bunratty Castle Banquet

Burial cairn - Connemara

Carrick a rede rope bridge - Antrim - fishers' bridge

Cashel cemetery - Tipperary

Celtic cross - Connemara

Church at Tara - site of crowned kings of Ireland

Irish Authors quoted
in this book:

All the authors quoted are representative of Ireland's penchant for inspiration. They have inspired me and others. As you read their works, keep in mind that their goal was to inspire a love for Ireland and its peoples. Each has brought his "Irishness", his own perspective, to the page. My interpretation may or may not be what he intended, but I want to pass on the inspirations I received from their works. Below, I append a brief 'bio' of each author so that you can appreciate his background.

Seamus Heaney: was born in County Derry in 1939, raised near the town of Bellaghy where today you can see a museum dedicated to him. He established himself as a great in 20th century poetry. He won the Nobel Prize for literature in 1995. He resided in Dublin and Wicklow from 1972. In August, 2013, he passed away after a fall and a 6 year battle with a stroke.

William Butler Yeats: lived from 1865 to 1939 and was born and educated in Dublin. He moved to England at 22, but returned to Ireland in 1896. His poetry is based on Irish folklore and nationalism. He died in France but asked that his remains be buried in Sligo where some of his poetry is set. He won the Nobel Prize for Literature in 1923.

Louis MacNeice: was born in Belfast, Northern Ireland in 1906; his father was the Bishop of County Down. He was educated in England and went on to become a Classics professor and lecturer in the USA, at Cornell University. Between 1941 and 1949, he produced radio plays for the BBC. He died in 1963.

Patrick Kavanagh: was born in 1904 in Co. Monaghan to a shoemaker. Patrick worked on the farm before moving to Dublin in 1939 where he was treated as a country bumpkin. His lyrical poetry, however, found its place in literature. He transformed the ordinary into the significant. He was diagnosed with lung cancer in 1955 and died of bronchitis in 1967.

Oscar Wilde: was the son of an eminent Dublin surgeon. He was schooled at Trinity College Dublin. Oscar was known for his eccentric dress and habits. He married and produced children's books, but soon took another tack when he published The Picture of Dorian Gray in 1891. Wilde's fate took a bad turn when he was accused of and jailed for homosexual behaviour in 1895. After his incarceration, he moved to Paris where he lived out a bitter life under a pseudonym.

John Montague: was born in Brooklyn, NY, of Irish stock. He returned to Garvaghey, County Tyrone at 4 years old. In his later education, he learned of the inspiration of Irish poetry and of the melancholy of Ulster and of Dublin. He returned to the USA, but has since moved back to Ireland to live in Cork. He has written extensively, one of which is The Book of Irish Verse.

Thomas Kinsella's: family was employed by the Guinness organization. He was educated by the Christian Brothers at the O'Connell schools. Kinsella then went on to become a civil servant; in the USA he lectured at Temple University. He retuned to Ireland in 1976 and lives in Wicklow. Kinsella brought modernism to Irish poetry.

Paul Durcan: was born in Dublin in 1944. He studied archaeology and mediaeval history, but soon became an acclaimed poet, winning the Patrick Kavanagh Award. Durcan is known as a critic of Ireland and of its emergence today. He is an intensely lyrical poet.

****

It is not intended that you, the reader, follow any pattern in this book nor that you read consecutively each entry throughout the year. As you feel inclined, find a topic which interests you and be inspired. Or, if you wish, be more organized and choose a passage from those entered for any given month. The goal is to foster inspiration!! Enjoy!

Yes, radiant lyre, speak to me; become a voice.
(Sappho, Greek poetess)

Classiebawn - Sligo - Mountbatten home

Cliffs of Moher - Clare

Cliffs of Moher

Cliffs of Moher

Croagh Patrick - famine memorial

Dingle Peninsula - Kerry - coastal path

Downpatrick Head-Ballycastle- Mayo

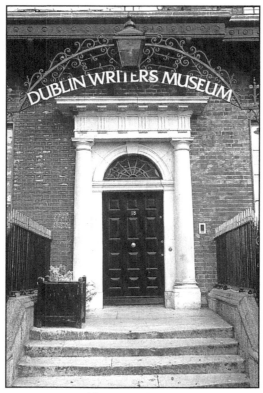

Dublin Writers' Museum

Dunbrody famine ship reproduction - New Ross-Wexford

Famine emigrants' flame - Cork

January

Fisherman's wife beckoning to sea- Rosses
Point - Sligo

Florence Court - Fermanagh

Autumn Journal (Louis MacNeice)

Why do we like being Irish? Partly because
It gives us a hold on the sentimental English
As members of a world that never was,
Baptized with fairy water;
And partly because Ireland is small enough
To be still thought of with a family feeling,
And because the waves are rough
That split her from a more commercial culture;
And because one feels that here at least one can
Do local work which is not at the world's mercy
And that on this tiny stage with luck a man
Might see the end of one particular action.
It is self-deception of course;
There is no immunity in this island either

The last two lines of this excerpt cause the speaker and reader to plummet back to reality. Without those express doubts, I believe that he has something for all of us. I believe that the sentiments of the true Irish spirit belong in every soul. That, I acknowledge, is improbable since the Irish are sublime and unique – inspirational. Nonetheless, try today to harvest some of the riches of the Irish mind – a "family feeling", an indomitable superiority over adversity, a singular and immediate goal, a sense of non-materialism and a citizenship beyond this world. That is the Irish inspiration.

Did you know that there are two Yeats: W.B and J.B.? Most of us have heard of William Butler, Ireland's famous Nobel poet, but fewer have heard of Jack, a celebrated artist. His works were on display in the Sligo Museum and Art Gallery on Stephen Street. I stood before "Leaving the Far Point" and read of Jack Yeats' love of Sligo County. Evidently, even William Butler complained about how Jack was a favourite with his grandparents. When W.B. went to London, Jack stayed behind in Sligo for his schooling. There, his indulgent grandparents gave him free rein to tramp the city and countryside absorbing the enchantment of people, mountains, rivers, woods, sea, and skies. In fact, Jack's formal education was insignificant to him. He wrote, "Sligo was my school and the sky above it." He learned well, for "Leaving the Far Point" catches the ambiance of sky, sea, hill and relatives. It is a scene depicting Jack himself, his wife, Coltie, and his uncle. In the early 1900s Jack and Coltie had returned to Sligo and the three took a walk at Rosses Point. Jack matched the sentimentality of landscape with that of relationships in the painting. It was so dear to him that he presented it to his wife on her birthday in 1947 and then again to Sligo in 1954 on Coltie's death. Both his family and his environment had benefited from his inspiration.

As I strolled through the rest of the gallery with Jack B. Yeats' permanent collection, I knew that I had to leave a far point to reach a near point and then again return. Our natural lives consist of two compass points: our family and our environment. We leave the one and go to the other, to return again. Back and forth and thus receive our bearings. It is the same spiritually. Two points: our Father God and Brother Jesus and our "new man" environment. Take your spiritual bearings today.

The Hosting of the Sidhe

The host is riding from Knocknarea
And over the grave of Clooth-na-Bare;
Caoilte tossing his burning hair,
And Niamh calling *Away, come away:*
Empty your heart of its mortal dream.
The winds awaken, the leaves whirl round,
Our cheeks are pale, our hair is unbound,
Our breasts are heaving, our eyes are agleam,
Our arms are waving, our lips are apart;
And if any gaze on our rushing band,
We come between him and the deed of his hand,
We come between him and the hope of his heart.
The host is rushing 'twixt night and day,
And where is there hope or deed as fair?
Caoilte tossing his burning hair,
And Niamh calling away, come away.

(W.B. Yeats)

The mystical powers of the *sidhe* (banshee), as portrayed in this poem, leave the blood cold – rushing gales surrounding these she-devils who deny dreams and deeds as they swirl in the twilight over the grave of Clooth-na-Bare, a faery grown weary of her life and who drowned herself in Lough Ia in Sligo. I shudder as I imagine the banshees described here, and turn away quickly. Yet, there is mythical beauty in this poem, too. Caolite was a legendary Irish warrior, nephew of Finn McCool, who lived for 300 years and Niamh was a golden haired maiden who seduced Oisin to go with her on a white horse to the land of eternal youth.

What shall it be, Yeats, the fearsome or Yeats, the romantic? Yeats, you include both in your poem. As for me, I want reverential beauty and inspiration today, not abject fear. "I believe in one God–" (the beginning of many credos). I have a credo, and darksome creatures created in occultic minds of Celtic paganism cannot unsteady me.

I picked a shamrock I had found at Glen Wood. Illegal perhaps, but I was hungry to experience and handle Ireland's motif of positive thinking. Close by the copse of trees (so I read in the guidebook) is Hunger Rock where hundreds sat down to rest, then to die during the 1840s Famine–another less known negative motif of Ireland. The Irish always are upbeat. I wanted to connect the image of the shamrock with the ill-fate of the Famine. It goes this way: In Irish folklore, if you throw a stone at this rock, you will never again be hungry. Finding Glen Wood was not a challenge for me, nor was it hard to notice the spreads of shamrock. They proliferated everywhere; I was motivated. Usually, I am a pretty pessimistic person, so the ease with which I came upon this symbol of Ireland surprised me. What would not have surprised me was to have lit upon Hunger Rock without any ado. But, I traveled back and forth along the road several times until I finally spotted the table rock overgrown with grass, moss and weeds; and here is the connection– beneath it was a fine growth of shamrock. I scaled the rock and sat on it with my imagination at full-bore. I could see and hear the poor emaciated souls who could go not further. They sat down before my eyes to die. They had no strength, either to throw a stone or to see in their shamrock what a grand country they had. I wept for those who had lived over 150 years ago and yet, who were the fortunate ones, to die in their homeland, free of English dominance.

We can choose today to be positive or negative, to stroll or sit, to succumb or fight. At day's end, will you be able to say that you have fought the fight and finished the course? Be hungry for that.

Sung by the people of Faery over Diarmid and Grania, in their bridal sleep under a Cromlech

We who are old, old and gay,
O so old!
Thousands of years, thousands of years,
If all were told:

Give to these children, new from the world,
Silence and love;
And the long dew-dropping hours of the night,
And the stars above:

Give to these children, new from the world,
Rest far from men.
Is anything better, anything better?
Tell us it then:

Us who are old, old and gray,
O so old!
Thousands of years, thousands of years,
If all were told.
(W. B. Yeats)

{Grania was a folklore heroine who was won in love by the old man, Finn after her first love, Dermot was killed in Sligo. This song was sung at a dolmen (a cromlech), actually a burial stone.}

What do we wish for others or for ourselves today? Silence? Love? Rest? Awe at the universe above? Seclusion? Is anything better? No! Is it possible for us who are old to experience those qualities? Yes! They are not restricted to the young, nor even to the departed. Search out a "faery" existence today, in other words, a spiritual existence. We will not deny you this joy in singing.

I asked why the stone gateposts at the entrances to farms were topped with conical caps. The answer came quickly, "Sure, now, we wouldn't be wantin' to have the little people sittin' on them, would we?" Yes, Ireland is the land of the Hounds and Leprechauns, Faeries and Banshees. And there is lots of superstition too. You wouldn't interfere with a hawthorn tree, or bad luck would come. You wouldn't disturb a mound in a field. That's where a faery lives, not a mole. You wouldn't kill a swan, under pain of persecution. It's illegal. A swan represents the legend of the four children of Lir whose wicked step-mother turned them into swans.

The most dreaded faery is the banshee (*'Bean Sidhe'* in Gaelic, the women of the hills) who haunts some families as she wails and keens when a death is approaching. Her long trailing tresses and red fiery eyes are fearsome. The general faeries are capable of anything, bringing on any mischief their little hearts see fit. As they dance the nights away, their shoes are worn out. Then, the leprechaun, the spritely little man in the green tunic, sits under a tree and repairs these shoes, but just one at a time. The leprechauns, in addition, possess a crock of gold and if you can outstare the small bearded man, you get his gold.

The oversized in legend takes the Irish mind to Cuchulainn, the Hound of Ulster who, with his javelin, fought off an army single handedly. The actual Irish wolfhound (at one time almost extinct) is an awesome sight – 150 pounds of pure hunting power with a precious metal chain around its neck

Despite the humour and intriguing attractions of Irish folklore, I'd rather look to another spirit or hope for today. I'd rather have another do battle for me than a hound. Approach today from the perspective of God, not from a superstitious fear. The peace of God passes and possesses all understanding.

The image of a fairy godmother is one of genuine grace and kindness and benevolence. Not so, the faeries of Ireland. As a matter of fact, Irish mothers used to guard their newborns from faeries by placing tongs across the cot/crib to ward off the mischievous little people who were known to replace the human child with a faery child or 'changeling'. Shakespeare surely had the Irish faery in mind when he penned "A Midsummer Night's Dream" where Puck and his band wreaked havoc on lovers. In Ireland, the farmer's wife was sure to pass on to her husband the inbred fear of faeries, but he knew well enough himself what they could do. On the farm, the faery would interfere with seed growth or make the cow dry. The farmer would mutter to himself, "Avoid the tree in the center of the field; it's a faery tree." And when summer came, the children were denied access to the fields where faeries sported on faery beds, outdoors! Disturbing a faery in its environment brought sure ill-fate.

I am glad today that God has allowed me free will. I do not need to ward off malevolent beings or appease someone out to cause me disturbance or harm. I am accountable first and foremost to God. With this inspiration in mind, I will go out to care for children.

The Errand

'On you go now! Run son, like the devil
And tell your mother to try
To find me a bubble for the spirit level
And a new knot for this tie.'

But still he was glad, I know, when I stood my ground,
Putting it up to him
With a smile that trumped his smile and his fool's errand,
Waiting for the next move in the game.
(Seamus Heaney)

Chase a rainbow, a bubble, a knot today. You too will smile on what might seem to be a "fool's errand." You will be inspired by being naïve and knowing it. But, you will be no fool. 'He is no fool who gives up what he cannot keep to gain what he cannot lose' (Jim Elliott).

Castleblayney in County Monaghan is another of those intriguing towns which has connections to Saint Patrick. He purportedly visited the village, raised an ancestral chieftain from his grave, baptized him and promptly reburied him! That's a classic Irish gem which begs for a chortle, at least a smile. It's Irish goodwill and practicality of life mixed together. But, Castleblayney is known for a much greater gem. At Hope Castle one learns of the family Hope who bought the lovely lakeside pastoral green and white mansion from the Blayney family in 1853. The Hopes fell on hard times in 1916 and sold out to return to England, all this despite the fact that Henry Philip, then Thomas Hope had owned the Hope Diamond found in India in the 1600s. At over forty five carats, this diamond was cut from the largest blue diamond in the world. The gem is worth a fortune. It had formed part of the French Crown Jewels, was stolen during the French Revolution, then bought by the first Hope owner. He divested himself of this fortune in 1867 because of its reputed status as the harbinger of bad luck. His nephew's grandson, who had the diamond in his care, auctioned it off in 1901 to pay his debts. If he had only kept it, you say!! The Hope Diamond now sits in the Smithsonian Museum and is owned by the USA. It has been ogled by thousands who have come from across the globe.

I am inspired today to hang on to family treasures and not to be forced into rash decisions.

Hugh O'Neill had been informed of the movement of English troops from Newry to Monaghan in order to re-supply the English garrison under siege in 1595. O'Neill played cat and mouse with the army, even allowing the enemy to complete the mission and lulling them into thinking they had circumvented O'Neill's attack en route home. At Clontinbret, Co. Monaghan, O'Neill set an ambush and won a resounding battle. Over two hundred years later, in 1834, John O'Neill of Clontinbret emigrated to America where he reached the rank of Colonel during the Civil War. After the war, he organized ex-Civil War vets in a force of 600 Fenians which invaded Canada at Buffalo. They occupied Fort Erie and humiliated much superior British forces at Ridgway Heights. It is evident that a fighting O'Neill spirit was in the genes. If any generation could down an English uniform, then inspiration was involved. A simple rock in a field inscribed with two crossed swords and the message "Clontinbret 1595" might have given John his inspiration to take up arms.

A simple symbol or image can be all that is needed today to inspire you to continue the great work given to you to do— a verse, a cross, a family crest, a face, a logo, a motto. Look at it and be inspired.

The Irish are famous for their folk heroes. One such legend centres on an awesome geographic monument, Benbulben, a table mountain in Sligo of gigantic proportions. Two members of Fiann(Irish warriors), one the leader, Fionn and the other, younger, Diarmit met fate. The daughter of the neighbouring high king, Grianne, was to be wedded to Fionn, but she fell in love with Diarmit and the two eloped. Fionn vowed revenge, but after some pursuit, the two warriors supposedly made peace and Grianne and Diarmit settled in Ballymote. One night, Diarmit went in search of a bothersome boar, but met with Fionn and his Fiann warriors who challenged Diarmit into attacking the boar on the top of Benbulben. Diarmit slaughtered the boar which in turn, as it died, dealt a death blow to Diarmit with its tusk. Dying, he pleaded with Fionn to pour his magical healing waters on him. Fionn fetched the water, but tantalizingly let it drip slowly through his fingers onto the rock beside Diarmit. Despite a late change in heart from Fionn, his competitor in love died. Fionn's vengeance was complete when he beheaded Diarmit and sent the head to Grianne who promptly died too. The two are buried in a cave on Benbulben. Such an incredible, gory tale requires a vivid imagination, not to mention a close following of a circuitous plot.

The torturous drive and hike to Benbulben's height are worth the reliving of Irish folklore tale.

As I stood there, I was led to contrast this with the real love triangle where Jesus and Satan vied for the love of the "Bride" on another hill. It too was a fight to the death when Christ, our suitor, won over death and sin. No hatred, vengeance, intrigue, elopement, cruelty. And, best of all, the "Bride" does not die. We live forever with our Eternal Warrior. Now, that's legendary!

Ireland boasts about 400 megalithic monuments called "court tombs". The early Irish named them "Giants' Graves", simply because their outline resembled burial sites for very large people. In actuality, they are circular or semi-circular uncovered spaces which provide access to a smaller gallery or raised area; they were not tombs at all. Historians tell us that for about 3000 years in Ireland (until 1500 BC), the superstitious or religious population used these court tombs for community, religious, assembly halls (much like our churches) where rituals aligned to the rising sun were held. If this is true, it begs the question why they were in any way connected to death. You just have to walk the side passageways of European cathedrals, or better yet descend to the crypt. These churches abound with the images of death: sarcophagi, skulls, bones and bodies of important people. Plus, outside most churches is a graveyard. Even today, many funeral services are held in churches. Hence, is it any wonder that people were cremated or buried in Neolithic times in these "churches"? So, archaeologists found human remains in court tombs. These monuments, which housed ritual worship by a living community, remained and survived. In Keadue, there are 3 such "assembly halls" in close proximity, bearing testimony to a sizeable population and interest in religion 6,000 years ago.

Cathedrals inspire me by their beauty, awe and silence. If you get the chance today, drop into a "place of worship" to silently pray and appreciate the devotion needed to build or design such a place. Don't wait to go in until it comes your burial time.

Archaeologists have uncovered most ancient remains in Ireland in Counties Mayo and Sligo. They reason as follows: the earliest settlers on the Emerald Isle arrived on these daunting looking shores after sailing up the western shores of Europe, then venturing or being blown further west. Sligo and Mayo would have been their first stop, based on winds and tides. Experts state that they came all the way from North Africa, Greece or Phoenicia! They were farmers and the Ceidhe Fields in Mayo show they used the same farming techniques as Mediterranean farmers. Then, disaster struck; the population numbers fell because of some climatic change. Scientists say that some sort of earthquake or volcanic eruption in about 500AD threw up a dust cloud to blot out the sun and bring on a wetter climate which Irish people are used to today. So, the Irish bog came into existence during this climate shift. Many Neolithic wooden roads and implements were preserved in these bogs. Presumably the wetlands took over previously inhabited and farmed land. Many left Ireland in search of a better life (so, the Great Famine was not the first exodus from Ireland).

I'm always inspired by the grit, and determination of the Irish spirit, despite the odds or circumstances. Let's include a bit of the Irish pluck in our actions today. We all fail from sin (it goes as far back as the first man and woman); we suffer and lose. However, there is a remedy and God is its source.

A Call

'Hold on,' she said, 'I'll just run out and get him.
The weather here's so good, he took the chance
To do a bit of weeding.'
So I saw him
Down on his hands and knees beside the leek rig,
Touching, inspecting, separating one
Stalk from the other, gently pulling up
Everything not tapered, frail and leafless,
Pleased to feel each little weed-root break,
But rueful also...
Then found myself listening to
The amplified grave ticking of hall clocks
Where the phone lay unattended in a calm
Of mirror glass and sunstruck pendulums...

And found myself then thinking: if it were nowadays,
This is how Death would summon Everyman.

Next thing he spoke and I nearly loved him.
(Seamus Heaney)

**Make that call today, before Death calls your dear
"Everyman". Do tell someone that you love him/her. That
person may be busy, but the call or visit is expected. The
weeding can wait until after your call. The weeds are so much
more insignificant than you and yours.**

As an island nation, Ireland has been both susceptible to and isolated from foreign invasion. Its coastline provides a plethora of bays and beaches upon which to come ashore. In contrast, a promontory fort such as Doon high on the side of Corrie Mountain would have been enough to bar inland access to the land of the green. It commands views of the whole Arigna Valley. A priest undertook excavation of this mountain fort and discovered ramparts, elevated walkways, and a cave used for defensive refuge or escape. All of these were about 400 years old. The network and massive central mound spread over much of the mountain top. The tourist can experience such history at Doon as well as hike over to an amazing 200 foot waterfall which seems to fall into a black hole. The falls inspire wonder in nature's glory, but the legend of Doon embodies the spirit of the Irish. Doon is reputed to be the headquarters of the *Tuatha de Danaan* who fought at Moytirra nearby. This race of people gave credibility to one of the fairy myths of Ireland. The faeries evidently began the practice of the "changeling" for they would snatch children from their beds and leave in their place small dark-skinned sickly ones. The *Tuatha de Danaan* is the clan which originated the stories of faeries and leprechauns.

There is just no possible way today that you need to sit or lie in a vulnerable state. Around you there is better than a promontory fort. There is someone who changed places with you when you were vulnerable and he did not do it out of malice or evil intent. Rejoice in a Saviour today who has stood in the gap and won a battle so this can be as victorious as any day in Christ.

Away out on the far western promontory of Sligo Bay is Knocklare Fort. This conical hill could date, they say, from the Iron Age (700-450 BC)! It is surrounded on three sides by the sea and protected on the east by ditches and banks. The purpose of such a fort is unsure, but it surely is virtually impregnable. On the peninsula, just southeast of the fort is an awe-inspiring cliff pounded by the Atlantic. Here is the 'Derk of Knocklare', home of the banshee. The actual howl of wind and sea are said to be Letitia Gore (Banshee Bawn), wife of one inhabitant of Lissadell House. Letitia was a free spirit who just pushed her wildness one step too far. She is supposed to have forced her coachman, at gun point, to free wheel along the cliff's edge. Alas, both catapulted over the brink to certain death on the rocks below.

What are you protected from today? Certainly not death. No unassailable fortress ensures longevity, in any era. Nor can we flirt with death or fly in the face of an overriding will. A famous hymn inspires today's title. Who is the Fortress? God is. Today, don't build walls; neither should you live on the edge. God does not want you to be a hermit nor a scallywag. Today is a day for moderation, feet up and in the Fort of God.

Ancient traditions die slowly, if at all. In pagan times in Ireland, the gods were worshipped at sacred wells or trees. Faeries and leprechauns frequented those sites too. When St. Patrick 'converted' the island, it was not overnight. Many pagan practices were worked into a Christian context. St. Attracta's well near Monasteraden in Sligo is one of these adaptations. St. Attracta was a local saint, baptized by St. Patrick even. She had 8 praying stones set on a wall above the well. A pilgrim visiting her nunnery would turn the 8 stones and so secure a blessing. In the 17th century, a crucifixion plaque was erected at the well, the Penal Cross, to welcome parishioners to come to mass. It is also said that St. Attracta blessed the water as a cure for warts and rickets. What was the difference between the pagan beliefs in the efficacy of a holy site and those Christian values enshrined by the church at the samewell? In essence, nothing. Religion is built on faith. The well at Monasteraden became a tangible symbol for someone's faith, but the force behind the faith, and in front of it is what proves the efficacy.

Decide for yourself whether miracles were effected at St. Attracta's well, in any era. However, faith in our time does inspire most to a higher plane of the miraculous. It's a faith day. Work a miracle by your belief in things unseen.

That's the Irish Tourist Board's motto and, indeed, the Irish can be the most welcoming and hospitable people in the world. A tip of the hat and a smiling hello from a passer-by on a street in Dungannon, Northern Ireland. Acceptance into a musical jam session or chat at a pub in Belfast. A farmer in County Armagh waving from his tractor to a total stranger flying down the road in his rented car. They all reflect the joy the Irish have in 'inclusiveness'. Let's go back to St. Attracta, the Sligo saint, she of the well. This holy woman built a nunnery where she could practice the art of Irish hospitality. She had the convent constructed, not to keep out the world, but to include it. The place was set where 7 roads meet, just so that she could exercise a wide range of hospitable resources. I, of the fertile imagination, can picture this sweet coiffed woman standing at the crossroads roundabout offering assistance: clothing, a meal, a bed, advice, directions, a cooling drink, shelter from a sudden Irish rain storm. Seven forms of welcome on seven roads.

I'm sure there are more ways of expressing our willingness to have an open door or heart. Inspire someone else today. Pour out 100,000 welcomes and your day will be full of blessing.

A prison wall is round us born,
Two outcast men we were:
The world had thrust us from its heart
And God from out His care:
And the iron gin that Waits for Sin
Had caught us in the snare.

(The Ballad of Reading Gaol – Oscar Wilde)

Inclusion and a sense of community are two vital components of a well-adjusted heart. But, Wilde's two characters felt not only ostracism and separation, but also a spiritual void. I want to repair such damning thoughts in my own heart; I do not wish for the sentiments of the two men Wilde is relating to. I do not want those thoughts in others. I want all to feel loved and wanted. To enable this environment, evil and sin must be scaled out of life's process. They are the aspects of life that need imprisoned and ensnared. Work at inclusion today. The smile of the accepted one inspires.

First, my apologies for the above pun to C.S. Lewis, himself Irish. The beach at Buncrana, gateway to the Inishowen Peninsula, is a conglomerate of scenery and action. To walk the strand south of Buncrana is not a straight-forward stroll. To reach the beach, a climb up and over dunes is necessary, with a final slither down the sandy slope to the water's edge. We encountered stretches of open level sand, streams trickling into the sea to cross, rotting crabs and starfish, heaps of cottage sized rocks acting as breakwaters, flying golf balls, narrow defiles between land and sea and noise and air pollution of tugs and lorries. At times, we had to backtrack and pick our way gingerly. The line was not straight. At either end of the beach workmen interfered with our peace of mind. A small freighter plied by and turned into one dock and a winch began to offload crates into a shed on the pier. At another pier a trawler ran to and fro endlessly from the middle of Lough Swilly to port to bring in some kind of catch of the day. Then, snaking in a sliver of land between highway and sea were the golf links. To golf at this course would be a challenge to the 'slicer' or 'hooker'. And, there was a permanent gale from the sea offering its own direction to the ball. At least the view was phenomenal if one took his or her concentration off the ball. But, no one did; no one hailed us from the course to the beach.

The strand at Buncrana is a microcosm of what God challenges us with in life: in play, work and obstacles. All are vital to Buncrana's existence. All are vital to our spiritual life.

The Coming of Wisdom with Time

(W.B. Yeats)

Though leaves are many, the root is one;
Through all the lying days of my youth
I swayed my leaves and flowers in the sun;
Now I may wither into the truth.

Yeats presents an interesting metaphor here. One might suspect that the root is the origin of truth, but Yeats tells us here that the root is the end product of truth. The youth radiates optimism and growth, but the evidence, produced in the 'spring' and 'summer' of life is found to be what it really is: flowers and leaves which wither and fall. What appeared to be the bulk of the plant is, in reality, temporal. Yeats feels that wisdom comes from withering (ironical, is it not?) back into the ground.

It is difficult for the young to acknowledge that wisdom comes with age. But, it is true; today, look up to an elder. He or she will inspire you with a bulk of truth.

An obligatory stop in Ireland for a Yeat's fan is Drumcliff where the poet W.B. is buried. Even in death, Yeats is an interpretive and religious enigma. He died in 1939 at Roquebrune on the French Riviera. He declared a last wish–: "bury me on the mountain (Roquebrune) and after a year or so, dig me up and bring me privately to Sligo." In 1948, his wish was fulfilled – his body was laid in Drumcliff cemetery, later than he had wished because of WW 2. Interpreting his poetic epitaph is a challenge too – "Cast a cold eye on life, on death. Horseman, pass by!" In his death wish and in his epitaph, there seems to be a ring of a resurrective apocalypse. It all smacks of a desire to cheat death, to meld life and death and to overcome the inexorable nature of death. One cannot treat life or death callously nor can one forego the effects of death, no matter if the image is of a Grim Reaper or of a Horseman. Our heritage teaches us that there is a raising of the body, but not in Yeats' way. It is ironic that Yeats wished to be buried in a graveyard at a church where his great grandfather had been rector. Yet, he did not wish the visit of the Horseman.

Inside the church a text on the side wall preaches a clear message of eternal life in Christ Jesus. One wonders if Yeats ever saw it or pondered it. It would have inspired him.

I have written elsewhere of another inspiration from the city of Armagh. I am also inspired by its motto—"a city built upon belief". When I visited St. Patrick's Trian, I learned of Armagh's 9000 year-old history – portal tombs (dolmens) and a court tomb welcomed me. Perhaps these were symbols of the belief of the ancient Celts—a gateway to a world beyond. Close by, Emain Macha (Navan) was built in AD 94 as a temple of belief in some god. Then Saint Patrick arrived in the fifth century; he believed that Armagh was to be the house of Christianity in Ireland. Over centuries, this bulwark of faith inspired a large monastic community (a Franciscan friary in the 1100s). Faith kept Armagh and its religious communities joyful despite raids and fires. Today, dating from the 1800s, two spires pierce Armagh's skies as symbols of belief. The towers of the Church of Ireland on one hill and the Roman Catholic Cathedral on the other are like two arms outstretched in a prayer of faith to God. While at the Trian, I saw another, more materialistic result of the belief and faith of Dean Jonathan Swift. He was a religious prelate who in 1726 published *Gullivers Travels* (his own copy is in the Armagh Public Library).

To read how this man of faith was also down to earth enough to write about Gulliver saving the Empress' burning palace by "making water" in the palace grounds made me chuckle. Swift was a man of the cloth who was taught to pray before he acted. Belief and practicality are complementary. Today I believe I can apply my faith in practical ways and be inspired.

Just west of Limerick on the Shannon estuary sits "Bunratty Castle and Folk Park". The entrance to the castle is not over a traditional drawbridge above a moat, but up a flight of twentieth century stairs. The castle itself was built in 1425. It was authentically restored to become a complete, real, working castle where medieval banquets are held each night in the Great Room. Tapestries and serving "wenches" and smoking tapers add to the atmosphere and authenticity. Guests even eat with their fingers! One sits almost in expectation of the alarm call to the sentry to drop the postern gate and flee to the tower because a Viking raid is imminent. I became a medieval knight that evening.

Earlier in the day, I was fast-forwarded five hundred years as I walked around donkey carts, sheep, jaunting cars, thatched cottages and milkmaids. I was now in Bunratty Folk Park proper which recreates both urban and rural life in the 1800s (minus the Great Famine years). I looked in a druggist shop window and almost saw myself in a black top hat and suit. No, it was jeans, a t-shirt and Nikes! Time and what it creates and changes inspires me. Its kaleidoscope of settings brings both variety and stability to my life.

Live as if everyday was your last. Tomorrow will be a vast improvement on today.

One day while staying with my sister-in-law in the Moy, my wife and I set out on a walk. The Argory, a county house built in 1824, is in the area. We had seen the old place before, but thought we'd visit it again. Shortly after setting out, we asked an old man how far away the Argory was, "Och, just a wee dander." By that he meant "not far." Four hours later, and even without time to stop at the Argory, we were back home! If that's a short walk, I hand it to the Irish for the power of understatement. The Argory is also an understatement, for it is a time capsule and it understates what luxury is. In 1824, it was a luxury gift to Walter McGeough's great-grandson. Yet, it stands today as it always did—no electricity, a central wood stove, a sundial, an oxy-acetylene plant in the courtyard to make gas for lighting. There is also a laundry and mangle room, stables and bullock houses. The home still evokes the palatial lifestyle of the family as one walks through the rooms, furnished as though it was one hundred and fifty years ago, decked out with the treasures of four generations. By today's standards, austere, but having a grandeur nonetheless. Our modern creature comforts inspire me, but so too does the grand age when life was harder.

Enjoy your cell phone and all that the twenty-first century has to offer. At the same time, however, appreciate the understated elegance of the past.

Dublin is a literary city. My first stop was the literary Museum and the Abbey Theatre to reacquaint myself with the facts, but I had to live the *Dubliner's* life of James Joyce. So, I wandered the streets (the Quays of the Liffey, O 'Connnell, Grafton, Mary, Henry Streets, Temple Bar). Trinity College which holds the gospels copied and decorated by monks in AD 800 (Book of Kells). Later, I was in Duke Street, and stopped for I had to visit The Duke, a true "Irish Pub", a "cult pub" whose ethos and design have inspired replicas in Europe and North America. Here there is music, spirited conversation, excellent food, and pints. I saw Joyce, Behan, Kavanagh and "The Ginger Man" reflected in the brass, polished mahogany and glass and I engaged them in literary debate. Invigorating! Then, I took the 'Intercity' out to Sandy Cove, toward Joyce's Martello Tower, and had dinner at the South Bank which also welcomed Joyce. My last pilgrimage that day was to enter Saint Patrick's Cathedral and stand silently at Jonathan Swift's tomb. Compared to these literary giants of Dublin, I was a literary Lilliputian. Conversely, they inspired me to continue writing.

I encourage you to write or to create today—a sketch, a diary, a diagram, a note, a card, a story, a poem. You will be inspired.

The Great Famine of 1845-1847 was, bluntly, a misnomer. In fact, there was an abundance of food in Ireland in those years. It was the potato blight (some problems beginning in the 1830s) which denied the staple food only to the lower and middle class populace. If the other abundant crops had not been shipped to England (for example, 200 tons of grain from Donegal in one year), no one would have starved. As it was, several measures were invoked to care for the hungry. In Donegal, the local priest made appeals from the pulpit. Visitors to the Spa Baths donated; shopkeepers gave to those with identity tags on "help day", Monday. Some, but few, landlords like John Hamilton or St. Ernan's and Lord Aran became benefactors. Finally, there were the food lines. A few hundred meters from Lough Eske stands an open stone structure with a massive cast-iron black pot sitting on a hearth. It is far from any town, but I am told that thousands queued along the road in those years, in silent patience, to have soup ladled out to them from the Famine Pot. The pot stands five feet high and measures three feet across—that's a lot of soup! One night, I had my photo taken beside the pot, and then hypocritically went inside Harvey Point's five-star restaurant to gorge myself on a five course meal. The irony! I had to queue for a table and then wait for forty-five minutes until I could be seated. I did enjoy the meal, but wondered whether the mendicants at the pot were more satisfied.

Line-ups don't inspire me, but the satisfaction of completion in the end does. Today, don't fume and fret in a line-up. It'll all come together at last.

"Fifteen thousand years ago in Ireland, the Great Elk wandered through the fields and mountains. It was a land of sweeping mists, gentle rain and soft sunlight. A land of pagan carvings and mysterious rituals. A land where the soothing lilt of the harp or pipe floated over cool, clear crystal lakes and rivers. It was the time of Cuchulainn, Queen Maeve and the Red Branch Knights. This was indeed the Celtic Twilight."

I quote from the Island Turf crafts and Bog Museum brochure—a place I felt inspired to visit. There I found an indoor bog and had an interactive experience with the bones and antlers of an Irish Great Elk. I was able to bring home replicas of pieces of ancient history—a Celtic cross standing two feet high, carved from bog oak and a piece of turf which tells time! Actually, it's a desk clock carved from hardened and polished turf.

Each time I touch those pieces of art from the Turf Craft Factory shop, I remember that the oldest, ugliest, and dirtiest can be made into something of beauty and usefulness—people or things.

I had driven alongside the walls of Benburb Castle numerous times, but a couple of years ago I finally stopped by to enquire as to its purpose and history. The King of Ulster, Shane O'Neill used Benburb as his main residence, but it wasn't until the early 1600s that Wingfield, Viscount of Powerscourt (Co. Wicklow) was given nine thousand acres and Benburb in recognition of his services to the British crown. The castle and bawn rose. In the 1800s, the Bruce family, of distillery renown abandoned the castle to build a new manor and to renew the town. During World War II, the castle was requisitioned by the army as a hospital. The Servile Order used it as a seminary to train priests, but they relocated to Dublin and the castle fell into ruin. At present, Benburb Castle is a Historical Monument, and one can tour the west keep to learn of the castle's storied past.

I am inspired by most castles, but by Benburb particularly, because it makes me think about serving others—to operate a loving home, to honour and respect authority, to care for the physical needs of others, to pass on training and to interpret the past to those who ask.

One of the most picturesque spots I have ever seen is Horn Head in Donegal—for its wide green spaces. (Of course, I find all of Ireland picturesque for a variety of reasons.) As we left the seaside town of Dunfanaghy, we broadened horizons exponentially until we reached the headland one hundred eighty metres above the valley. We were driving a single lane trail past sheep and rocks. At one point, as I reached the peak of a hill, all I saw was sky ahead. Straight out west—I turned and the headland moor spread and rolled east, north and south. My view was unimpeded by building or cloud. The sheer openness inspired me. I could have drunk in the scenery for hours. As I peered out to sea again, I saw Tory Island. The inhabitants there have an independent spirit equal to the green splendour around them. They have their own monarch, a non-hereditary king, whose only goal and power as to attract tourists. The subjects even refused to be resettled to the 'mainland' in the 1970s. A local artist opened a school of primitive artists who claim superiority over conventional artists.

Such open resistance to conformity inspired me too as I scoured the island's cliffs and rockeries. It is a people and a place which provide us today with motivation to be free and different.

(a real link to the other side)

I used to live on Ferry Road. People asked me if I lived near the ferry terminal—actually I do, about a five minute drive now, but that's not why our former street is called Ferry Road. Once, many years ago, a small ferry used to run across the Fraser River so that business could be done from south to north. The ferry is gone, replaced by a busy tunnel.

Okay, I'm getting to Ireland—Belfast—'B'eal Feirste' in Gaelic means "approach to the shallow ford." It was here that Irish bards crossed the Lagan River. Such a natural spot called a natural community together. In 1306, one of Belfast's first buildings was built, the Chapel of the Ford, so that travelers could enter and give inspired thanks for a safe crossing of the river. Saint George's Church on High Street now occupies the spot. Belfast has always had a hand in linkages—a ship building and rope making capital of the world.

I am inspired when I see community and personal bonds. It takes a physical, mental or spiritual crossing, by ferry or on foot or by word, to float such linkage. Each sets out to maneuver the waters at the shallowest place, and when the other side is reached, we can give thanks. Thanks to Belfast for its inspiration.

Gallarus Oratory - Kerry

Giant's Causeway - Antrim

(or, Do You Understand English?)

Overlooking Sligo Bay are the Ox Mountains or Slieve Gamh. Under circuitous etymology we might see the connections between the two names. *"Gamh"* in Gaelic sounds like *"Damh"* which in turn means "ox". So, can you follow how the English living in Ireland gave the mountain range its name? Basically as a result of an unfamiliarity with the local's language and in an attempt to be open to the local culture. Let's go back to *"Gamh"*, evidently a servant to one of the Celtic invaders of Ireland. The poor servant was beheaded at Tullaghan ('hawk', in Gaelic) and his head thrown into a well. The faeries cast their spell upon the well and it produced salt water at one time, fresh water at another. The well was hard to find, but ultimately I came across the stones surrounding the spring topped by a cross. There I sat down to think about oxen and miracles.

God's messages are never obscure or double-edged. In fact, they are miraculous. At one point in time, God instructed Moses to throw a branch into bitter water so that his people could have fresh water. The miracle ensued and the people got the point. God was saying to them," I care about you, even about the water that you drink." Today is a day to thank God precisely for every small gift. God does not equivocate with you; it's not time to dissemble with him by language couched in vague terms. Thank you, Lord for You and me.

In Emyvale, County Monaghan, I visited Father Moynagh's grave, a pilgrimage site for many Prince Edward Island families. It's a moss covered stone, topped with a weathered crude Celtic cross. The link to Canada's smallest province is inspiring. In 1820, some Irish families from Emyvale emigrated to Glasgow, Scotland, but found that working in factories ill-suited their farming heritage. Their priest advised them to move to Canada where his father owned large farms in PEI. They took the good Father's advice. In due course, Fr. McDonald was in PEI too as their pastor and landlord after his father's death. The Irish had settled in comfortably and were so prosperous, though illiterate, that they sent a letter, via Father McDonald, to Donagh, Emyvale. In it they encouraged a mass emigration from Ireland. Sixty families took up the offer after Fr. Moynagh read the letter at Mass one Sunday. The priest then was good enough to arrange for this second wave of emigrants. The descendants of the families have been forever grateful, for they escaped the Great Famine and have prospered ever since.

The pioneering spirit has always inspired me and today I want to break new ground. No matter what I try, though, I sense that it will not be as daunting as crossing the Atlantic in the 1800s and clearing ground in a cold and hostile land so that my children can have a brighter future. My hat is off to the inner drive of those Irish and for their inspiration.

Templepatrick stands on the Sixmilewater River just off the M2 to Belfast in Antrim. The name refers to the Church of Saint Patrick. The saint has seemingly been omnipresent in Ireland. At this particular site, he baptized converts in the ancient holy well waters in the fifth century. In order to give the new babes in the faith a church setting, he founded the stone church in the centre of a graveyard. Now, one can see only a monumental mausoleum where the church once stood. It is a sacred place and God and Saint Patrick set it up to secure its sanctity from any inroads of industry. In the last century, developers began to blast limestone from the land adjacent to the graveyard. This quarry was to supply rock for the new homes. Initially, the blasting was set to be investigated, even blocked by authorities when the graveyard sexton hurried to announce that the holy well had dried up. The bureaucrats' attempts to save the site from development would prove unnecessary since it appears that God/Providence/Patrick/the Faeries took their own definitive vengeance. The 'pit' that had already been dug, for the quarry was flooded and all equipment ruined.

As I walked over to the pit, I was motivated to put the sacred first in my life. Profit over Providence never succeeds. Patrick saw to that.

One does not go far in Ireland without meeting Finn McCool, and at Lough Neagh there is another legend relating to the giant warrior. He is evidently responsible for the creation of Lough Neagh. The story goes this way: Finn was in pursuit of the Scottish giant who had stolen his lady friend. The Scottish warrior had a skill superior to Finn's – his speed. He was outrunning Finn and had almost reached the coast to escape to Scotland. In anger at his loss, McCool scraped up a fistful of rocks and let them fly. Alas, he overthrew his target and the Scot leaped home. The hole made from Finn's handful of rocks filled in and became Lough Neagh. What's more, the Isle of Man is supposed to be part of the land mass which Finn threw. I'll let a geologist rule on the similarity or difference between the land strata in Northern Ireland and on the Isle of Man. I'm impressed, however, with the results of this tantrum – a gorgeous natural habitat in the form of the lake and a pristine hideaway on the Isle of Man.

If anyone around you loses his or her temper today (or, if you do), let some benefit derive and devolve from it.

I am always taken by the intriguing and imaginative tales of ancient Ireland. This one tops all, perhaps. In ancient times, Ireland was a utopian splendour; it boasted luxurious homes, fine castles and towers, peaceful glades and an abundance of food for all: an Irish Eden, if you will. The land consisted of little perfect fiefdoms which never went to war. At the heart of one of these kingdoms was a magical spring. The waters provided fresh sustenance and healing for all. In time, the inhabitants turned to greed and thievery. The spring watched this declension with alarm, and at first did not act. At last, it could bear it no longer. In dudgeon, it rose and inundated the kingdom – with Lough Neagh as the boundaries of this now evil fiefdom. Locals will tell you that fishers have said that on a calm day, they have spotted the glimmering towers far beneath the surface of the lough.

I can tell you that there was a real Eden which fell as a result of sin, and also that there is a perfect kingdom which will never fall or decline. That's heaven, and I'm inspired today because I'm going there.

was lost deep in the Clogher Valley in County Tyrone, searching for the 'Carleton Country Trail'. William Carleton was the "people's novelist" in Ireland. The scenery was stupendous, but I wanted to learn more about the author whom Yeats called "the greatest novelist of Ireland." That's heady praise coming from the master himself. I wanted to know more than the fact that Carleton was born to a tenant farmer in 1794, one of fourteen children and that he moved to Clogher near Dungannon to write of his youth. I never did find the Carleton Summer School, but I did get bogged down in mud on a steep hillside track. I pulled out his three novels (*Traits and Stories of Irish Peasantry, Paddy, Go Aisy, The Black Prophet*) and read excerpts as I waited for the RAA to rescue me. I have chosen lines from "Traits" for today's inspiration:

Enjoy and ponder deeply.

There never was a more unfounded calumny than impiety to the Irish peasantry in indifference to education (The Hedge School)

"Women , if they bring us into many an unpleasant scrape, can succeed in getting us out of others that are as bad." (Legend of Knockmany – Finn McCool)

"Bill was obliged to "travel' – in other words, he fell asleep, or still plainer, he died." (the Irish penchant for the gift of the gab)

Your first reaction is probably to tell me that I'm away with the faeries, that I've got the wrong country. "Sure an' begorrah," you're wrong. There have always been links between Scotland and Ireland. It is true enough that one of these has been the root of Ireland's deepest problems. When the Scottish plantation owners and farmers were transported to Northern Ireland, there began the deep-seated hatred existing between Catholics and Protestants. However, we are inspired by the lilting presence of Burns in County Meath at the Agnes Burns Cottage on the Stephenstown Estate where her husband, William Galt was "Confidential Manager." Agnes was the sister of Robbie and a dairymaid on the Fortescue Estate. Agnes Burns-Galt lived in the eighteenth-century cottage on the Stephenstown Pond, Carp Fishery and Nature Park. Inside the cottage today one can see panels and displays of the life and works of Robbie and scenes from Agnes' rural life. The montage brings Agnes and Robbie to life as the two relate, through actors' voices, accounts of their daily chores. Should Auld acquaintance be forgot and Days of Auld Lang Syne?

I'm not certain if Burns had a question mark, but I'll insert one to make an inspiration for today concise. As I stood at the cottage door, we sang it, even though it was not January 1st. Wherever I am, I will recall my friends and my past.

Mirror in February

The day dawns with scent of must and rain,
Of opened soil, dark tress, dry bedroom air.
Under the fading lamp, half-dressed – my brain
Idling on some compulsive fantasy –
I towel my shaven lip and stop, and stare,
A dry downturning mouth.

It seems again that it is time to learn,
In this untiring, crumbling place of growth
To which, for the time being, I return.
Now plainly in the mirror of my soul
I read that I have looked on my last youth
And little more; for they are not made whole
That reach the age of Christ

Below my window the awakening trees,
Hacked clean for better bearing, stand defaced
Suffering their brute necessities,
And how should the flesh not quail that span for span
Is mutilated more? In slow distaste
I fold my towel with what grace I can,
Not young and not renewable, but man.

(Thomas Kinsella)

Some things come as a shock, none more than the realization of the passage of time. The mirror is an honest friend, both the actual, physical glass, and the mirror of the soul. We accept with frustration and fear the "mutilation" of our bodies from the arrival of middle and old age, but we are loath to look into the mirror of our soul and admit and we are mutilated by sin unless Christ has stepped in. If we have let Christ enter in order to care, we become more than a mutilated man or woman—we become eternal beings. We must not forget that February will soon become July, if we are faithfully patient.

Hyphenated names are a feature of many names in the British Isles and Ireland. In some cases it's pure snobbery of the nobility: James-Smith sounds ever so much 'posher' than just Smith or James. Or, the hyphenated label derives from the need to define geographical setting: Stow-on-the-Wold, Grange-over-Sands, Hetton-le-Hole, Barrow-in-Furness. Hence, I want to re-name the strand at Rossnowlagh to something more poetic. That late March mid-morning it was the expanse of sand, the rolling waves and the mist which inspired me. We drove right down on to the beach. The tide was at ebb. We began to walk – for two hours, on the same beach! And, we did not reach either end. The sand was tawny tan, level smooth some places, hard rippled others. Not one rock marred the continuance of the stretch until we viewed the basalt framework of the bay. It was truly a ribbon of silicate undulating between two supporting cliffs. This aura was emphasized by the mists created by the sun-warmed air meeting the sea. The rollers could be heard but their origin was shrouded in fog. It floated in and out like a wraith. The sea fog stood to the west and the veil of condensation on land to the east. The dunes and cliffs were visible as if through a gauze. The beach house and hotel at Rossnowlagh appeared surreal within a misty sheer. Above, only rosy brilliant sunlight. Man, woman, child, beast did not exist there except a handful of companions strolling the strand. The world was far away.

Sometimes God's creation allows an imperfect glimpse into heaven. This site was that glimpse. Where God is there is a never-ending strand of love encompassed by His Cloud of Unknowing perfection.

My love, we will go, we will go. I and you,
And away in the woods we will scatter the dew;
And the salmon behold, and the ousel too,
My love we will hear, I and you, we will hear,
The calling afar of the doe and the deer.
And the bird in the branches will cry for us clear,
And the cuckoo unseen in his festival mood;
And death, oh my fair one, will never come near
In the bosom afar of the fragrant wood.
(from the Gaelic)
W.B. Yeats

The desire of the human soul to draw aside from the natural activities of life is strong. And to withdraw into the realms of nature with a loved one is even stronger. The images here of scuttling through the morning grassy fens kicking up the dew and staring into pools filled with salmon and responding to the calls of birds in festive mood is exhilarating. Today would be a grand day to set aside plans and seclude oneself in the woods, would it not? However, even there we cannot escape the claws of death. Of that too I am certain today.

Since I am old enough to have endured the sixties, I hold the Beatles in a special place in my heart. So, when I heard that Paul McCartney had booked Castle Leslie at Glaslough, County Monaghan for his wedding, I just had to go there too to capture the romance of the place. In fact, I had looked into booking a weekend at Castle Leslie some ten years ago, but found it too rich for my pocket book. With some difficulty and after inquiring in Monaghan City, I found the County 'R' road leading to the castle. Glaslough is a sleepy but prosperous village, having existed only for the Leslie family known for its Nationalist leanings. I drove through the town on a summer morning. The streets were deserted at 11:00 am. I entered the castle grounds and was to be disappointed – the front door to the hotel was locked and the grounds were in need of care. The image was not of an Edwardian mansion in full splendour. Inside might have been different, but nothing about the exterior beckoned me to stay. I could envision the McCartney couple perhaps arriving by helicopter at the terraced side of the home. Their sequestered honeymoon at Castle Leslie was surely more memorable than my stroll in the parkland and my unanswered ring at the door.

Sometimes reality conflicts with fantasy, and disillusionment results. I know, however, that I will draw inspiration today from being realistic – oh, and from the Beatles too!

Death of a Naturalist
(Seamus Heaney)

All year the flax-dam festered in the heart
Of the townland....
There were dragonflies, spotted butterflies,
But best of all was the warm thick slobber
Of frogspawn that grew like clotted water
In the shade of the banks......
Swimming tadpoles. Miss Walls would tell us how
The daddy frog was called a bullfrog
And how he croaked and the mammy frog
Laid hundreds of little eggs and this was
Frogspawn....

Then one hot day when fields were rank
With cowdung in the grass the angry frogs
Invaded the flax-dam; I ducked through hedges
To a coarse croaking that I had not heard
Before. The air was thick with a bass chorus.
Right down the dam gross-bellied frogs were cocked
On sods; their loose necks pulsed like sails. Some hopped:
The slap and plop were obscene threats.

The innocence and ideals of youth are often destroyed in the raucous obscene and violent basics of life. Heaney paints an image of the quintessential Irish bog lake and stream meandering amid the production of linen. He lets us see the little lad collecting the eggs for tadpoles. Then, this perfect world of nature is shattered by what adults, and sometimes children maturing too quickly, come to know. What we see is rarely what we get. The bizarre invasion of the flax-dam would be truly off-putting, even threatening to a young naturalist boy. To him a monster has been born and he will never see the environment in the same way, but now in a sullied and perverted light.

Life need not be that way. We need not 'put to death the one we love', to paraphrase Oscar Wilde, just because we view from another facet now. Do not discard someone or something today just because you see him/her/it in a different light.

In his acceptance speech in 1995 for his Nobel Prize for Literature, Seamus Heaney recounted the following tale from the Northern Irish days of the "Troubles". One January night in 1976, a minibus full of workers going home was halted by armed masked men who ordered the frightened and tired men to make a line. All Catholics were commanded to step forward; but, only one man was Catholic. He began to move, but was detained in the darkness before detection. The split second hand of a Protestant colleague gripped his arm. The squeeze implied that the rest would not deliver him for murder to this group of supposed Protestant paramilitaries out for some tit for tat revenge for an earlier Catholic killing. The lone Catholic was not to be deterred by his friend's offer. He stepped forward anyways, bravely to face death. Instead, he was pushed aside into safety and the whole lot of Protestant workers was gunned down, presumably by this band of IRA Provos. Heaney concluded his story by commenting, "History is about as instructive as an abattoir; Tacitus (Roman poet and historian – *my addition*) was right ... that 'peace is merely the desolation left behind after the decisive operations of a merciless power.'"

Peter, Paul and Mary and Pete Seeger used to sing, "When will we ever learn?" We plead today for mercy and peace and tolerance and understanding, and yes, love, not sectarianism, violence, murders and revenge. Don't "get 'im back" today. Give 'em love.

We'll continue with an excerpt from Heaney's Nobel speech, another of his stories. Once upon a time, Saint Kevin was kneeling in prayer at his retreat with his arms outstretched in the form of a cross. This monastery to Saint Kevin can be found a Glendalough in County Wicklow and is also a retreat for wildlife: birds and beasts in a natural setting. The story goes that Kevin was so engrossed in his prayer and meditation, so long that a blackbird mistook his hands for a nesting roost. The bird swooped down and laid her eggs in his hands! There she rested and there Kevin displayed a simple practiced faith and love. He stayed immobile for hours and days and weeks until the fledglings hatched and flew off independently. Heaney went on to question Kevin's common sense, but not his idealism. Heaney wanted to "make space for his reckoning and imagining for the marvelous, as well as for the murderous." When all around him were losing their heads, Heaney wanted to marvel at "the positive in the work of art."

I like Heaney's and the Saint's philosophies, and I love Heaney's poetry. When it comes time to just sit and enjoy what is around us, what we read or who others are, that thought transcends the moment. The moment may extend into hours or days, as it did with Kevin. That's okay. Today, I am going to be a Saint Kevin.

Spanish Armada captain, Don Alonzo Martinez was on the run in the Girona. He had 1300 on board a ship built for 130. Events had not turned out well for the Spanish fleet of warships in their battle with the English and Martinez was trying to find refuge for as many of his fellow countrymen as he could. He felt he could do so by sticking close by the Antrim coast, for he believed he could find a haven there. He knew that the McDonnells of Dunluce Castle, who hated the English almost as much as he, could and would provide safety in Sorley Bay. Martinez, therefore, turned his swamping Girona around to stagger toward the chimneys of Dunluce Castle. They beckoned the chance of what he thought was warmth and life. Instead, only nine men survived the shipwreck which ensued. Martinez, instead of spotting the chimneys of the castle had really spotted the "chimney stacks" of basaltic rock of the Giant's Causeway. Today that bay is called Port na Spanaigh in honour of the deceived Spanish captain. From our tour zodiac which took us along the coast, it was easy to see how Martinez was led to believe in a fake impression. Dunluce is only a few kilometers to the east and its chimneys do resemble the natural rock of the Causeway.

What did inspire me from this story was Martinez' faith. The only trouble was that he had placed his faith in an ephemeral fake which was real. That's Irish logic! As for me, I've faith in a real God who is in the right place for me.

Glenarm Castle is just one of hundreds of gorgeous castles in Ireland, but its "barbican" (a form of architecture designed to represent or create defences) gateway holds a special story. The choirmaster of Wells Cathedral in Somerset, England had married the Countess of Antrim who owned Glenarm. Unfortunately, the dear Countess enjoyed the bottle too much. As well, the castle did not sport an attractive gateway to impress visitors and guests. Phelps, the chorister, made a deal with his new wife. He would provide her with a gateway worthy of the castle and of her position in life if she would stay "on the wagon". The ornate gateway at Glenarm is a testament to her perseverance to give up drink. She was given defences against her addiction; the gate is a symbol of her strength to overcome.

I find this anecdote inspiring because the husband's offer was more than just a "carrot", or an incentive offered to change behaviour. The gateway was a permanent reminder. If the Countess should ever have regressed, Phelps need only have taken her down the path to the entranceway and shown her the mark of his love and faith and of her courage and strength. That would have set her on the rails again, I am sure. Is there someone near you whom you can motivate today in a similar way?

We engage in a complex trip today with letters in a name, so hang on. The Gaelic word *Muineachain* meaning "little hills" has given to one of Ireland's counties its name: Monaghan. That's its nickname in tourism brochures – the County of the Little Hills. As I drove into the county for the first time in 2002, I could see how the name fitted. The county has a history dating back to the Bronze Age, and was once the heart of the Kingdom of Oriel. In fact, some believe the County should be called Oriel. Muiredach or Muineachain aka *Colla da Croich*, was the son of *Dubhlen* (Dublin) and Alechia, daughter of King Alba of Scotland. Hence his name: *Colla* of the two Counties. Oriel or Uriel was the King of Ulster, and from his name, many noble Irish family names descended: Malone, MacHugh, McGrath and MacMahon to name just four. The County of Monaghan was Colla's home lair, so with this origin of Irish culture, perhaps there is an argument for renaming it Oriel. I have not checked the etymology, but I see a link between Ireland and Oriel. That link widens the rationale for titles and patronyms from all over Ireland being linked to Monaghan. Let's start a campaign to rename Ireland Monaghan!

What we cannot do with a name, or without a name. You may not have the romance of a name from 'the hills beyond', but let your name inspire you today – if nothing else than to be yourself. I am reminded of John Proctor in *The Crucible* who shouted, "Give me my name; it's all I have."

The Londonderry air is one of the most recognizable tunes around the world. This love ballad, supposedly written by Thackeray about the love of a barmaid, Peg or composed by an English lawyer called Weatherly has a storied past. The most accepted one goes like this: in 1851, Jane Ross was listening to an itinerant fiddler in Limavady, poor blind Jimmy McCreary. He sat between the cart shafts in the Limavady High Street and serenaded merchants at work. Jane lived above these shops and was so enthralled by this one tune that she transcribed it as Jimmy repeatedly played the air. Ross offered Jimmy a coin (royalties?!), as it turned out a valuable florin, instead of the usual penny given to buskers. Blind Jimmy rubbed the coin against his lips to determine the denomination and then began to chase after Jane to return the florin. Naturally, Jane refused. It is said that Jimmy got his inspiration from the faeries which still were around from 250 years earlier when they had picked up the tune. Irish immigrants brought the tune to the US, where evidently one Margaret Weatherly of Colorado heard Irish gold prospectors humming the tune. She sent the melody to her brother-in-law, Fred Weatherly who matched his lyrics to it.

The stuff of Irish magical lore, to be sure! Take time out now to sit back and allow some simple tune to inspire you. And, oh, as well offer a coin to a busker!

Of Difference Does it Make

(Tom Paulin)
*During the 51 year existence of the Northern Ireland Parliament only one Bill
sponsored by a non-Unionist member was ever passed*

Among the lovers and the stonechats
protected by the Wild Birds Act
of nineteen-hundred-and-thirty –one,
there is a rare stint called the notawhit
that has a schisty flight-call, like the chough's.
Notawhit, notawhit, notawhit
- it raps out a sharp code-sign
like a mild and patient prisoner
pecking through granite with a teaspoon.

Have you ever asked the question as to the reason for your existence? This satirical poem addresses the same question about bureaucracy or sham lip service or politics. What was the reason for the existence of the non-Unionist members, or for that matter, of the Northern Ireland Parliament? Maybe"notawhit". Any attempt by ingratiating power-brokers to include others in decision-making leaves a hollow or even meaningless feeling of success, or worse a sense of fruitless effort – like "a patient prisoner pecking through granite with a teaspoon."

Look around you today and watch out for those who seem to wish for inclusiveness, but really don't care – "notawhit".

You would hardly expect to find a shrine to such a goddess in a small agricultural and industrial centre in Northern Ireland. Dungannon is an unlikely spot to have on one of its hills a chambered cairn called, Knockmany. On the stones at this large cairn, some chiseler carved concentric circles which some scholars say can be traced back to a cult of a Mother Goddess in Syria in about 3000 BC. How is that for the bizarre!? Knockmany means "Hill of Aine" in Gaelic and Aine was a popular goddess of love. Whichever tribal chieftain set up this cairn in Dungannon, he must have had some link to the worship of a deity dedicated to love or to a loved one. Did he find love in Dungannon? I knew that I personally expressed my vows of love just outside Dungannon (my wife's home town is Dungannon). I did not raise a cairn or worship the stars, but I did acknowledge that day that human love is based on godly love as outlined in 1 Corinthians 13 and John's Epistle. As I voiced my vows that day, sectarian violence raged in Northern Ireland where there was little love.

'If I don't love, I am nothing' – 'faith hope and love and the greatest of these is love' – 'God is Love.' You can find love anywhere, you know. It's not hard to locate it today. It is in God and God is everywhere.

But the life of man is sorrow,
And death a relief from pain;
For love only lasts till tomorrow,
And life without love is vain.

(Ye Shall Be Gods – Oscar Wilde)

The memories of yesterday's love are precious, but it is true also that today's love, left over for tomorrow becomes stale. Today, yesterday and tomorrow cannot exist without love, but each only lasts the length of that day. So, inspire yourself to love today and always amid the pain and the death of this world. Renew it each day.

Love is all around you.

No, I don't mean Dolly, the sheep clone. I refer to a small town in County Monaghan which is proud of three of its hometown boys. First, Barry McGuigan was the "Clones Cyclone" who defended the WBA Featherweight title several times until 1989. On another athletic front, James Cecil Parke was arguably Ireland's greatest eclectic athlete – capped in rugby, # 4 ranked tennis player in the world, an internationally scratch golfer, first class cricketer and sprinter, as well as a child prodigy in chess. He died in 1946. The final son of Clones was Sir Thomas Lipton, he of Lipton tea fame. Lipton's family moved to Glasgow in the Famine times. He went to America later, but returned to Scotland to set up a tea shop. He bought up tea plantations in Sri Lanka and now his distinctive tea boxes grace kitchens everywhere. Lipton returned to Clones regularly until his death in 1931.

One could "pun" that these three men were not "clones", but unique one-of-a-kinds. They did put a small economically poor town on the map and serve as role models. Surely those men inspire me to excel in my field.

Man and Hound Escape in Blinding Snowstorm

So could have run the village paper's headline in Derrynamuck, Knockanacarrigan, in County Wicklow. This is one town which I just had to visit, simply for its name. Once on Main St, however, I realized that this insignificant spot holds a place in Irish history. A pristine, whitewashed and thatched cottage (the Dwyer McCallister Cottage) drew me in. Inside on the walls, also whitewashed, is the tale of Michael Dwyer. This storied rebel was holed up in Connell's Cottage on Hoxie's Farm in a snowstorm in February 1799. He tried to evade the pincer movement of British soldiers who had been informed of his presence and who overran his sentinels. McCallister would not surrender, although others had been burned alive in their hiding places on the farm. Despite the designs of the Brits to capture and hang Dwyer, he escaped over the snow-covered Imaal Mountains and Glen as his relative, Sam, drew fire from the open cottage door. Legend has it that the rebel's mascot, an Irish wolfhound, went with Dwyer. I pulled into the town square in Baltinglass and found a pub to take a pint. In the square, I came across a memorial statue to Dwyer who laughs up at the sky. In the pub, I overheard the locals talking about the present use of the Glen of Imaal. It is a shooting range for the Irish army. Dwyer would have enjoyed the irony.

The Dwyer McCallister Cottage inspires me to defy the odds, to win, and to be honoured for that courage.

Mountstewart, near Newtonards, County Down is a majestic historic home with outstanding renowned gardens, on the banks of Strangford Lough. It has been home to important characters, one being Lady Londonderry, the designer of the gardens. She established an Art Club in her home to which leading politicians of the 1800s came. She assigned each character the name of an animal and the club members enjoyed their time playing roles in the animal's character. As well, in that same parlour where games were played, Lady Londonderry had a stained glass ship hung in her window so that she could permanently picture a sailing vessel on Strangford Lough. The stained glass replica is hung exactly at sea level. The kitchen at Mountstewart is actually called the "still room", not because it was silent, but because of what they brewed there. I also saw the "wake table" during my visit. The table was used uniquely to "lay out" the newly deceased one so that the rest of the family could celebrate the life of the dead one, with a copious flow of Irish whiskey. A wake table is not unique to Mountstewart, but it rarely is on display as it is here. Finally, our very entertaining guide recounted how Lord Castlereagh (a chancellor in the British Parliament and owner of Portstewart) called two very illustrious men to his office. This was the only time in recorded history that Lord Nelson and the Duke of Wellington came face to face. The two military geniuses each had an appointment with Castlereagh that day. They arrived together and it is said that Nelson turned to an aide and curtly asked, "Who is that man?"

So much for fame! Today is not the day for mundane or stilted behaviour. Cut loose and do something bizarre. You might even meet someone famous.

The wee town of Cushendun on the Antrim Coast was modeled after a Cornish town to make the town's most important wife feel loved and at home (she was from Cornwall).While we are on the topic of love, let's see how a simple Irish town can become a love nest. Cushendun was visited by two famous men, visits which made it a feature for our drive through today. In the town one can find Cave House, a secluded retreat. To reach Cave House, one must traverse an 18 meter rock tunnel. Inside the cave, two men courted at different times in history. If you guessed that St. Patrick was one, you'd be right. The dear saint stopped to pray at many places and Cave House was one where he prayed with such fervour that he wore two hollows in what is known as Gleonan Stone, on view at the cave. There he courted God's ear over and over until his knees indented the stone and God was caused to listen. Much later, in 1820, a more earthy love took over. The great poet, John Masefield, used Cave House to court his lover. Such a place would provide maximum privacy for the pair, to be sure.

Give yourself two luxuries today. Inspire yourself with a little private love nest, but don't forget the spiritual. Draw aside alone and court God's ear. Inspire Him by your faith in fervent prayer and your own soul will benefit. The answer will come.

To make the Body and the Spirit one
With all right things, till no thing live in vain
From morn to near, but in sweet unison
With every pulse of flesh and throb of brain
The soul in flawless essence high enthroned,
Against all outer vain attack invincibly bastioned.

Somehow the grace, the bloom of things has flown,
And of all men we are most wretched who
Must live each other's lives and not our own
For every pity's sake and then undo
All that we lived for – it was otherwise
When soul and body seemed to blend in mystic symphonies.

(Humanitad – Oscar Wilde)

Wilde's idealistic stretch is not an impossibility, nor an improbability despite his postulation that the sense of unity of Body and Spirit is lost when we act only out of pity for others and not from an innate interest to create a "flawless essence" in both parties. Oscar, I have that symphony playing in me because I have let God join my body, soul and spirit, in Christ.

In the time of the Crusades, almost any atrocity was committed under the guise of bringing Christ to the infidel. Other equally horrific examples have been perpetrated over history, almost none as hypocritical as what the "church" has done in Ireland. For centuries, the Catholics and Protestants have 'waged war'. In 1695, the Penal Laws existed stating that there was to be no other religion in Ireland other than the Church of Ireland (the Irish equivalent to the Church of England i.e. Anglicanism). The question comes to mind how one can legislate faith. In 1784, "enlightenment" came and the Penal Laws were abolished. In Lagg, an unincorporated area in Donegal, the first Catholic church came into being in 1784. Before that, Catholics had to meet outdoors at a Mass Stone in the dead of night for fear that the 'purer' followers of Oliver Cromwell's Puritans would purge them of their Catholic evil! An intriguing offshoot in Lagg resulted. The church graveyard has two segregated sections, the top tier for Catholics and the lower one for Protestants. Segregation was alive and well before its entrance into North America. Was there a hidden agenda in Lagg? Was it a hope that one section would rise first from the dead, or that the other lower one would not rise at all? Or, was it a fear that one dead body would contaminate the hopes for resurrection of the other if they shared the same dust? Or, was it political correctness?

Tolerance is our theme today. By all means, hold on to your doctrine, but , in so doing, don't trample that of others. In resurrection, God will judge the living and the dead. Your religious medal will not matter.

We mar our lordly strength in barren strife
With the world's legions led by clamourous care,
It never feels decay but gathers life
From the supreme air
We live beneath Time's wasting sovereignty,
It is a child of all Eternity

(Athanasia – Oscar Wilde)

Will you fight time today? You cannot, for it marches on inexorably towards Eternity. If you're anything like me, you are concerned by the constant tick of the clock to the next appointment, class or duty. Today, however, I set aside the watch or clock and let Time listen to itself. I will not listen to it; I will hear God's timepiece. That's sunshine and that does not mar my lordly strength.

...**d** own to the sea." Those are the lyrics of the nineteenth century song writer, Percy French. If you look at a topographical map, you can see how Slieves Marth, Muck and Donard sweep along the landscape like waves toward the Irish Sea. Two other vantage points offer a similar perspective – from the north, at a viewpoint at the Spelga Dam or from the peak of the 2800 foot Slieve Donard, you are given the inclination to repeat French's words. We hiked up Slieve Donard and on the way experienced a microcosm of Ireland's climate. Within two hours, it rained, snowed, hailed; then the sun warmed the late winter air such that we took off two layers of clothing. At the top, we looked across to the Silent Valley and I experienced the inspiration of width. The expanse before me was a thrill. After, we worked our way to Newcastle for lunch on the promenade. The guidebook referred to the beach at Newcastle as "sweeping sandy." I thought that the choice of words was appropriate considering my mountain top experience.

It's wise today to give a sweeping perspective to all facts in a situation. Perspective is everything.

> Some love too little, some too long
> Some sell and others buy
> Some do the deed with many tears
> And some without a sigh
> For each man kills the thing he loves
> Yet each man does not die.

(Ballad of Reading Gaol – Oscar Wilde)

Individual differences are what make for an interesting life trip. It would indeed be a shame if we all were from the same cookie cutter. Love and business and daily life and death need unique perspectives. Those perspectives must, however, be in the light of two facts – that each is part of the whole fabric and that each person's existence does not end at physical death.

Live for yourself today, but also in an acknowledgement that you touch others for eternity.

Glendalough - St Kevin monastic site-Wicklow

Glenveagh Castle - Sligo

One of the most sacred sites to the Irish is Tara, former "seat of the high kings of Ireland". The hill rises 300'above County Meath, and on it one can still hear the bangs and roars of the people as they engaged in the inauguration and acceptance of a new ruler. Corresponding to the Stone of Scone, the regal inauguration stone of Scotland, there is the "*La Fail*" on Tara, a stone which roared when the new king was crowned! Royal feasts and assemblies as well, took place at Tara. As I stood atop the hill with a wild Irish March gale snapping at my coat, I heard the roar too of the call to arms. I knew then that the Irish would always be strong. That spirit of rallying was to rise later in history on Tara when the patriot fighter for Irish independence, Daniel O'Connell came to Tara. He held a political rally on the hill when one million Irish attended to pledge allegiance to this "king" of the revolution. One reason for this congregational fighting spirit in the Irish is their desire to procreate; indeed, large families have always been a symbol of Irish power – more of us born, more of us to fight. This urge is displayed at Tara too, for in a nearby graveyard, St. Adamain's cross has carved into it a fertility symbol – a "*Sile na Gig*". It's as if the cross is telling the Irish to value their right and ability to bring on more little Irish to crown more leaders, to lead a great people.

In company there is strength and continuance and encouragement. Don't be a loner today. Congregate!

A hike through the Peatlands in County Tyrone inspired me. The Peatlands is a masterful development which educates the visitor about Ireland's famous peat bogs. One can either walk or ride a train which takes you over hundreds of acres of heather-covered peatlands. Interpretive guides and signage instruct the visitor on soil, plant life, and animal life. When I visited, it was late March, and just the trails were open. Remember, this is bog land, so it was mucky and wet. I was alone until I saw two ladies and two hounds approaching. The dogs were acting, well, dog-like. Back and forth, in and out, and in time, they bounded towards me. One woman shouted, "Youz'll not git eeate, youz'll jest git dorty." Spoken in the broadest of Irish brogue, the words had to be translated slowly. "They won't bite; they will only jump up on you." With a friendly wave and a "Cheerio!" we parted. I was left to contemplate the pitfalls of miscommunication and the excitement of understanding. I was inspired by the joy of the moment in two strangers sharing nature and camaraderie.

I was also inspired by a drive to be sure that what I say to people has a clear message, passed on with a happy smile and without rancour.

When I was in Dublin, a visit to Dublin Writers' Museum was de rigueur. In awe that in three hundred years Dublin could produce literary geniuses like Oscar Wilde, G B Shaw, James Joyce and Samuel Beckett, I entered 18 Parnell Square with reverence. Moving through the collection of these authors, among whom are numbered Swift, Sheridan and Yeats as well, I read books and letters and viewed portraits and personal items, like a rough table and chair complete with teapot, mug and oil lamp. I moved on to Merrion Square where Joyce lived (remembered now by a modernistic statue in the square) and then to Synge Street, where Shaw was born. The trip to Sandy Cove made the circuit complete. There, I climbed Joyce's Martello Tower, now a museum which opened in 1962, once a tower built to withstand Napoleon's attacks. The tower is the setting of the opening of Joyce's monumental novel *Ulysses*, which some say is the most influential novel of the 20th century.

To read any of these great men provides inspiration for the mind. That they could pen such images is meat for the mind and soul and a motivation to other writers.

Just off Main Street in Randalstown, Antrim is John Street, now relatively quiet and unused after New Street became the main road to Toome. So what, you say—doesn't smack of the stuff of hounds and leprechauns! Patience. John Street is known as Tay Lane and in that is our inspiration for today. The pronunciation for "Tea" in the Irish brogue is "tay." According to legend, the local ladies in this street spend their days leaning over the half-doors, "shannocking" and drinking tea. The remains of the pots of tea were thrown onto the street until it because tannin-stained—Tay Lane. There is another explanation. The Tay Fencibles were stationed in Randalstown in 1798 to quell disturbances and used the land to reach their quarters. This regiment from Scotland was sent into Northern Ireland as an unusual measure since the situation called for an outstanding armed presence in the region. The Tay's were rarely, if ever, sent overseas, seen particularly at home in Scotland as a "homeland security" force.

I stood in Tay Lane and sensed the skirl of pipes and the smell of tea leaves and I was inspired. The tea led me to believe it was beneficial to take life more easily—just to sit and drink a "cuppa" and chat. The Scottish pipes leading the soldiers then led me to appreciate when it is necessary to spring into action and defend the values I hold.

Lough Neagh, at three hundred eighty three square kilometers, is the largest freshwater lake in the UK, and was the center of life for ancient human civilizations in Ireland. There are three legends about this lough. The fact brings about today's inspiration. Where Lough Neagh now sits was once a simple well with charmed waters under the faeries' influence. An old woman, believed to be a witch, was the well's guardian: her role was to lock the gate of the iron surround to the well after any visitor came to fall under the faeries' realm. One fateful day, the old dame forgot to lock the gate and as she walked home, she turned at a rushing noise behind her. It was a "tsunami" emerging from the well. The lady ran terrified toward Toome where the townspeople captured her. In anger at her carelessness and in fear of the flood, they tossed her into the rushing torrent. She was like a sacrifice forfeited to save the land. At last, the well ceased its overflowing and a giant lake remained—Lough Neagh. Toome sits at the far north end of the lough and is today the centre of the eel-fishing industry. Its people seemed far less aggressive to me that those who sent the "witch" to her death. I would assume their approach to any chaos today would be far more rational and judicious.

Today, I will not allow hysteria to cloud my judgment. I will be as peaceful as the Lough Neagh which I viewed that early March morning.

The catamaran journey from Wales to Ireland was over, and we had a hotel to find in Wexford, just north of Rosslare. Entering the city, I must have made a wrong turn, because I found myself in a rather unsavoury residential area. I made several attempts to get out, but succeeded only in returning to the same intersection, where a car and two motorcyclists lingered in an Irish *ceilidh*. Trying to keep easy lines of communication open, I asked my Irish wife to ask for directions to the hotel. One cycle-rider fired up his machine, popped down the visor of his helmet, and waved me to follow. After a multitude of turns, there we were, at the hotel carpark, five minutes later. I offered him some money, but he waved me off, and roared into the gathering darkness. Now, that's going out of your way to help. Another scenario crossed my mind as I sat in the hotel. I had a British rental car, the Troubles still raged, hatred of anything English seethed, and the area in Wexford had been clearly Republican. The hotel manager commented to me that we could just have easily have been escorted to our deaths, down an alley to the Wexford Harbour. I trusted the goodness of a Samaritan Irishman, and was rewarded.

This young man inspired me to go the second mile to help someone in need, even at cost to myself. And he reminded me of the love and goodness of the Great Samaritan, Christ, who traveled to Earth to guide me to Heaven.

Whinlands
All year round the whin
Can show a blossom or two
But it's in full bloom now.
As if the small yoke stain

Hills oxidize gold
Above the smoulder of green shoot
And dross of dead thorns underfoot
The blossoms scald.

Gilt, jaggy, springy, frilled
This stunted, dry richness
Persists on hills, near stone ditches,
Over flintbed and battlefield.
(Seamus Heaney)

I'd just arrived in Ireland the night before and swung up the M1 to Dungannon tucked in the hills of Tyrone, west of Belfast. Now, as far as my eyes can rove – an uneven splattering of brilliant yellow on the hillsides outside the country house hotel on the outskirts of this seat of the O'Neill clan. It is March, after St Patrick's Day. These yellow splotches have been added to the fresh green palette. The Irish call this the "whin bush" which is responsible for producing this saffron covering. The very way the word is pronounced by my Irish family attracts me. Something about the throaty initial "wh", giving out a blowy, spirit-filled quality inspires me. There is something about whin's proximity to "win" that motivates me to a goal of success today even as the mists swirl in the early morning valley. Then, simply by lifting my gaze to view the expanse of whin bushes on those hills, I am completely uplifted. I say the flower's name aloud, "Whin bushes", and am thrilled. The gold, back-dropped by the emerald green, makes of God a Master Decorator and Creator. The whin's flower has no scent, but its beauty is sufficient to make my heart race. Step up with me on my morning walk, closer to the whin's blooms. The bush itself is straggly, coarse, scratchy and ugly (a bane to the sheep), but each bloom is an exquisite cup of yellow, a cup holding a golden promise for today.

Today is a "whin-whin" situation. Stay close to God's creation and you'll see and stay a winner.

The Battle of Drumbonagher on March 13, 1688 was the Irish equivalent of Custer's last stand, for the McKenna clan in County Monaghan. At that time, James II, England's Catholic king, was beginning his war with the Protestant Williamites (to come to a head at the Battle of the Boyne). James appointed a Catholic, John McKenna as Sheriff of Monaghan. The Protestants objected. In retaliation, the Jacobites took up positions in Monaghan City; the Williamites hunkered down at Glaslough. Foolishly, the Jacobites took the offensive and attacked Glaslough. They wasted all their ammunition in the assault. The Protestants then easily ran the retreating Irish down and captured McKenna. He was beheaded and his wife was presented with a gory gift – her husband's head on a pike. From then on, the McKennas were a powerless clan.

I can either be inspired or dismayed by the stand someone takes on an issue. Inspired if that stand is worthy and viable. Dismayed if it is foolishly conceived or stubbornly maintained in the face of defeat. I want inspiration from God to know when to fight and when to fold. God, grant me inspirational courage from You.

There are two places in Ireland famous for the hard stuff and they are not Guinness and Bushmills. One is Urris near the Gap of Mamore in Donegal which achieved top rating for its 'poteen' (whiskey) in the 1800s due to its medicinal qualities. And, Glashedy Island has the distinction of being a haven for the dark side of Ireland – the continuance of the illegal still. Glashedy won its fame because the distillers could hide from the Revenue Man who had the job of enforcing several prohibition laws. But, the makers of the "dram of the hard stuff" had a more intangible adversary: the faeries. Those involved in the trade were superstitious enough to follow the demands of the faeries or else their brew would supernaturally disappear or the Revenue Man conveniently heard where the still was located. To appease the faeries, to gain their loyalty and to belay any practical joke from the faeries was so necessary, for, you see, the faeries knew of every location of every still. To gain the faeries' support, the brewers believed they had to throw away the first glass taken from each brew. I can well imagine the superstitious Irishman reluctantly discarding that first glass, but he knew he must, or forfeit all.

This reminds me of prayer, only antithetically. God does not demand appeasement or sacrifice for his loyalty or for his forgiveness of our sins. He expects a simple acknowledgement of our weakness and he forgives. Don't forget to confess today and every day. I am glad I am not superstitious of the faeries.

To me the swans seemed normal. All across Ireland ponds and pools and lakes are graced by the white beauties. I thought that this small pond beside the parking lot on the outskirts of Buncrana would naturally have been home to swans on March 27. There was Lough Swilly to the west and the highway to the east. A little oasis of a park, a short trail and the pond were the habitat of these swans. As we watched, the pair paddled close to shore to take food from a tourist family from Wicklow. In true Irish fashion, the grandmother struck up a conversation. After general banter, she revealed her knowledge of a swan's habits. "Ya know, now, dese swans should not be here at all. Tis a quare bit early in the year." Evidently the swans' early arrival on this pond, in late March, was an omen to this superstitious Irish lady. The fact that a family of swans was on the water now foreboded a super hot summer, so she told me. To her, the swans' instinct allowed them to settle in to nest at an earlier date than they would normally choose. The nest was made, somewhere in the reeds, and the female's instinct kicked in when a small child ran too close to the site of the nest. Wings spread, the swan rose and her feet and wings slapped the water in attack mode. Fortunately the child escaped the vicious beak. Mother settled back on to the surface to resume her stately glide on a day when she should not have been there.

Our eternal Father has instincts too: to love, to protect. He senses by his deific powers when he must move in alongside us: when the heat is on.

Saint Patrick was on the return leg of his journey to Donegal (to Griann Aileach) after converting Eoghan (Son of Niall) to Christianity. On the way, he founded more churches and took time out to meditate on an island in Lough Derg , County Fermanagh. Once back on the road, he stopped at Maghera Keel for a drink from a well. This act of visitation rendered the well with holy waters, they say. Henceforth, any person with a toothache who drinks from Maghera's well receives instant pain relief. I don't know what the dentists in the area have to say about this – I was hesitant to ask!

What is your source of analgesic/balm/relief/release? Is it in a bottle, a caplet, a powder, a needle? I believe that you can find true and lasting solace in a spiritual act of faith, a faith not in Lenten sacrifice or in Holy Water, but in Christ. Take him today, the One God. Then call on him tomorrow and every day thereafter.

Coda
(Louis MacNeice)

Maybe we knew each other better
When the night was young and unrepeated
And the moon stood still over Jericho.

So much for the past; in the present
There are moments caught between heart-beats
When maybe we know each other better.

But what is that clinking in the darkness?
Maybe we shall know each other better
When the tunnels meet beneath the mountain.

(A coda is a musical term which indicates a repetition or a refrain)

Maybe we knew/ maybe we know/ maybe we will know. Just maybe. It is profitable to accept this philosophy – that when time stood still in a love scene, we were lost that when a nano-second clicked by, our hearts stopped in confusion, that when the tunneling is over, the bore holes of our hearts' desires may not meet. All uncertainty repeats itself. That frame of mind forces me to be inspired by a force beyond me. Once in a while, today, I have to look beyond my self-assertion and my independence. I fall back on God with whom there are no "maybes".

Many years ago, Leon Uris penned a story of the birth of the state of Israel which also was a modern day version of the Biblical tale of the Children of Israel exiting from their enslavement in Egypt. Uris' account of 600 Jewish holocaust survivors aboard the steaming and heat-wracked ship in the Mediterranean is a chilling antithesis of the real exodus of over one million men women and children who followed God and Moses in a plan for salvation and renewal of his people. In Sligo City on Market Square, one man was well-known, a certain Peter O'Connor. He was a successful entrepreneur in retail goods and the importation of lumber. O'Connor had been observing the declension and degradation of Irish peasants during the Famine. He took action on March 15, 1846 by advertising the departure of a ship for the New World (New York via Quebec). His was the first ship to export the Irish spirit and desire for freedom to a "promised land". In the next year alone, over 13,000 souls sailed from Sligo on O'Connor's ships. Peter O'Connor altruistically set in motion an exodus. Others followed him in transporting the Irish from famine and slavery; many were not so benevolent or caring. The horrors of the "coffin ships" are legendary.

Human ideals for an exodus can offer temporary hope and utopia. God's offer always provides the perfect outlet. Human offers can be well-meaning, but often result in heartache and worse conditions. I am sure that Peter O'Connor had nothing but the best intentions and future in mind for his Irish confreres. So does our God, but only His promised land is purely perfect. Trust not in man today for an outlet. God will inspire you with one.

In 1850, some children were playing in County Meath near the Hill of Tara when they came upon a treasure in a field. It was a brooch dating from the 8th century, white bronze inlaid with a varied display of precious stones. This piece of jewelry is now one of Ireland's most famous treasures—on display in the Museum of Natural History—the Tara Brooch. During its original times, women did not wear it as an adornment; Irish chieftains and warlords wore this pin proudly as a symbol of their power. Today Irish dancers wear a version of this pin on their kilts to display their Irish heritage. I cast my mind back about 1300 years ago and envisioned the warlord/king seated in Shane's Castle in the Great Hall. He has just returned from battle victorious. He will rule this area of Ireland and proudly bears the Tara Brooch on his sash. One day in the future he falls prey to another warlord more powerful than he and in the fight the brooch is torn from his chest to fall unseen in the Irish mud. A thousand years pass and the children rediscover this symbol of power and give Ireland a focal point for its cultural arts. It is a joy to watch an Irish dancer perform and, as she sports the Tara Brooch, we appreciate the dauntless spirit of the Irish to turn a symbol of military power into peace.

Today is a day to set aside conflict. Bury it and instead raise up the grace to forgive, love, dance and sing.

The Ice Age carved several valleys into the Donegal Highland. At the head of one valley on the R251 is an area known as the Poisoned Glen. So the story goes, this label originated in one of the plants which thrives there. A wildly poisonous sponge (it causes nausea and vomiting in grazing livestock) has taken over the land and inhibits the growth of other flora in this secluded valley by depriving them of water. As I stood among the hills, I could well imagine the local shepherds passing on the warning to others to steer clear of this glade, despite its pleasant outlook. The bad reputation cannot be entirely valid, however, since sponge grows in many other Donegal villages without causing farmers to eschew a presence in them. The Glen itself is an idyllic site which ancient ice had passed through and sculpted into Irish beauty. The white marble native to the area was used to build a beautiful, though now ruined church. The marble contains a mineral rich in manganese and so the white marble takes on a telling black crust when weathered by the wind and rain. The black and white contrast is dazzling.

As I pondered the unfounded rationale for the oxymoronic name for the valley (the very word "glen" connotes peaceful safety, not deathly poison) and as I marveled at the effects of the elements on the marble, I found the inspiration to be less judgmental, to base my decisions on fact, not on rumour, to let time and truth spell out the reality of the blacks and whites of life. Let's make that our common goal today.

esterday we met one of the legends of the Poisoned Glen. There are two more, one steeped in folklore and Irish mythology, and one more logical. Balor, king of Tory had a ravishingly beautiful daughter, but because of this own misplaced ethical standards, he imprisoned her in a tower so no man could look on her. As with any restriction, Balor's law served to create the opposite effect. Several assaults were made on the tower, until one young man broke in and made off with the girl. Balor of the Evil Eye (Balor Na Suile Neimhe) pursued him until he reached Glenriagh and murdered him with a giant stone. This rock lies at the glen's entrance and in the evil or poisoned eye of Balor. That's an imaginative account, but here is something a little more believable. Neimhe means poison in Gaelic, but Heaven is neamh (only one letter difference in Gaelic). The Irish named it Heavenly Glen for its loveliness (sloping hills with wild deer and silent snowy Slieve Snacht above it), but an English mapmaker mistranslated the Gaelic and doomed the glade forever. Again, these stories inspire me to rethink my views and judgments. With people as with places, names stick despite truth to the contrary. People often try to imprison beauty instead of allowing its innocence to shine.

It is what is inside that matters, not how someone else presents a person or an issue or even a place. I want to see past another's interpretation, prejudice or analysis. I want to see the real you, the real environment: the person and place that God sees. That's what inspires me to approach this day with candour, honesty, and innocence.

I wondered why the ad for Irish linen depicted a woman dressed in the white and then the cloth spread from her in an endless line across the Irish fields. I had to learn about the process of linen making to answer my query. It started with a simple field of flax, blooming blue to the horizon. It's harvested, and in true old-fashioned manner the stalks are dumped into dammed streams to rot for one to three weeks. This mess is then sent to a noisy skutching mill to break down the stalks into finer strands of material. The spinning mills now receive the product and the yarn is made; then the weavers take over to weave the yarn on hand looms into cloth material. The woven material in bleached in lye and laid out on the fields in long ribbons so the sun and dew can increase the strength (linen actually becomes stronger when wet). And finally we come to the beetling process. Yes, sorry, I had to keep you in suspense! Beetling is that last step before we can enjoy Irish linen. I visited the Wellbrook Beetling Mill on the banks of the Balinderry River near Cookstown, the last such mill in Northern Ireland. A sixteen foot water wheel attached to the side of the pristine red and white structure powered the hammers inside. These hammers pounded the rolls of linen until it acquired its inimitable sheen. And so, now you know. As I learned about linen, I was inspired by the rough and sometimes crude processes followed in order to produce such a fine and delicate cloth. It reminded me of the processes of life.

Today might be a noisy skutching for you, or an overwhelming deluge of work or a long impatient wait in sun or rain or a hammering in reprimand or reproof. Whatever you may encounter, there is an end in sight—these unhappy events will lead to a finished product that is a strong, valuable pure person, the individual God wants you to be.

A rainbow spread over the Glenelly Valley below the Sperrin Mountains. The afternoon squall had given way to brilliant sunshine although black clouds still hunched over Clogherny Top and Mullaghbogh. We were trekking the Central Sperrins Way. I was in search of some kind of gold. It looked so a propos that the rainbow should seem to dip to ground at Curraghinalt. I almost expected a wee leprechaun to appear sitting on a stone wall as I came over the rise. But, there actually was a real industrial gold mine there in the valley. Not the pans and stream which I had experienced at the Heritage Centre that morning when the kids had enjoyed the drama of searching for nuggets in the sluiceway. This mine was a significant find in the bedrock in the 1980s. The rainbow soon vanished and there was no little leprechaun with his black pot of gold. The reality of this mine was in my face with the images of noisey machinery, filth and danger. I continued my hike along the Glenelly River away from the gold mine to Mount Hamilton where I rested and read of Saint Patrick who spent nights praying in solitude along this very path I trod.

I pray too for inspiration that I might find the gold in my life, in the right places.

I can recall being awed by my sisters' studies to become top flight secretaries. One course they took in High School was Shorthand. You guessed it – the Irish had a hand in the creation of this skill of creating squiggles and swirls out of vocalized words. John Gregg was born in 1867 at Rockcorry, County Monaghan. At 10, he suffered an accident which damaged his hearing. This disability provided him with inspiration at 21 to create his famous shorthand system when he thought that his ideas were superior to the then used Pitman system. The Gregg Shorthand system caught on in England and America where Gregg lived and taught. (I still remember my sisters' texts with GREGG prominently printed on the cover.) The system was then adapted to the learning of foreign languages. In 1939, John Gregg returned to Rockcorry to pay tribute to the setback in life which had been the impetus to make him famous.

There are so many other tales of people who have manufactured gain out of loss, and benefit for others of personal deficit. They all inspire at least for the moment, hopefully over a longer term so that, when we hit the wall as Gregg did, we can make something out of the unintelligible swirls of life.

Off the N5, the guidebook took me to the Glenariff Horseshoe (no, the horseshoe is not one of Ireland's lucky charms!). This horseshoe-shaped drive is on the wild side, through 500 and 600 meter mountains (Benbulben, Truskmore, Benaiskin) and cliffs (Annacoona) which are home to a rare alpine flower, Cushion Pink. It is the site of Dairmit's and Grainne's grave and of a ruined national school (who would build a school here?). But, it is the source of Glencar Waterfall. From the mountain and cliffs, a series of streams and waterfalls begin to cascade toward Glencar Lake. One stream is called "The stream against the *Wid-Sruth in Aghaidh an Aird*, because with a southwest wind, spumes of water are blown back against the flow of the river. Later, as the waters continue to descend, the rivers converge to create the idyllic Glencar Waterfall and pool, immortalized in Yeats' poem, "The Stolen Child". From the wild and wind-blown comes the artful peace of "the pools among the rushes that scarce could bathe a star."

There are always two sides to life and to any story. Today, try to see impartially and to assess where action and words have originated. Sometimes the highly strung volatiles produce the wispy softs of life. Have you walked a mile in another's moccasins? Only then can you MAYBE understand or assess the situation. Jesus said, "Judge not so that you won't be judged."

That's a typical request for a souvenir from Ireland. The warm, wooly, yet formidable symbol of Ireland came from the Aran Islands at the mouth of Galway Bay. Consider this Irish conundrum, however: On the islands of Inis Mor, Inishmaan and Inisheer there are no sheep—so go figure! The three islands are rocky limestone ridges of the Atlantic. One wonders how and why so many dry stone walls (one hundred miles of them on Inis Mor) until one is told that the only way the inhabitants could rid the land of rocks to create tillable soil was to pile the stones into walls, which also serve as windbreaks. The Arans were a refuge for Christians, authors, (J M Synge spent summers there, and wrote "Riders to the Sea" about Inishmaan) and victims of marauders. The seas, stone forts and forbidding cliffs would have turned away most invaders of privacy. The most impressive fort is Dun Aengus (Aanghasa), with four concentric stone walls and set with razor-sharp, pointed stakes. In contrast to the Arans' austere image are the people, or so I at first believed. There is a traditional costume. Women wear a red flannel skirt and a crocheted shawl. Men don a sleeveless tweed jacket, a colourful knitted belt and the inevitable cap. I watched two men decked out this way, as they prepared to unload their *curragh* (a low rowboat of canvas pitched with tar.) Yet even there, I sensed an austerity, for here were simple people, sixteen hundred in all on the island, who led a basic lifestyle.

As I caught the ferry from Kilronan back to Galway, I was inspired by these three islands. It's good to be austere today.

Now, don't laugh. It is easy to lump the Irish in with the Brits for bland cuisine—I jest! The Irish create grand, basic meals. There's the hearty Irish stew, hardly bland the way I serve it up. Salmon, oysters, mussels—and don't forget the Guinness or whiskey. And you haven't tasted satisfaction until you've had a plate of "champ." I've tried my hand at it too, but could not succeed like my mother-in-law. Hers was the lightest and creamiest potatoes whipped and mounded on my plate, welled speckled with green onions (chives). She helped me form a well in the centre and in there went pure, rich Irish butter. You open it up, dripping the potatoes into the butter well each time. Delicious! When I visited Drombeg Stone Circle in Cork, I learned of another traditional Irish culinary form. At the circle is a communal cooking pit. The Stone Age worshippers evidently got hungry here. They would pour three hundred and forty liters of water into the pit and then throw in five hot stones. It works! One Irish TV chef tried it out and successfully cooked a joint of meat in this gigantic pot!

It's a meat and potatoes day today. Be inspired by plain fare—but stay away from a fast food joint!

To Ireland in the Coming Times

Know, that I would accounted be
True brother of a company
That sang, to sweeten Ireland's wrong,
Ballad and story, rand and song;
Nor be I any less of them,
Because the red-rose-border hem
Of her whose history began
Before God made the angelic clan,
Trails all about the written page.
When Time began to rant and rage
The measure of her flying feet
Made Ireland's heart begin to beat;
And Time made all his candles flare
To light a measure here or there;
And may the thoughts of Ireland brood
Upon a measured quietude.
(W.B. Yeats)

Yeats begins his ode to Ireland by joining with a "company" of those who voice a song, the goal of which is to right wrongs. His first stanza ends with a wish for a "measured quietude" so that he and his country may consider Ireland's future. It sounds simple, and it really is.

It is important today to set issues right, and to do this, we need to inspire ourselves to withdraw into a quiet place to brood positively about where the righted wrongs can take us. To whom is your ode?

Unlike many inner-city cathedrals in large European cities, Saint Patrick's Cathedral in Dublin has an open setting with spacious lawns spread from the street up to its refined spired architecture. Named after the venerable saint because he baptized converts at a well *in situ*, the first wooden structure became a stone church in 1192. The cathedral has a unique feature because of the arrival of persecuted French Huguenots (Protestants) in Dublin. The then-Dean held out a hand of friendship and allowed the Huguenots to use the Lady Chapel as a place of worship. (Today Saint Mary's, not Saint Pat's, is the Catholic place of worship.) St. Pat's, however, is best known as home and workplace of Jonathan Swift, Dean in 1713. I found "Swift's Corner" in the cathedral. Kept there are his death mask, his self-penned epitaph and two brass plates marking his grave and that of "Stella" Ester Johnson, a young friend who, by her association with the Dean, brought severe criticism on the Dean. (There was another Hester "friend" at the same time.) Other relatives brought Swift more pain—his *Gulliver's Travels* is a strong satire on Anglo-Irish connections. My last stop was to see a door in the Chapter House with a hole in it. In 1492 Lords Kildare and Ormonde ended a feud by shaking hands through this hole. A bizarre way to call a truce!

Offer a handshake to someone today. Cold hypocritical relationships inspire neither side.

Now, I could not write this book about Ireland without more than one entry on the great Saint of March 17th. "Ego Patricius"—I, Patrick. The latest tribute to St. Paddy bears this name. It is an ultra-modern center, costing over $15 million, and can be found in Downpatrick, right beside the Saint's grave just twenty two miles from Belfast. It is a bold approach to preserving the Saint's words and mission. In addition, it honours the impact of Irish missionaries in the European Dark Ages. Patrick spent his latter years in Ulster on his mission of salvation. This began in 444AD. He was granted a site for a cathedral in Armagh. It was not to his liking, so he asked for the hilltop where the old cathedral still stands. Tradition says that while he was measuring the site, a doe and fawn came by. Patrick denied his friends the kill and took the fawn on his shoulders to another hill where he laid it down and announced that God would receive glory in all Ireland. The new Cathedral in Armagh stands on that site. The old man, now well into his seventies, continued his work until his death at the chieftain's fort near Saul and where the Downpatrick cathedral stands. Some say that for several days a heavenly light shone on coffin. This holy man, who sang one hundred Psalms each night, slept on bare flagstones in a wet quilt and used a stone as a pillow, achieved his goal—to free the fold of Ireland from the worship of the sidhe (faery spirits).

Semper Fidelis—Forever Faithful is the motto of my school. I would like that to be said of me today. Hodie Fidelis— today, faithful.

Christ be with me, Christ within me
Christ behind me, Christ before me
Christ beside me, Christ to win me
Christ to comfort and restore me
Christ beneath me, Christ above me
Christ in quiet, Christ in danger
Christ in hearts of all that love me
Christ in mouth of friend and stranger

"I bind unto myself today the power of God to hold and lead, his eye to watch, his might to stay, his ear to hearken to my need, the wisdom of my God to teach, his hand to guide, his shield to ward, the word of God to give me speech, his heavenly host to be my guard." (Attributed to St. Patrick as his armour when he set out to rid Ireland of Paganism.).

Just near Cookstown, County Tyrone is an impressive 17th century manor home, or plantation mansion, Springhill House. It was built by "Good" Will Conyngham. When the Upton family agreed to marry off their daughter, Anne, to William in 1680, the marriage contract stipulated that he build "a convenient house of lime and stone, two stories high with necessary office houses". Springhill resulted. The stark white limestone main wing, split by long narrow paired windows and flanked by rounded wings with conical roofs lead one to gasp driving up the entry lane. The gardens are a treat. I wandered the herb garden and down a bowered drive into the walled beech and rhododendron woods. I then strolled under 1000 year old yews as I wended my way back to the house. Inside, I toured the impressive Costume Collection – a display of haute couture from 300 years ago. Finally, I heard of the gentle ghost, Olivia Lennox-Conyngham who touches the faces of sleepwalkers. The builder, Will, fought in the honourable 'Defence of Derry' in 1689. I viewed his blunderbuss hanging in the gunroom. When Anne Upton moved into Springhill, she initiated a legacy that stands today in all its beauty and intrigue.

What contract will I sign today? Large or small, business or personal, I want to leave a peaceful and gentle legacy which all in the future can look at and say, "An honest heritage, well fought for."

Most of you will have heard of Robert the Bruce ("Braveheart") who was inspired to return to conquer his native Scotland. The story goes that Bruce, in great depression over his condition of exile, holed up in a cave, was ready to give up, until he saw a spider labouriously making successive attempts to reach its goal. Each time the spider would spin its filament out, but fall back in defeat. At last the creature not only reached the other wall of the cave, but also motivated Bruce to make his successful counterattack. That cave is on Rathlin Island (Raghery) just off the coast of Northern Ireland, but only sixteen miles off Scotland's Mull of Kintyre. The island is a glorious ecosystem and a testament to perseverance. Why was Robert the Bruce there? Well, the Scots lay claim to Rathlin and this was an outpost to which Robert could flee. The island is now linked with Northern Ireland for the simple reason that there are no snakes on Rathlin. Since Ireland has no snakes, Rathlin, ergo, is Irish.

Our most motivating times are when we make logical deductions from visible evidence. Bruce made his decision based on a single observation. The Irish consider Rathlin Island theirs based on a potent piece of evidence (humorously so, I admit). Today's inspiration comes not from the complex, but from the most seemingly insignificant person or object in front of us.

All that remains of Dunseverick Castle is two walls on cliffsides surrounded by water on three fronts. The castle was once a seat of royal importance on the road from Tara. It was, however, leveled by the Scottish in revenge for an Irish uprising in 1642. Associated with Cuchulainn and the goddess Maeve, Duseverick holds one story of a sad nature. A Druid divination in Ulster foretold that Deirdre, a royal daughter, "would be the fairest, wed a kind, but because of her, death and ruin shall fall on Ulster." Deirdre grew up to be the fairest and was betrothed to marry Conor, an aged King. Deirdre, however, fell for the King's bodyguard, Naisi. Naisi took Deridre away but Conor pursued and, in the end, slew the interloper. When Conor took Deirdre back to Dunseverick, it is said that she never smiled again. When asked by the King what she hated most, Deidre replied, "Thou." She started up from the chariot and dashed her head against the rocks.

That is, to be sure, a sad tale of a sorrowing lady. It inspired me to be certain of goals for marriage. Not convenience, not power, not money. Not tradition, but for love. There was another "Lady of Sorrows," as people of the Catholic faith call her. Mary, the mother of Jesus, lived and bore her child for love. She is an inspiration to many and her children acted out of love for God.

Just three miles east of Portrush, one of Northern Ireland's favourite holiday destination, is Dunluce Castle. The first time I saw it was at dusk, from the east, and the setting sun was silhouetting the stark ruins. It gave the castle a striking, romantic power. Dunluce had been one of a series of forts (defence sites) along the Antrim Coast. These were built by the MacDonnell family to permit them to rule the region for four hundred years. The ruins of the current castle date from the 17th century, but Dunluce has stood in defence of Ireland since 500 AD. One anecdote from Dunluce provides an inspiration for today. Because the castle sits on rocky outcroppings, there was always the danger of the fallout of erosion. Evidently the kitchen stood on the outside edge of the cliff. Indeed, one night as the MacDonnells were partying, the food stopped coming. The rocks had fallen away during the banquet, and the cooks and kitchen had plunged into the sea. That brought the end to the banquet and available provisions! At that hour, the castle became vulnerable to attack.

It is clear that without food, any other resource people may have in defence from outside dangers becomes meaningless. Food, finely prepared, inspires me, but food at its basic level sustains me. Thank God today for food—and its cooks! (Mum, Dad, whoever...)

We parked our car at the eastern outskirts of Portstewart, in County Antrim. Even in March on a Sunday morning the waterfront strand was alive. The cafes served tea and scones to full houses: the bandstand had musical entertainment, but a score of children ran about inside. Outside, others built sand castles. A wedding was in progress in the chapel. Young men matched wits in arcades. We climbed to the west past the austere Dominican Convent, dating from the 1800s, which stood at the highest point. We then headed further west until we reached the dunes and beach which swept around the by as if they would reach across the laugh to Inishowen. We took a detour off the beach to visit the well at Tubber Patrick. It sits in the dunes and is reputed to have been then water source of Stone Age cave dwellers. There is another surreal water ritual site at Lissoonduff where concentric circles retained water for a worship service. The wind had ripped at our coats through the course of our promenade and, at the same time, had catapulted us through centuries—from the vibrant holiday present to the silent, vague prehistory.

All peoples of all ages, of all eras inspire me. I want to meet as many as I can today, as I walk the strand of life—a reveler, a child, a couple in love, a secluded religionist, someone from another culture.

(bonus!)

One of the most photographed sites in Ireland is a round, domed temple perched on the edge of a cliff on the Causeway Trail near Castlerock. Mussenden Temple is one intact building of Downhill Castle built in 1780 by the Bishop of Derry, who had an obsession with circular buildings. The Bishop, Fred Hervey was one of the most flamboyant men of the 18th century. He lavished a fortune on Downhill's grounds, planting two hundred thousand trees. The temple itself is modeled after the Tivoli Temple in Vesta, Italy, and even today it can be rented for private occasions: I could imagine a festive reception taking place indoors while the revelers drink in the inexhaustible beauty of the Antrim Coast. I could also picture the Bishop retiring to this "folly" to pray and study and meditate on the power of God in the land and sea and air of Ireland. I saw irony in the inscription from Lucretius, Latin poet, around the dome. "Tis pleasant, safely to behold from shore, the rolling ship and hear the tempest roar." Where once there was space between the temple and cliff edge, there is now barely one meter of land before the precipice begins.

This temple on the hill inspired me to think big, to live on the edge, and even to dream in a circle, not in "a box." I'm a Fred Hervey today.

Golfers at Salthill - Sligo

Heritage center - Ferricarig - Wexford

When one industry drives a town's economy, and when that industry declines, repercussions can be monumental. I thought I'd only see it once in my lifetime when the farm machinery industry died in my hometown in Ontario. But I saw the same scenario in my wife's home in Dungannon. The linen factory there employed most all of her family. It was known simply as Moygashel; in fact, a mini-town known as Moygashel grew up around the linen factory—homes and businesses built and patronized by the employees. Homes ranged in quality from villas for the executives to row-houses for labourers. That central lifeline closed because of a decline in demand for linen. Now the factory is silent, and only a portion has been restored as a factory outlet mall—the Linen Green. The shops have become a tourist attraction. Apart from that success, acres of brick buildings decay and collapse. What was once a key Irish industry has been replaced by electronics factories all across Ireland. In Dungannon, streets are now home to mainland European and Asian immigrant workers, bringing a new fabric to the community. I was inspired by the ingenuity, creativity and bounce-back restorative powers of Dungannon and of Ireland in general. What could have become a ghost-town (as happened to the downtown core of my home city) is now an award-winner for its beautification projects.

When life hands you a power-outage, get on the treadmill and make your own electricity.

In pagan Ireland, each tribe worshipped its own deities. Revered above all, were the gods and goddesses controlling the plough (Earth), the hazeltree (Mysteries) and the sun (Spirit), children of the goddess Danu. At one point, Danu's children were defeated by the Gaels and had to hide in *sidhe* (shee)-mounds under the earth. Chief among the deities was Bodb Dearg, eldest son of Dagda. Another son, Midir objected to Bodh's rule and became god of his own underworld, lord of death and resurrection. Midir kept three magical cows and a magical cauldron on an island where he took up opposition to his brother. In spite of such rivalries, the gods held sway over humans because of the immortality of the deities, a quality to strive for by underlings of the Earth. What humans did not know was that the children of Danu had to hold a Feast of Age in which they continually revived their immortal state. They ate magic pigs and drank the ale of a smithy so as to remain an Everlasting One for the next year!

I'm not certain if belief in such fallible beings is credible or wise. It was, no doubt, gratifying for these pagans to hold some crutch. Some would say that any religion is a crutch. I suppose that, in a way, it is; it is a way of getting through life. A crutch is a tangible object, and as such, cannot be dismissed as ludicrous. I've got a real, immortal God. I know I've leaned on him and he has supported me. No one can tell me that my religion or my God is a figment of my imagination.

Only the Scottish and the Irish can properly master the guttural, German-like "ch" / "gh" sounds. It must go far back in linguistic history, and a regal tale confirms my suspicion. It runs as follows: Daghda, chief of the tribe of Tara invited Corginn, leader of Connaught, and his wife to visit. Very Irish, I must say. Unfortunately, Aedh (Hugh) fell in love with Corginn's wife. In rage, Corginn killed Aedh , but was not himself killed in revenge by Daghda. Instead, Corginn was ordered to carry Aedh's body on his back all over Ireland (from Tara to Donegal is a long way!) until he found a burial stone exactly the size of Aedh's body. Yes, you guessed it. He found it in Donegal at Lough Foyle at Aileach. Corginn set up Hugh's burial and promptly passed away himself, wailing "ach, ach" at his pain and remorse. Wouldn't you too after lugging a dead body that far? As the Scottish today would say, "Ach, it's a sair fecht." Or, the Irish would moan, "Ach it's quare and sad." Aileach (from Corginn's last words) is the origin of the name Griann Aileach.

Pain is a burdensome woe – we all endure it, almost daily. What will be yours today? It surely won't be carrying a dead body all over Ireland. What it will be is what God allows you to bear. Strength to endure will come in equal measure to the pain. No one endured pain as Christ did. He is our supreme example.

Saint Patrick:

* Patron saint of Ireland, a.k.a Paddy Magee (but teamed with Saint Brigid)– can be present at a Finnegan wake.

* Taught the Irish to make whiskey (now, that's a tale!)

* Brought learning and Christianity to Ireland (though history tells us that there were devout Christians before his time)

* Taught the truth about the Trinity by picking a shamrock (even he could not find a four leaf clover!)

* Rid Ireland of snakes – though there were none before his time anyway!

* He has been deputized to judge all the Irish race on the "Last Day"

This man has become a legend, 'beyond the pale' (an Irish term itself signifying "outside the area of accepted control" – i.e. Dublin's environs. He is truly bigger than the sum of his parts. In fact, we have only two samples of his writings. Some pad their resumes; others let friends or relatives glorify them beyond the truth. Today is not the day to blow out of proportion your own skills. Let others do that.

Patrick is said to have performed several miracles. On his return to Ireland in 433, he was accosted by Dichu, a Druid chieftan, who raised his sword to Patrick to do him harm. The aggressor's arm turned rigid until he allowed Patrick to proceed to see his former master to pay his ransom. The news of the miracle preceded the saint to Mount Slemish where Patrick had been enslaved for seven years under Michu. Michu, in a fit of fear, set his mansion afire and leaped into the flames. Another miracle is worth noting. On Easter Sunday in the same year, Patrick arrived at the hill of Slane to light an Easter fire in defiance of Druid laws. The Druids tried to extinguish the fire repeatedly, but could not. The Druids then called a cloud of darkness over the hill. Patrick dispersed the cloud and when Arch Druid, Lochu, by Druidic power, flew into the air to block the sun, Patrick dashed him to pieces on a rock. Finally, as Patrick and his eight men made their way to Tara, the King of Dun Laoghaire stationed soldiers to ambush them. All they saw were eight deer and a fawn passing by. Four miracles in one day!

Are there miracles today? Certainly! Any time evil is defeated by good, God works a miracle. He can use you to be a miracle worker too. Let God give you faith today to perform a wonder.

Like Dolmens round my Childhood, the Old People
(John Montague)

Jamie MacCrystal sang to himself,
A broken song without tune, without words;
He tipped me a penny every pension day,
Fed kindly crusts to winter birds.
When he died, his cottage was robbed,
Mattress and money box searched.
Only the corpse they didn't disturb.

Maggie Owens was surrounded by animals,
A mongrel bitch and shivering pups,
Even in her bedroom a she-goat cried.
She was a well of gossip defiled,
Fanged chronicler of a whole countryside:
Reputed a witch, all I could find
Was her lonely need to deride.

Ancient Ireland, indeed! I was reared by her bedside,
The rune and the chant, evil eye and averted head,
Fomorian fierceness of family and local feud.
Gaunt figures of fear and of friendliness,
For years they trespassed on my dreams.
Until once, in a standing circle of stones,
I felt their shadows pass

Into that dark permanence of ancient forms.

Montague speaks of two of the elderly whom he recalled. He was able to see the true sides of those whom others misunderstood or abused. Those characters represent Ireland to Montague. They are the eternal standing stones (dolmens) marking the grave of a great one. A circle of, and for, religious respect. Those stones must one day fall and pass. The dark and superstitiously fearsome past must dissolve into "dark permanence."

There is always room for a new beginning. Tradition must, at times, be set aside and room must be made for the child-like and the old.

126

Glenelly geese are prized in Ireland. In the nineteenth century, these geese were a common sight, and a source of income for farmers in the Sperrins. The farmers would raise the geese for Christmas markets in Strabane, Draperstown, and Derry. They actually walked the birds to market along the roads and, in order to harden the feet of the geese, the farmer would walk each goose through a trough of melted tar and then through another of grit. The soles of the birds' feet were now ready for their last journey. One of the towns in Glenelly geese country is Goles. In July 1690, a freak storm hit and the torrents in the mountain streams merged into floodwaters in the last mile of the valley. Goles was engulfed and the flood swept to their deaths more than a hundred people and animals. I imagine that some of the animals were geese. The region never recovered, and today it stands barren and wild.

As I stood on top of a burren, I imagined the final journey of geese and men and women and children. I was inspired to make every minute the best and most profitable it can be, for I never know when I will be "walked through the trough," unknowingly prepared for a higher calling. Or a cataclysm may engulf me in a second, without prior notice. I am ready, for the Holy Spirit "inspired" me to become a Child of God.

Recently two works by Jack Butler Yeats, William's brother, went on auction in Toronto, touted to fetch about $150,000 each. They had been owned by the Delay family of Victoria, B.C. and Toronto. In 1923, Alfred Delay, a top dean and professor at University of Toronto, was in Ireland recruiting students. He met W.B., and then J.B. Yeats, and bought The Boat Builder (in Galway) and The Mail Car, Early Morning (in Ballina, Mayo). From 1923 to 1955, the paintings moved from Toronto to Ottawa to rural Ontario. The family farm was sold off and the next generation let the paintings slip from memory until an American family member reminded them of their existence. The great nephew and his dad spent a weekend searching the farmhouse for the two masterpieces and brought them to be with their mother in Toronto. In the end, they have been put up for sale. At the time of writing, it was estimated that they would be going home to Ireland. With the booming Irish economy, it seems that some rich Irish connoisseur who reveres Yeats (as many do) will pay top dollar to bring back the paintings across the Atlantic.

To steal from Jack's brother's poem, "The Second Coming," these works have spent a long time "slouching towards" home. I am inspired by the recognition that everything and everyone ultimately finds its rightful place. I will be home someday.

You'd hardly connect this name with one of Ireland's famous towns, Armagh, unless you had a passing knowledge of Gaelic. *Ard Macha* (Hill of Macha) is Romanized as Armagh. Macha was Ulster's most influential woman. Legend says she came as a faery bride to a wealthy Ulster farmer/ widower. She lived with him, but she also forbade that her name be spoken by mortals. When, however, she was mentioned and forced to race horses while nine months pregnant, she placed a curse on all the people of Ulster, even Queen Maeve, because she sacrificed her dignity in giving birth to twins in public. She was also Queen *Macha* and her bare-breasted pagan statue sits in a crypt in Armagh Cathedral. St. Patrick's statue stands opposite, frowning at *Macha*. As for *Emain*, the word refers to *Macha's* neck brooch. The queen marked out the ritual site of Navan Fort, just six miles from Armagh, with the point of the brooch. Armagh has been both seat of kings and site of holy pilgrimage in pagan and more modern times. It is now a vibrant business and tourist town, famous as well because of Jonathan Swift and his story of Lilliput.

**   *Macha* and the city of her namesake inspire me to stand out above the crowd and to stand tall, even in disgrace and humiliation.**

Novelist Willam Carleton nicknamed the jail in Monaghan City this way in his book *The Fair of Emyvale*. Short was the prison-governor in town and was a little less than upright. He would release thieves and pick-pockets from the jail on fair days in Monaghan and surrounding towns such as Emyvale. On these occasions the rich farmers came to town to ply their wares and crops; Short knew that the light fingered workers would have a heyday amid the bustle of the fair. When the inmates all came safely back to cell, checking back into their "hotel suites," Short insisted that they provide him with a percentage of their take that day. History says that both Short and the prisoners did well for themselves, but the history I read does not tell if Governor Short ever met justice.

Does graft and extortion inspire or repel you? Despite the clever and devious intelligence of evil men, most of us will be inspired today by clean, honest men and women, a breed all too rare in our society.

Excerpt from: A Welcoming Party
(John Montague)

.... Our parochial band of innocence
Was all we had to give.

To be always at the periphery of incident
Gave my childhood its Irish dimension;
Yet doves of mercy as, doves of air,
Can falter here as anywhere.

That long dead Sunday in Armagh
I learned one meaning of total war
And went home to my Christian school
To kick a football through the air.

Montague's reaction to the events and close of World War Two, as concentration camps were freed, was "How was that possible?" His Ireland was at the periphery, supposedly isolated from the horrors. Despite his Christian school education , and childhood, he was not immune to war, nor was his country.

It is valuable to educate ourselves beyond our four walls. A "parochial brand of innocence" does no honour to self or country.

One feature which marks out British and European culture is the use of rail systems for daily travel. Another is the ubiquitous pay toilet. Both of these cultural norms provide our inspiration for today. The Ulster Railway was a key transportation network in the late 1800s and early 1900s. Sadly, few trains run in Ireland today compared to the Irons Horses' heyday. Indeed the branch line of the Ulster Railway to Monaghan closed down in 1957. Before that time, there was a stationmaster in the 1920s in the old railway station on North Road who was sent a letter of reprimand. The scolding came for not making "financial returns" from the public toilets in the station. Here is his reply to his superior: "The inhabitants of Monaghan have been inflicted by a severe outbreak of constipation." That can be none other than the Irish wit!

Sometimes a "drying up" (mental or spiritual constipation) does occur in our lives due to lack of demand, a change in goals, or a physical or mental depletion. I will not shut down or become blocked today. My ideas and creativity flow.

"Cu" means hound in Gaelic and "*chulain*" can be anglicized as "Cullen." So, this is a story of the hound of Cullen—well, actually, two hounds. The human Cuchulainn was the son of faery maiden, Dectera. She offered her newborn son as a gift to Ulster after she had lured warriors to her palace. They returned to King Conor's place with the boy, Setanta. There he was raised. One day, the court was invited to Cullen's home for a feast. Setanta told Conor he would come later, but by the time even the main body arrived for Cullen's merry-making, it was dusk. Cullen barred the gates upon their entry, and set out his fierce mastiff to guard his lovely mansion (Cullen feared a marauding army). In the hilarity of the moment, they forgot about Setanta's impending arrival. Outside in the blackness, a baying hound and then the howls of combat were heard by the partiers. They rushed out to find the lad, Setanta standing over the dead hound, its throat torn open and its head dashed against the stone gateposts. Cullen was grief-stricken, but Setanta promised him that if the boy was given the hound's pup, a shield, and a spear, he would become Cuchulainn and guard the house. The pledge was kept and Setanta was called Cuchulainn until he died.

The thought of a brave pet defending the master to the death inspires me to offer my dog or my closest friend an extra special treat. And a supportive and courageous child, steadily facing an opponent, motivates me to appreciate my children's love.

Ireland's fabled prehistoric geological events have resulted in an Irish industry that has placed it foremost in quality and demand. Millions of years ago, when eruptions and pressure formed Ireland's rock, large amounts of silicon, sand and litharge were deposited. They are now extracted, fired up to 1400 degrees Celsius, polished, carved and chiseled into different kinds of fine crystal—Waterford, Donegal, Galway and Tyrone. Most have heard of the first three, but it is the last which I love the most—not just for sentimental reasons, but for its style. The Tyrone Crystal Factory sits between Dungannon and Coalisland (now sadly closed). It was modern and attractive. Bus tours stopped regularly to allow visitors to view the artists at work, sample Irish fare in the café and, naturally, buy the exquisite pieces. Tyrone Crystal was the first crystal of Ireland. In 1771 Father Austin Eustace began a crude factory. Today, Tyrone Crystal is an art form which employs many. As I sit and write, a notepad and pen holder of Tyrone Crystal graces my desk.

From the earth to the office involved many steps until I admire the smooth elegance of a little piece of Ireland in my home. I also have an exquisite set of Tyrone crystal wine goblets. Whenever I lift a glass at a formal dinner, I am transported back to Ireland. From the muddy earth to the festive board involved a linkage of tasks until I am able to toast my friends and my inspiration, Ireland. My inspiration is not clouded by the past—it is crystal clear.

Malin Head, on Inishowen, is wild and forsaken. A lighthouse marks the path into the North Channel from the Atlantic. I have already commented on my pilgrimage along the coast at Bamba's Crown. There's more. As I stood looking out to sea, I spotted a speck bobbing on the 20 foot high rollers. It took 30 minutes before I realized that the object was a fishing trawler making its way around the head, perhaps to enter Lough Swilly for port. I could not even hear its engine above the sea as, at last, it was even with my vantage point. That progress had been slow and difficult as the boat fought the tide and winds. I became bored with its battle and looked closer in to shore. A head caught my attention. It was a sea creature, a lonely seal which was scooping up lunch which had been pushed too close to shore. The seal's progress was swift and certain. At one moment I saw its snout at 10 o'clock; it disappeared below the surface and reappeared hundreds of meters further on in just a few minutes. It ran with the tide and enjoyed its environment. The seal was surrounded by the same dangers as the trawler (rocks and oceans), but it seemed as if it was lolling about in a swimming pool. It basked in the sunlight and fed on its surroundings.

We have the choice of being a seal or a boat. Do we fight our circumstances with our own might and make slow progress, or do we make advances by using the provisions which God gives and which are all around us.

The Travail of Passion
(W. B. Yeats)

When the flaming lute-thronged angelic door is wide;
When an immortal passion breathes in mortal clay;
Our hearts endure the scourge, the plaited thorns, the way
Crowded with bitter faces, the wounds in palm and side,
The vinegar heavy sponge, the flowers by Kedron stream;
We will bend down and loosen our hair over you,
That it may drop faint perfume, and be heavy with dew,
Lilies of death-pale hope, roses of passionate dream.

The master's poem evokes timely images for Easter – the Passion as it is called (as Mel Gibson has so forcefully reminded us in the movie) in some circles. Let's be passionate about Death, Burial, Resurrection – a cycle that Christ perfected, but which we can experience each day. One author spoke of "little deaths" (Killing Mr. Griffin – Lois Duncan) we endure each day; the character was inspired by Hamlet's Ophelia and her "nonny, nonny". You may go through these, "daily rejections of our well meant offerings that render the soul lifeless." The "little deaths", however, are followed by little burials and little resurrections"

Life is more than about death. It's about living in and beside God.

Road rage brings on a variety of responses, one of which is the universally known "finger salute," It's a crass way of reacting to another driver's insult, budging, or impediment to our own progress. Ah, but that's not my topic for today—I just wanted your attention! Another gesture surprised me and has never ceased to amaze me. I can be driving down an Irish county lane and there is a farmer ploughing or working outside his barn. With a wide smile, often toothless, he waves a grand hello and tips his cap. Two strangers passing, but connected. I have been walking along a similar Irish lane and a car approaches. The driver slows and waves, then calls out a joyful "how are you?" from his window. I have never encountered such a willingness to engage in another's life for a fleeting moment. What causes our world today to be so cold and distant? Yes, I believe that there is a great deal of danger and we need to be circumspect as to whom we speak with. I do believe, however, that we have taken our discretion too far. There is nothing which need deter us from friendliness to others.

I encourage you today to smile and wave to a total stranger. He or she may think you're 'daft', as the Irish would say, but most will appreciate such a gesture. Try it—don't stop till you get a wave and hello back! It will inspire you.

Standing tall against the Sligo horizon is Classiebawn Castle near Mullaghmore. Later to become Prime Minister of Britain, Viscount Palmerston (1784-1865) began this castle for a residence for his tuberculosis stricken daughter. He was told that the fresh air of Sligo would promote a cure. Palmerston was a benevolent man to more than his family; he supported both Catholic and Protestant schools. He died before the castle was complete and it was finally finished in 1874. Ironically, the home passed through marriage to Louis, Earl Mountbatten murdered by the IRA in a naval explosion. So much for religious tolerance practiced by Palmerston! As I viewed the profile of the castle in my rear view mirror and headed out to Mullaghmore Head, I was in a pensive mood. What causes one person to be caring and tolerant and loving and another to be evil, cold and murderous? Where is the fine line which the soul can cross? I thought of this as I walked the headland and peered out at Inishmurray Island straight out west to North America, nothing in between. I found the answer in that vast expanse.

God's creation opens mind and hearts. The evil live dim closed lives in dingy quarters to plot attacks and explosions. Sit by open water today, if you can, and drink in God's love. You too will then become tolerant and kind and insightful of others.

> I will arise and go now, go to Innisfree,
> And a small cabin build there of clay and wattles made:
> Nine bean-rows will I have there, a hive for the honey bee
> And live alone in the bee-loud glade.

So begins Yeats' virtuoso poem, "The Lake Isle of Innisfree". Yeats wrote about the material that his father had read to him from William Henry Thoreau's *Walden* (the chapter on the Bean Field). At Walden Pond, Thoreau learned that the solution to man's problem is via peaceful existence, not the consumer treadmill. Thoreau's imagery remained with the boy and he set in motion plans to live on a cottage on the island. The shoreline point is difficult to find and the island itself is hardly an idyllic looking site. It is a small treed knoll some 500 meters offshore in Lough Gill. The views from the island would hardly be spectacular when compared with the gems of the world. He might have seen Cloghereevagh House set on the opposite shore from where I stood. It is now a girls' school. The only other striking aspect on the horizon is the profile of the Sleeping Giant in the Dartry Mountains. Yeats though, could see the inner strength of this haven. That power was in the simplicity of the "small cabin", thatched and whitewashed no doubt. His sustenance was equally basic: beans and honey, supplemented for sure by the ever present Irish potato and bread. Yeats' company was hardly raucous – the little bees would be the loudest influence on his ears.

Yeats teaches us to withdraw, at least temporarily, and appreciate our simple God. Yes, His complexity makes Him simple. He is so far above us that the only avenue to Him is by simple faith. Arise and go to 'Innisfree' today. Innisfree to me is Christ. He is better sustenance and solitudinous company.

The Jewish people in the times of the patriarchs centered their life around a small rectangular box made of acacia wood and overlaid with gold. Inside were several items to remind them of their past and to center their focus on their God. This Ark of the Covenant was housed in a sacred place where only God's Highest representative could enter, only once per year. It was the very presence of God. It seems the Irish have a similar box called the Misach. This ornate "ark" holds a holy book, evidently a calendar of the lives of the saints. Outside of its religious significance, and parallel to the reason for the existence of the Israeli ark, the Misach was carried into battle as an icon of protection. Many an Irish warlord appealed to the saints' protection by toting the Misach along with his soldiers. Whether it was as successful as that of God's people (sometimes the Ark of the Covenant brought victory; other times it did not), we will never know;

...however, both boxes underscore a need for a focus or an icon in our lives to inspire us. And, I mean a physical, tangible one. Whether we have a box, a person, a book, a photo or whatever is immaterial. Place an image in front of you today. Do not, please, worship that image, but use it to recall and ponder your spiritual past and existence. God used a box for his ancient people; the Irish used a box to dedicate themselves. Work within your box today. God is inside it.

Novelettes III

The Gardener

(Louis MacNeice)

He was not ale to read or write,
He did odd jobs on gentlemen's places
Cutting the hedge or hoeing the drive
With the smile of a saint,
With the pride of a feudal chief,
For he was not quite all there....

He would talk to amuse the children,
He would talk to himself or the cat
Or the robin waiting for worms
Perched on the handle of the spade;
Would remember snatches of verse
From the elementary school
About a bee and a wasp
Or the cat by the barn door spinning;
And would talk about himself forever –
And you would never find his like –
Always in the third person;
And would level his stick like a gun
(With a glint in his eye)
Saying 'Now I'm a Frenchman'-
He was not quite right in the head.

**MacNeice's image of the gardener puts a little smile on
our faces, but it is not mocking or discriminatory. This gentle
fellow truly enjoys life.**

**If you meet a mentally challenged person today, savour life
in the simple way that he or she often does (or could live simply,
if someone did not come down too hard on him or her). Life is
simple, for it's not quite all there.**

The same Bishop McNally who inspired the building of Saint McCartan's Cathedral in 1858n in Monaghan set in motion in the same year another Monaghan institution, Saint Louis Convent and Saint Louis Secondary School. McNally knew that several Irish girls were at school, in France under the care of the Saint Louis Order of Sisters. Reports of the educational endeavours and successes of the girls reached McNally, so he invited three sisters to move to Ireland to establish a similar school. First, classes were given in a hotel, then in a home on Mill Street. Finally, once so many girls had signed up for this fine Catholic education, funds were provided to purchase an old brewery from an Italian transportation manufacturer, Charles Bianconi. The building was converted from suds and spirit production to mind and spirit mentorship. For over one hundred years it was one of Ireland's finest schools. The Sisters were invited to other Irish towns to replicate the success, and they did carry on.

To be educated by God-inspired people is a blessing and a motivating experience. I've been on both ends of the educational paddle, we'll call it, and I can attest to the inspiration of learning from a godly sister, or brother or lay person: French or Irish or?

It always amazes North Americans that tourist sites are so old in Europe and, vice versa, many Europeans are not impressed by what North Americans call history – it's just too recent for them. I was impressed by Sligo's medieval Dominican Friary. It was founded in 1252/3 by Maurice Fitzgerald, then Chief Justice of Ireland. The Dominican monks fulfilled their vows there until 1642. Over the almost four hundred years, three of the eight lancet windows were blocked off by a tower built in the 15th century and then by a memorial in the seventeenth century. It survived a fire in 1414 and a siege in the 1500s. The day of our vist, we admired the high altar and the medieval grave monuments still with their original beauty. We could feel the reverential qualities of the friary as we pictured monks strolling the cloister in meditation. Or we heard chanting in the choir and praying before the altar. We envisioned them serving in the sacristy. It was truly sacred ground. Were there impure friars and was there evil in the church? To be sure! But all that came to a vicious end when, in the name of God, Sir Frederick Hamilton and his Puritan soldiers sealed up the friary and massacred all the monks. They left the monastery in smoldering ruins. Yes, in the name of God in their "sacred grand" perspective. Is that hypocrisy? I can believe there were believing priests in the order at that time who were pure souls. Legend has it that the silver bell of the friary was thrown into nearby Lough Gill and at times it rings out for the pure in heart to hear. One or two Dominican friars hear that bell, I am certain. Does any Puritan soldier hear it? Maybe?

Atrocities have been committed in the name of God and "on the horns of the sacred altar." We must be so careful that what we label as sacred may be in fact sacrilegious. Christ's words are succinct, "Judge not that you be not judged."

Down by the salley gardens my love and I did meet;
She passed the salley gardens with little snow-white feet.
She bid me take love easy, as the leaves grow on the tree;
But I, being young and foolish, with her would not agree.

In a field by the river my love and I did stand,
And on my leaning shoulder she laid her snow-white hand.
She bid me take life easy, as the grass grows on the weirs;
But I was young and foolish, and now am full of tears.
(W. B. Yeats)

This wonderful country love poem is Yeats' way of saying, "Stop and smell the roses." But, it says more. It deals with the consequences of not taking life easy. A stubborn stance against this philosophy of Yeats and of others results in separation, conflict and grief. Today, I will enjoy the salley (willow) gardens and the snow-white innocence of youth and the advice of others who love me. Speed is not worth it. Slow down and be a leaf or a blade of grass today. "God loves you and I love you; and that's the way it should be."

Ireland has its famous author, Maeve Binchy; it also has its famous queen Queen Maeve, Queen of Connaught. Her grave is atop Knocknarea Mountain in Sligo. The mountain itself is impressive enough, a massive flat topped dome, but to catch sight of Maeve's cairn on the summit from far away is even more striking. First, Maeve's life – she was the warrior queen in the *Taoin*, Ireland's legend of *Cuchulainn*, the hound who beat Maeve back from Ulster. On a higher plane, Maeve was the female goddess of war and sexuality. Her task was to promote the art of war and the continuation of the Irish race through reproduction. Maeve's death (despite being a deity) is bizarre – she was killed by a lump of cheese shot from a slingshot by her vengeful nephew. Her last resting place is this huge passage tomb on Knocknarea dating back to 3000 B.C. It is 55 meters in diameter, 10 meters high. Her alignment in death with the sun and stars north and south is marked by two large stones. Nearby are several oval hut sites containing arrowheads, axes and pottery from about 3300 B.C. The climb to this hilltop is steep but exhilarating.

That feeling reminded me of another hill and another divinity, a real god. Our King, recalled today, glorified war in his pitched battle with Satan and by that battle, he preserved the eternal species. His death was not bizarre at all, but a criminal's crucifixion. By that death, he aligned creation with God. He has left behind a heritage of tools to fight sin. Relish your king today.

We just had to find the Killevy Straining Stones in the grave yard. It was difficult enough to find the cemetery itself along the road to Innisfree. Twice we did three point turns on the Irish lane until at last we pulled close to the stone wall and onto the grassed knoll. Even then, we were in danger of being hit by a passing farm wagon. In any case, we took the risk to search for the seven egg-shaped stones surrounding one rectangular stone with seven threads or strings tied from the central stone to the others. If one takes one string and replaces it with another, one takes away with him/her an infallible cure for aches, pains and strains. Before departure, we must lift each stone in turn and repeat a prayer as it is turned. It is a uniquely Irish blend of the Christian and the pagan. I did not try the cure. In fact, we did not even find the stones. We were called away by something much more mundane – two farmers were at an impasse and called us to move our car so that they could continue on their jovial way. The images in the tour guidebook were enough for me. I imagined myself pulling one string and replacing it with my own. Then feeling the seven rocks warm on my hands in the late spring sunshine, I turned them in my mind.

I actually use a different method of curing my ills and straining out my aches and ills today. I place them on the Rock, Christ and replace them with His warmth. He is the perfect Rock of Ages. He takes all my strains and I try to see everyone with a minimum of criticism and hypocrisy. I don't 'strain out the gnat and swallow the camel' as the Pharisees did.

The first line from another of Yeats' poems reveals one more of his enchantments. The Wynne family owned most of Lough Gill's land and planted most of its trees, indigenous and transplanted from afar. The family made other prolific additions to the landscape: islands, moss and rock houses, a windmill. The trees, however, were their crowning contribution, so much so that the fine view of the lake from the house itself is now blocked and the house is not visible from any trail in the woods. One of the trees imported by the Wynnes was the Strawberry Tree, with only 36 known species in Hazelwood. It is a protected species and must also survive the winds and cold of Ireland, away from its native South of France. The Latin name is "unedo", 'I eat only one' because its fruit resembles a strawberry, but is virtually unpalatable. Yeats says in his poem that he went to the wood because "a fire was in his head". He picked a berry (one of the "strawberries") and with it on a line, caught a trout.

These three images from Yeats' Hazelwood remind me of the alluring and tempting nature of misplaced, though honourable goals or mysteries. Like Adam and Eve, we can be drawn into activities or habits which hook us, block us or deceive us. Only a look at the real "tree" of Calvary can unmask the blindness of sin. Deception is not inspiration.

I was staying at the luxury country house hotel near Castlebaldwin (the actual castle is just a ruins but a modern town thrives on the N4 north to Sligo). From the hotel, I could walk to an enormous portal tomb or dolmen, Labby Rock erected sometime around 3000 BC. The dolmen is massive with its capstone weighing in at 60 tons. It got its name from "*leaba*" Gaelic for "bed" since Diarmit and Grainne slept here while running from Fionn, to whom Grainne had been promised. Its history is another story. Inside/below is a burial chamber over which the limestone cap rests on four stones. Cremated remains were taken out last century. But whose? Locals have concocted a tale that in the dolmen was buried Nuada of the Silver Arm, a king of the gods killed in the battle of Moytirra by Balor of the Evil Eye. That fictional imagery sets my heart racing. As I stood in front of Labby Rock, I pictured and heard swords sweeping and clashing. I saw Nuada mourned and laid to rest here after the battle and as a result of the Herculean effort by his mourners to erect this rock memorial.

Then I read of a different true historical account of a burial, though denigrated by past and present experts and officials. I believe in that grave site far away outside Jerusalem. It is not nearly as large as Labby, just a small cave with a sliding or rolling cover stone. It was the property of a rich man and the tomb for just three days of a true king, Jesus. Jesus was not cremated, but raised by the power of God. Upon His resurrection the Christian faith is built. Because He lives again, I can face tomorrow and the Evil Eyed One has no power. Inspire yourself with that.

Who says the Irish can't spin a good yarn! Balor of the Evil Eye was finally killed too in the battle of Moytirra, in its closing stages. His own grandson, Lugh, who was fighting on the other side, fired a rock from his slingshot through Balor's single monstrous eye. That eye had brought instant death to many with one glance in earlier times. Now, the light was extinguished. But, the horrific eye hole opened again and its existent power burned a great hole in the ground. The hole filled with water and is now Lough Nasool (Lake of the Eye), just north of Lough Arrow. But, the incredible yarn is not over. Because of its dire origin, locals live in fear and awe of the lake, for the water of the lake disappears every 100 years! Yes, it did in 1833 and in 1933. Somehow the timing went cock-eyed, as the vanishing happened again in 1965 and 1985. Scientists have explained the phenomenon as complex hydrology or climate variations. Whatever! It's an edge-of –the –seat tale, to be sure. Begorrah!

I prefer to read equally awe-inspiring accounts of the miracles of the Son of God. He spoke of moving mountains. He could have. He walked on water. He calmed tempests at a word. He dried up a tree instantaneously with a curse. Those are just as earth shattering as the story of Lough Nasool, but they are 100% believable to fundamental Christians. If God can perform such miracles, that belief inspires us to have faith in similar occurrences in modern times. Join that inspiration today.

Trevane Bay in Donegal is a small community, but it has assisted "Young Ireland" rebels, just like many towns and villages which have been home to repression and persecution of Ireland's racial or religious groups. In 1848, during the Great Famine in which millions of Irish died (despite the fact that there was indeed plenty of food to go around), one young man, Thomas D'Arcy Magee from County Louth joined in the "Young Ireland Uprising". In festered anger, locally by the horrific conditions, largely fostered by the British, and internationally because of the other revolutions in Europe, Magee and hundreds of others were pushing for justice. They were brutally quashed and Magee escaped the court, but fled to Trevane Bay where townspeople sheltered him as "Father John". With a 300 pound bounty on his head, Magee had to leave Ireland. Off Trevane Bay lay the "Shamrock" where Magee was spirited one night. He joined other refugees and made his way to Philadelphia and on to Canada. Thomas D'Arcy Magee became a noted politician in Canada, one of Canada's Confederation Fathers and a Minister of Agriculture. He labeled his involvement in the insurrection as "the folly of youth" and paid with his life for a dimmer view of rebellion in later life. He was shot to death in 1868 by Fenians in Ottawa, a group he once supported, but now opposed. Magee is an example of a man who takes his views strongly, is open to persecution and is adaptable over time.

Such a man may inspire me to act similarly. Jesus Christ was of the same ilk. He took up a heavenly cause against the injustice of sin, paid with his life for a bounty of 30 pieces of silver. But, praise God, he never regretted his involvement.

(bonus!)

In the heart of Belfast is one of its landmarks, the Albert Memorial Clock, rising some fifty meters into the Belfast skyline. It has been lovingly restored to its Victorian original condition and looks splendid. Along with decorations like crowned lions (very British), and carved floral designs, it naturally sports a statue of Prince Albert, consort to Queen Victoria (she's just a wee ways off at City Hall right now!) The clock was erected in 1865 to honour Albert, who meant so much to Victoria, as well as to memorialize Albert's personal penchant for punctuality. Despite all this attention to exactness of time, fate caught up with the clock to make it imperfect in another way. The land on which the clock was built was reclaimed from the Lagan River which flows through Belfast. Engineers did not account for land subsidence and hence the clock leans one and a quarter meters off the vertical. Imagine, Belfast vying with Pisa for having a leaning tower! I took a photo which lined up the clock with the 90 degree wall of a building in the foreground just to prove the lean. I was moved that day by the concept of precision. Like Albert, I am a punctual person.

Today is one time when we all can consider others and respect their time by being on time. It's an imposition on them to make them wait. We know, however, that eventualities arise (like unforeseen subsidence or risings), so we do have to be tolerant and understanding if someone does make us wait. "Do unto others……"

(bonus!)

The Great Hunger IV
(Patrick Kavanagh)

Maguire knelt beside a pillar where he could spit
Without being seen. He turned an old prayer round:
"Jesus, Mary and Joseph pray for us
Now and at the Hour." Heaven dazzled death.
"Wonder should I cross-plough that turnip ground."
The tension broke. The congregation lifted its head
As one a man and coughed in unison.
Five hundred hearts were hungry for life-
Who lives in Christ shall never die the death.
And the candle-lit Altar and the flowers
And the pregnant tabernacle lifted a moment to Prophecy
Out of the clayey hours.
Maguire sprinkled his face with holy water
As the congregation stood for the Last Gospel.
He rubbed the dust off his knees with his palm, and then
Coughed the prayer phlegm up from his throat and
Sighed:Amen.

This is the tale of Patrick Maguire, the poor overworked, 65 year old bachelor farmer protagonist of Kavanagh's epic. In this scene, Patrick finds himself unhappily in Mass. Outside, 1000s are dying in the potato famine, but the 500 in the congregation raise a prayer for life amid the death of the Great Hunger. Patrick is the antithesis of the congregation – the realist but also the faithless. I find ironic humour in his devolutionary prayer, in his inattention, in his secret and almost anonymous presence, in his exaggerative action with the Holy Water and in his bored Amen. But, the most significant line is "coughed the prayer phlegm up." The action and the meaning are contradictory. Phlegm: an irritating waste mucous product to be expectorated is lined up beside a prayer – a communication of hope and desire to be breathed out gently. God would have received mixed messages from Maguire that day.

Today is a day for being straight up and true. No equivocation.

Hook Head Lighthouse-Wexford

Kylemore Abbey - Clare

And here you thought Coney Island was in New York! No, it's in Sligo. The original name was Irish, Mulclohy, but it was renamed for its horde of rabbits (coneys). To get there, you need to follow 14 pillars set in the ocean, or you'll get swamped by tides. It's serene and gorgeous. New Yorkers got their island's name from Captain Coney from Sligo who worked timber boats plying the Atlantic. When he set eyes on the island overrun with rabbits, he baptized it Coney Island too. What a contrast between the two islands – pristine rural versus industrial urban. On Ireland's Coney Island, St. Patrick has had his influence. At one spot is a boulder dropped in glacial times and it is called St. Patrick's Chair. I sat on it and was informed that I could have but one wish to be fulfilled that year.

Fortunately God is not like Captain Coney. He does not see human 'rabbits' and do nothing but apply a label, "sinner". He sees real value in his human race and restores us. Today, like every day, you will have sinned, many times no doubt if you're like me. We have more than one chance a year to come to God and it's more than even a wish for forgiveness. In spite of our label as inveterate sinners, we can constantly ask for forgiveness and it's granted. At any time during the day, stop and request forgiveness once you are aware of your sin. God is faithful and will forgive you. That's an inspiration.

Gerry Adams' face is recognizable in many parts of the world as the political representative of Northern Ireland's Republican Sinn Fein movement. He has received acclaim for brokering dialogue and peace activities. Born in 1948 in Catholic Belfast, Falls Road area, Adams went to Saint Mary's Christian Brothers' School. He is personable and articulate. He has published at least eight times. He politicks well, having been elected even to a seat in Westminster in London. Most recently, he was one of those who negotiated the Good Friday Accord and is acknowledged for his skill in making deals for ceasefires and disarmament. One cannot help but feel that Adams is an honourable man. Yet, there is a dark side to Gerry Adams. He has been tarred as an IRA terrorist. Authorities have jailed him in all of Northern Ireland's infamous prisons (three) where he wrote and made escape attempts and, some say, arranged IRA bombings. Some Unionist leaders refuse to speak to Adams and allege that he should be in jail again. There has been an assassination attempt by the UFF. Clearly, Gerry Adams is a political and social idealist who fights and feels strongly.

That fact about Adams inspires me. There have been activists who have championed their cause as strongly as Adams. Jesus Christ was one such man; however, so were Hitler and Stalin obsessed with their causes. They were inspired by other socialist authors and leaders. I challenge you today to inspire others by your consuming drive; but, do it loyally, gently and peacefully, and in love. Follow Jesus' cause.

Knighted Rollo Gillespie (Rollicking Rollo) came from quiet Comber, County Down, but he led a magical military life of world wide adventure. To begin his rollicking ride, he eloped from Comber and his privileged life style, but ended up in a duel for the woman. During the contest, Gillespie was miraculously spared when a bullet bounced off his brass button. His opponent died. He fled to Santo Domingo where he was arrested and sentenced to execution. His membership in the Free Masons saved him when his jailer gave him the Masonic handshake. Rollo responded and was spared again. He arrived back in Ireland at Cork and was soon involved in more chaos. During a brawl, Gillespie was arrested, but escaped again, dressed as a nursing mother. When he arrived in the Bosphorus to hide, he was promptly kidnapped. While held for ransom, he escaped the clutches of death once more. His captor released him after Gillespie cured him of a fever. At last, Rollo met his end, shot through the heart in India in a doomed military skirmish. His last words were reputed to have been, "One more shot for Down." These words are inscribed on a fifty five foot tower and statue in Comber. Maybe it refers to his ability to always have one more opening for survival.

Risk takers always inspire (and scare) me, since I am assuredly not one. I enjoy the fantasy of such adventure and vicariously ride with it. Only to realize that I have but one life, but the imagination was worth it. Today, be inspired to dream a risk, but keep your feet planted firmly in the knowledge that you have only one life and it will soon be past.

He wishes for the Cloths of Heaven

(W. B. Yeats)

Had I the heavens' embroidered cloths,
Enwrought with golden and silver light,
The blue and the dim and the dark cloths
Of night and light and the half-light,
I would spread the cloths under your feet;
But I, being poor, have only my dreams;
I have spread my dreams under your feet;
Tread softly because you tread on my dreams.

I applaud the idealism expressed by the Irish genius. Even if the perfect trappings of heaven are not available to pass on, Yeats can at least extend to us the ideals of his dreams. He does warn us also that, since he is being open enough to us to display his idealistic goals, then we must respect the dreams he has.

Isn't it comforting to be around a realistic idealist who desires to share his/her optimism with us? Be that someone today. Shed the pessimistic just for a moment and wish for the cloths of heaven to fall on a loved one, a close one; if not that, at least wish your dreams to another.

Derry (Londonderry) is known as the Maiden City because her seventeenth-century walls have never been breached. Despite the violent and bad reputation, in my opinion, Derry has a strong and soft image. In the Tower Museum in town, we are faced with the might and stability of the fortifications that still exist today. Derry was, and still is, a hotbed of Catholic and Protestant rancour. In the Tower is a reprise of the Derry Apprentices Boys struggling to close the gates of the city against the Earl of Antrim's troops. The largest siege the walls endured lasted one hundred and five days in 1688—a long time to hold out against aggression! The keys to the gates are on display in the chapterhouse. Taken over by London in the 1660s, Derry was largely developed by the British and, according to its new rulers, re-named Londonderry. However, the city has a long history before that: it was founded by Colmcille in 546 AD. When the saint went off to Christianize Scotland, he was homesick and referred to his dear "oak grove" as *doire* in Gaelic, thus giving the city its name. In modern times, Derry has acquired renown. In World War II she was a key port to welcome and shelter convoys reaching the end of their hazardous Atlantic missions. Also, Amelia Earhardt landed unexpectedly in North Derry on May 21, 1932 after her solo Atlantic flight.

Derry inspires me as a symbol of security and safe refuge, a warm spot unbreached by a rapacious, pillaging, materialistic world.

Long ago, in Falan in Inishowen lived St.Mara, but it is not the Catholic saint who provides our inspiration this day. It is a Protestant church in Falan. [As an aside, Protestant churches are common in Donegal, for the province was once part of Ulster. Religion knows no geographic boundaries.] Within the graveyard wall of Falan's church is a wishing stone. Legend has it that if you stretch out your arm before closing your eyes, and if you then walk toward the wishing stone and are able to fit your hand directly into the center of the stone, presto, your wish comes true. Sounds like Irish 'pin the tail on the donkey'! Such a story conjures up all the fascinating images of leprechauns, faeries and superstitions too. In contrast, it also emphasizes the human spirit's desire to risk, to gamble. None of these activities are based in reality, nor in Biblical principle. God does not reserve his will for any one race or religion. He does not ask us to take risks today. He does not ask us to close our eyes and engage in tenuous hope. God has no wishing stone in any graveyard.

He asks us to express 'eyes-open' faith, to walk with Him, not alone. It is ours today too place our hand in His , not to grope for a stone's hole. One writer puts it more succinctly than I can. "Put your hope in God, for you will yet praise Him." I look forward to praising God today, not going to Falan.

The wild nature of Malin Head on the Inishowen Peninsula sits in contrast to the exact neatness of Malin Village. This town won Bord Failte's assignation of Tidiest Town in Ireland and proudly flaunts its award on large signs as you enter the village. It also does all it can to maintain its reputation. The village green is manicured and spotless. The homes and businesses ringing the square and on its few other roads and lanes have polished door knockers and hinges, newly and brightly painted doors, sashes and walls. As if on cue on my arrival, a garbage truck came into sight as we parked outside Malin Hotel. Bins were whisked away and not a wrapper or bottle dropped onto the street in carelessness. Malin Hotel was our chosen site for lunch. Despite the antique and dark interior of the reception and lounge, the hotel lived up to the "tidy" image. Magazines were on display in neat piles, chairs were arranged in linear exactness and the lunch was a "tidy" size without the "tidy" price. We tucked into generous portions of trout or salmon accompanied by 'veg' and 'taties' enough for four. (Doesn't English have a wonderful paradoxical connotation of words? What does "tidy" really mean?)

God is a tidy God. Order is of paramount importance. He expects clean hearts and pure minds. He also spent a "tidy" sum on our salvation and we are a "tidy" group of believers worldwide, the Church, the Body of Christ. If God had an earthly village, he would win the award of "Tidy Town" outright. He already has that eternally, the community of Heaven.

Ireland is not known for its unlimited hours of bright sunshine—just an average of six hours a day in June, five in July and two in December in Dublin, with even less in the North. That's pretty bleak! Not much to inspire me, but the Irish can have the brightest of personalities and smiles. They resurrect positivity in me. That sunny spirit reminds me of a visit to *Bru na Boinne*—the place of the Boyne—Newgrange, Knowth and Dowth. Here thousands come to be amazed at the prehistoric passage tombs (dating from 3200B.C.). There are about forty mounds holding traces of the oldest human activity in the area. It is a UNESCO world heritage site, eight miles from Drogheda on a loop in the Boyne Rive. Professor M.J. O'Reilly was one of the archaeologists who excavated the site in the 1960s and 70s. He discovered the roof box through which the midwinter sun floats and strikes the tomb but once a year. O'Reilly wrote on December 21, 1969 (the Winter Solstice): "At 8:58 hours the first pencil of direct sunlight shone through the roof box and along the passage tomb, sixty two feet, to reach across the tomb chamber floor as far as the front edge of the basin stone in the end recess." It happens only once a year!! Did the ancients feel that the sun had resurrective powers?

Let sunshine inspire you today. And remember that the Son of God will resurrect the faithful one day. If you die, will you be raised by Jesus' power?

Our engineers and technicians pride themselves in our times on their skills and achievements – and rightly so. But, remember that what is accomplished in technology, space, travel, engineering has had access to mechanized machinery and computers. As I toured the cemetery at Monasterboice in Co. Meath, I went back 1500 years (no cranes or computers). The remains of the Round Tower of the monastery of St. Buite mac Bronagh (of St. Patrick's time) are a tribute to the learning and skills of men BC (Before Computers). The tower stands in ruins but about ninety feet still exists – a perfect stone column which acted as a lookout tower. Ultimately, the monastery fell to the Vikings, but not before it had produced some of Europe's top scholars and artists (listed in the Irish Annals). One piece of art, an extravagant high cross containing carved New Testament and Old Testament stories, is a masterpiece. Tucked away in rural simplicity is a tribute to the genius of men and women "back then".

I would like you today to build, create, produce something without the aid of a computer or motorized or mechanized machinery. Tough! Then, appreciate what resources we have. At last, do not denigrate the backward "backthenners".

O Do Not Love Too Long

(W. B. Yeats)

Sweetheart, do not love too long:
I loved long and long,
And grew to be out of fashion
Like an old song.

All through the years of our youth
Neither could have known
Their own thought from the other's ,
We were so much at one.

But O, in a minute she changed-
O do not love too long,
Or you will grow out of fashion
Like an old song.

I don't believe that Yeats is being critical in this poem of extended relationships. He is not advocating the "butterfly in love" approach. What can happen, though, in a prolonged love is what I call "presumed continuity". Or, the clichéd "familiarity breeds contempt".

Please, God, that we do not take anyone for granted. When you do and when you least expect it, you will 'grow out of fashion'. As this spring time of the season of love progresses, do not love too long, that is, in the same way. Instead, inject new passion, new lyrics, new music, new youth into your love today.

Booking into the Lodge was like experiencing how the other half live – well almost. The intensely personal Irish *failte* – welcome impressed me. We were being treated like stars. Our upgraded suite was truly luxurious; I sat at an antique desk to make some author's notes and I stared in peaceful reverie over Lough Arrow, above hundreds of Irish hills and lanes and out on to the Bricklieve Mountains where royalty was buried thousands of years ago. This was the Emerald Isle at its diamond best. Our dinner time was set for 7:30 and what an exquisite culinary feast it was – seven courses of the finest in Irish style served by a most attentive and friendly young man. The Old Baileys Irish Cream was the ultimate top off to the day. At last, the rural silence and blackness provided the atmosphere for deep slumber. The mountain loomed inky at midnight and then became a bloody purple as the sun rose at 4:30. At that moment the bubble burst and the nectar spilled to the ground. We were given a spartan breakfast, a curt disagreement re the final bill and no farewell.

What shall I choose to recall? Of course, the glory of the stay inspired me, not my disappointment of the departure. Fine food and a well-appointed cozy room will always inspire me.

K eshcorran was not only a home for animals and humans, but for hags too. Didn't Fionn MacCumhaill find that out! Fionn and his band of warriors, the Fianna, were hunting in the mountains and the plains below Keshcorran. Fionn, so the tale *Bruidean Cheise* goes, sits down to rest on the cairn on the summit and is lured by three hideous witches into one of the caves and is bound there. Whatever attracted Fionn, we don't know. Did the witches change form in their seduction? His Fianna come to his rescue, but they too are tied up with cords woven by enchantment. Sounds like a faery tale, doesn't it? Part of the actual story runs this way: "Their eyes were bleary and red, their mouths were black and twisted...a hedge of curved, yellow fangs. They had mustaches poking under their noses and woolly bushes growing out of their ears." That's enchantment? Fortunately, Fionn and his mates were rescued by Goll MacMorna, and the hags were slaughtered.

Temptation is rife around us in today's society, and we can be lured and trapped by what, in reality, is sheer ugly sin. I remember singing a childrens' song, 'Yield not to Temptation', and the truth of that phrase is timeless. Today will no doubt bring its own version of temptation. Bypass it, shun it, stamp it out, and at day's end you'll feel better.

Jamsey and Bessy Coleman had ten children. The youngest, Michael, was born in 1891 near Gurteen in Sligo. In honour of this international star of the early 20th century, music workshops and performances are held each year in Gurteen. Michael learned music from his father, who was no mean flute player, and Michael took up the fiddle. At twenty-three, Michael left for New York just as WWI began. There he became renowned at many concert halls and in seven years was cutting records. He recorded hits like, "The Grey Goose," "The Green Fields of America," and "Lord McDonald." Coleman died in New York in 1945; his home is now a tourist attraction called Coleman Country. Yes, there was another brother, Jim, eight years older than Michael, but Jim stayed in Ireland. In fact, Jim was the more gifted fiddle player of the two; he could have outshone Michael. Ah, the turning points of life. "Two roads diverged in a yellow wood," says Robert Frost. Perhaps Jim regretted not following his brother to America for fame and fortune. Perhaps he was glad he stayed at home.

Contentment with our lot in life is paramount. Was Michael happy? Only he could say for sure. God, not fate, is serving up our lot for today. Be content with it; that is inspiration enough for the day's needs.

On the N4, I noticed a sign, Kilcullen's Seaweed Baths. Ever the maverick, I had to investigate, so I drove on into Enniscrone. The bathhouse was the exclusive domain of Christopher Orme in 1750, but the Kilcullen clan saw entrepreneurial potential and expanded on Orme's site in 1910. Originally, the seawater was heated by turf fires and a tonne of turf was used on a busy Sunday. Nowadays, one can luxuriate in this Edwardian bath, sinking into steaming hot water and seaweed. The water is pumped directly from the sea nearby and heated electrically. The seaweed is then added and this gives an oily consistency to the water, not unlike olive oil. The "patient" is directed into what is really a domestic bathroom. An Edwardian style bathtub awaits you amid luxurious wall hangings and towels. You literally slide into a yellow-orange tinged water. The first reaction is repulsion at the colour, but you remind yourself that you have been informed that this shade comes from the intense iodine content of the seaweed. Enjoy the therapy for the skin, which in the end, is as soft as a baby's bottom.

There are millions of cures in the world for thousands of ailments. Some are realistically beneficial; others are placebos. Feel better today; indulge yourself in harmless physical luxury. We all need a pick-me-up. But don't forget about eternal "health and welfare." Spend time in God's bath of love too.

Just off the strand near Enniscrone is a full-sized statue of a black pig. Children were playing on its back and tusk as I read its history. The town is called Muckduff, Black Pig in Gaelic. Beside the boar's likeness is a cairn of stones to honour the poor souls which it devoured. In Donegal to the north, a black boar ran rampant for months, killing and eating defenseless children, and mutilating men and women. Finally, a posse of brave souls chased the pig from Donegal Country south into Sligo via the sea. The wicked beast came ashore near Enniscrone at Muckduff, and was met there by a second vigilante group who overtook the pig, cornered it, and watched it perish. The county was saved from the fate of Donegal, and the townspeople erected the cairn in memory of Donegal's casualties. The statue of the boar came later, as a tourist attraction, and don't tourists love such a story!

How selfish and territorial human nature is, but some display a higher virtue. They even respect those who have tried to keep their own skirts clean in passing the buck, or in sliding the dirt under the carpet. Can I encourage you today to face the beast in your life? Don't ignore it, but slay it. At our own peril, we slide a problem onto others.

Within this restless, hurried, modern world,
We took our heart's full pleasure – You and I,
And now the white sails of our ships are furled,
And spent the Lading of our argosy.

But all this crowded life has been to thee
No more than lyre, or lute, or subtle spell
Of viols, or the music of the sea
That sleeps, a mimic echo, in the still.

(My Voice – Oscar Wilde)

It can be heart-rending to look back on an event, a day, a holiday, a task, a life and assess failures and successes. Music is a bonding agent for life's experiences that is appropriate, for it is fleeting, yet eternal; intangible, yet corporeal; an echo, and a wave. I sense and suspect that when Wilde uses his "but" and his "no more", he does not share the same positive interpretation which I have on life. Look at this day with the lilting pleasure that music gives; sing and play.

In Banada, Sligo, a graveyard caught my attention. In it were the remains of the first Irish house of the Augustinians of Regular Observance, Corpus Christi Priory. Donnchach O'Hara founded it in 1423, but during the conflicts of the 1600s, the property was handed over to a Protestant family, the Joneses (Irish names are so much more poetic, aren't they?). During the many confrontations between Catholics and Protestants, the fight boiled over at the priory, now in Jones' hands. One of Mr. Jones' family raised his hand to strike a priest, but his arm was instantly paralyzed. Next day, the Jones clan converted to Catholicism at this display of power and retribution. Not only that, but Mr. Jones donated the property to the Irish Sisters of Charity. The sisters opened the school in the form of a monastery, but the school was closed in 1987. There were no more women who wished to take on those Holy Orders.

I wonder why people adhere to certain communities or religions. Is it tradition? Is it fear of family displeasure? Is it faith? This day, examine your motives for your belief. Once you're sure you have the correct basis for your credo, don't ever let it die out. Pass it on.

When Christianity came to Ireland, its job was to bring the gospel to the Celts. The Pope sent Palladias in 430 to begin this task. St. Patrick founded the first church in Armagh in 455 and St. Columba was the first indigenous missionary in 563. Ancient monasteries dot all of Ireland: Glendalough, Clonmacoise, Devenish Island were some of the earliest. In Donegal City there is one of the earliest, actually founded by a woman, the wife of Red O'Donnell, one of the Celtic Irish warlords. This woman founded a monastery/abbey near Donegal Bay in 1474. Its ruins are still visible, just down from the noisy main road. Such religious fervour of the past was taken up again in Donegal Castle and Abbey. Four Franciscan friars began to write the Annals of the Four Masters in the 1630s. It was to be an historic account of the history of the Gaelic people. And, it begins with Noah's grandmother, 40 days before the Great Flood! These four men who wrote this massive work are depicted in bookstores in Donegal as cute, tonsured, smiling, chubby monks hard at work in scribbling down these annals. Their job was to take the historical account all the way to the 1500s. It truly is a definitive work.

It reminded me of a much wider read book by four men, the Gospels in the best selling book in the world, the Bible. It's not dry annals of history. It is the living word of God. Derive your drive today from a book. Read anything which improves and empowers you. Reading is good for the mind and spirit. Once all that is done, don't neglect the best book. Read Psalm 23 or John 17, or both.

The O'Hara family is legendary in Ireland. The clan founded abbeys and their finances were instrumental in preserving Irish lore in poetry. They and another great Irish name, O'Connor in Sligo became patrons of the O'Huiginn family, professional poets. From the O'Higgins came one of Sligo's first bards, blind Tadhg Dall O'Huiginn (1550-1617). The relationship became strained when the O'Haras took advantage of Tadhg's hospitality and , in turn, he composed a satirical retort in song. Six O'Haras arrived on Tadhg's doorstep from their Castle Carragh, beat the poor sightless bard and then cut out his tongue. To lose two senses was just too much for the old man. He died from his wounds and from a broken heart. Admittedly, the verse was very pointed. Here's how it went: "I beseech God who shed his blood, since it is but decay for them to be alive – it is scarcely to be called living – that none may slay the group of six." That really cuts in sarcasm, for it implies that death is too good for those O'Haras. What atrocities have been committed in the name of revenge. Why must we engage in tit for tat? Why must we try to one up those around us? As I rounded Killala Bay and read of the clan's actions, I recalled reading a novel set in Killala Bay. Hundreds set out from the port here during the Great Famine for the New World. Why? Because one race had to prove to another that it was superior by depriving the other of its livelihood.

Our motivator today should be meekness and humility. It is not wrong to turn the other cheek, to let bygones be bygones. We are stronger for it.

Certain Irish family names are recognizable by the world at large. O'Dowd is perhaps one of those names, the leading family in Connaught from 1000-1600. They owned twenty four castles. But, have you heard of the MacFirbises? Highly unlikely. This clan ranks undisputedly in Irish/Celtic scholarship and were the hereditary poets and history-writers for the O'Dowds. The MacFirbis boys inaugurated O'Dowd chieftains, instructed in history and compiled tomes of basic importance to the Irish: The Book of Genealogies of Ireland. Let's narrow the clan to one, An Dubhaltach Og MacFirbis (that's a mouthful – imagine him at a book signing session!). This MacFirbis was the most famous of the clan and was murdered near Skreen in Sligo at an old inn/pub. The reason for his demise is unclear. Did he antagonize another drinker over his presence, his writings or his name? I am sure his death brought mourning to both the O'Dowds and to the MacFirbises, but he still maintains his place of importance to the Gaelic people.

Your identity and mine give us a unique nature – to be loved, admired, despised, rewarded, attacked. Reflect upon your clan and your identity today. Have they prompted and motivated you to be supportive. Be proud of family, especially of a spiritual family. Revel in being a child of God and brother/sister to the greatest "clan", belonging to the name Jesus.

An unassuming little town, Culdaff, in Inishowen provides for us a telling insight as to "what's in a name". Shakespeare introduced us to this question in Romeo and Juliet and he has Romeo convincing himself that "a rose by any other name would smell as sweet" as he agonizes over falling in love with Juliet. He fears the consequences of his love because Juliet is a member of the family which is an avowed enemy. The Irish too have declared sides over the centuries, to the death. Culdaff has its player in this drama of supposed religious conflict. In 1690, an actor and writer, born and bred a Catholic, played the part of Shylock in another of Shakespeare's masterpieces, The Merchant of Venice. This role solidified Charles Macklin's substantial credibility as a famous actor in London. But, but, Charles Macklin was not Charles Macklin. He was Culdaff's Cathol MacLochlainn who wrote a play, "The True Born Irishman." Cathol, in order to further his career and improve his status, set aside his Gaelic name for a more "acceptable" Anglo Saxon sounding name. Furthermore, Cathol turned from Catholicism to Protestantism. Charles/Cathol's signature role as Shylock should have been enough to have taught him that an undue attention to one's identity or beliefs can end in disaster and disgrace.

We thank God for offering a clear identity in Christ. However, we too will get a name change (written on a stone), but ours does not originate from a personal desire for advancement, but from an act that Christ has effected to position us closer to God. Praise God! No identity crisis – you can be His child with His name. That's inspiring.

eltown, near the historic city of Kells is called *Tailte* in Gaelic and was the site of *Aonach Tailteem*. In pagan times, the Irish tribes would gather for Olympic-style games. Various unusual competitions were held such as swimming horses through the river at dawn. Now, Irish Olympics would not be complete without song and dance, would they? Recitations and music invited dancers to whip up a beat in honour of pagan gods. One ritual always received major audiences. A young maiden would stick her finger through a hole in a door. If the man on the other side admired the finger, then seized it, the woman became his wife; the union was valid only for a year and a day. So, he and she were free the next year to make another attempt at a longer lasting marriage. Meanwhile, much more seriously in Kells, the monks were at work. They had fled the Viking raids on Iona Island and were creating a more lasting heritage than the games at Teltown. They were writing and illustrating the Four Gospels, as found in the Book of Kells (the original is in Trinity College in Dublin). These monks painstakingly copied out the gospel accounts and the sketched and drew the most beautiful images around the Scriptures.

I am thankful that there is no vestige of Irish Olympics around today. I am, however, appreciative of the effort of the Ionian monks who preserved the gospel stories which inspire me. The image of Jesus telling a story of a father forgiving his wayward son gives me a warm feeling. Forgiveness is a motivating factor to create a permanent bond that leads to a relationship of more than a year and a day.

It was a challenge to find, but well worth the effort. The instructions in the guidebook were not at all clear ("Turn right in Carrick") and the road was not signposted once we were in Carrick. At last, we were on track. The one lane road switchbacked and wound over desolate mounds. On numerous occasions I honked at sheep ruminating in the middle of the lane. Other sheep dashed in front of my hood. I climbed on until I met with probably the most awe-inspiring sight I have ever seen. Bunglass or Slieve League (League Mountain) is really a set of massive cliffs dropping into the Atlantic, the highest cliffs in Europe. I was alone, suspended on the edge of a deathly precipice, six hundred meters above the Atlantic. We decided to risk walking a portion of the trail leading up even further. It is not recommended for inexperienced hikers. At first, the path was a series of roughly placed stairs of flagstones; then, it became a one person track worn in the grass, just one meter from oblivion straight down over ochre and amber rock. Ahh, the colours. Yes, the colours! The cliffs take on a variance of colour and shade depending on weather and time of day. They are an Aurora Borealis in stone.

Here there is no sound except the wind's howl and the rollers' crash. I have rarely been so touched by the works of nature and God as I was that day. I stared out over the Atlantic and was inspired at the world in which we live.

To kiss the Blarney Stone is the goal of so many people, but it is also death-defying. It was pouring on that day we visited and only I in our group was either foolish or courageous enough to attempt it. I lay back three stories up, hanging over empty air. An attendant covered me with an umbrella, but I was still soaked. To boot, I am no more loquacious now than I ever was! I guess the reason is simple. The Blarney Stone is only half there, according to legend. – the other half is the Stone of Scone in Westminster Abbey. The Stone of Scone, over which all Scottish kings were crowned, gave regal powers to the king of Scotland. In 1314, however, Robert the Bruce gave away one half of the stone in gratitude for military support from Cormac McCarthy. This Irish lord (yes, you guessed it – he lived at Blarney) engaged in "subtle diplomacy" with Queen Elizabeth 1 when she tried to hoodwink Irish lords into a watered down brand of ownership under her legal aegis. McCarthy saw through the queen's ploy, and she likewise. She is rumoured to have said that McCarthy gave her "a lot of Blarney" as he negotiated with her.

Our goal today should be to cut through the "Blarney". There is enough dissembling in the world today without our contribution. Our spiritual roots teach us that God has made his goal clear: he does not "shoot the breeze" (nor any other euphemism you can name it). Nor does he attempt to "con" us. Today, take God at his word and give your own unequivocal word to all you.

Along the Quay Road, from Enniscrone to Ballina, I came across a little glade. In it was an earthen mound and some boulders. It seemed an unassuming sight, but let me quote the actual story of the Mermaid Stones found there: "Thady O'Dowd was the Chieftain of his clan. One day while walking along the seashore, he saw a beautiful mermaid wearing a cloak which shimmered like the scales of a fish. Without the cloak, the mermaid would remain human and unable to return to the sea. Thady stole her cloak and asked her to become his bride (rascal!—my observation) She knew he would never relinquish the cloak, so she went to live with him. They lived happily for many years, and she bore him seven children. One day, her youngest saw her father hide the cloak and she told her mother. While Thady was away at battle, she took her children and the cloak to Scurmore. The children tried to stop her from returning to the sea, but she could not resist its call, and turned six of the children into stone, taking her youngest with her. It is said that every time an O'Dowd dies, the rocks weep." That's better than I could have said it.

I was moved as I stood silently before these six stones. We are all called to a mission, and we must obey that calling. What is your calling today? Don't waver from it, nor should you deter someone from his or her calling. A calling is from God, and insertions of our own will do not assist in its fulfillment.

Who dreamed that beauty passes like a dream?
For these red lips, with all their mournful pride,
Troy passed away in one high funeral gleam,
And Usna's children died.

We and the labouring world are passing by:
Amid men's souls, that waver and give place
Like the pale waters in their wintry race
Under the passing stars, foam of the sky,
Lives on this lonely face.

Bow down, archangels, in your dim abode:
Before you were, or any hearts to beat,
Weary and kind one lingered by His seat;
He made the world to be a grassy road
Before her wandering feet.
(W. B. Yeats)

The world can be considered from varying vantage points. Is beauty eternal in the world? Is there anything new to wonder at and ponder in the world? Are we just passing through this toilsome world, reflective of a lonely face? Is the world a "grassy road" which meanders for its and our enjoyment? It is all of that and more than that. This world gives us a meaning for our existence. Today, by seeing my world from a different perspective, I can see how my life contributes to the whole of this universe that God created. I am important to the life of this world and to the life of God.

In Memory of my Mother
(Patrick Kavanagh)

I do not think of you lying in the wet clay
Of a Monaghan graveyard; I see
You walking down a lane among poplars
On your way to a station, or happily

Going to second Mass on a summer Sunday –
You meet me and you say:
'Don't forget to see about the cattle –'
Among your earthiest words the angels stray.

And I think of you walking along a headland
Of green oats in June,
So full of repose, so rich with life-
And I see us meeting at the end of a town

On a fair day by accident, after
The bargains are all made and we can walk
Together through the shops and stalls and markets
Free in the oriental streets of thought.

O you are not lying in the wet clay,
For it is a harvest evening now and we
Are pulling up the ricks against the moonlight
And you smile up at us eternally.

My own mother passed away in this month. She did none of the things that Kavanagh remembers of his mother. In fact, I recall very little of my mom's activities (shortbread making was one) for she led a simple at home lifestyle. What she did in life was precious, but what she is now is infinitely more. She is eternal, not from memories, but because of her faith in God and her existence among the angels. Many years after she had gone to that eternal state, I wrote a short story in honour of her (it appears in an anthology of stories). I urge you today to sit down and, like Kavanagh and me, write an "In Memoriam" to mother– but, unlike us two, give it to her before she passes on.

Dooney Rock, just outside Sligo City, was immortalized by W. B. Yeats in his poem, "The Fiddler of Dooney". "When I play on my fiddle in Dooney; Folk dance like a wave of the sea; My cousin is priest in Kilvarnet; My brother in Macharbuiee." I can picture Yeats or any Irish fiddler bowing up a storm for a folk dance by the lake and inviting any and all who could come, be they priest or brother. Indeed, annually, a traditional music contest is held in Sligo named for the well in Dooney. The rock was the site of many a celebration of the ancient fiddle, I'm sure, for Dooney Rock is named from the Gaelic – Carraig Dhun Aodh – the Rock of the Fort of Hugh. The 'cashel' or fort, atop the rock was no doubt an impregnable fortress which withheld enemy attacks. Afterwards, the fiddlers feted the victory. Another story fits with Dooney. From the rock I spotted an island which the people of Sligo call, "Beezie's Island". Beezie Gallagher was a quaint, garrulous woman who lived alone on this island. She rowed daily, until her death in 1951, across from her home to Dooney's Rock and then walked into Sligo to shop and ceilidh with any who would stop and chat. As I stood and viewed her old house across the expanse of lake, I wondered if she ever heard the fiddler at the rock. Did she stop to dance with her brother or her priest? She did it simply because she was Irish and because the rock was there.

Why can't we stop and dance today? The idea reminds me of King David in the Bible who danced and played just because his Rock, God, was there, symbolized by the Ark of the Covenant. Enjoy Christ today. Dance or play or sing. He's our brother and our high priest. He invites us to celebrate our spirituality.

Oh, loved one lying far away
Beyond the human moan,
Can coffin board and heavy stone
Turn god-like man to senseless clay?

Or, hast thou eyes to see the light
And feeling quick with joy and pain?
Alas! I think a less than gain
Is mine, if thou canst see me right.

Alas! How mean we must appear
When looked on by the holy dead!
I trust the glory round thy head
Hast kept thine eyes from seeing clear.

(Untitled – Oscar Wilde)

Wilde addresses the aged question of whether there is an afterlife. There is! It is indeed a "far far better place to which I go... a far far better rest" (Dickens – A Tale of Two Cities). Our human lives do now moan and endure a pendulum of joy and pain. It is a mean existence, for sure, with little gain – at least when compared to the place of God. This day, I want to understand and capture what is in store for me beyond this life. I have more than Wilde. I have pure and perfect ecstasy in Christ.

At the moment we reached the summit, it was anything but sunny. No, I lie; I have to admit that there was sunshine, but it was visible miles away across Lough Swilly. Ireland was serving up its usual smorgasbord of weather. Where we were parked beside Griann Aileach, the hail was bouncing off the windshield and the wind was whipping the rain in horizontal sheets. I read the guidebook. Aileach means 'sunny rock' in Gaelic. If I waited long enough, the sun would reach us. I did wait, and our tour of the Bronze Age fort was pleasant. For two hundred years, the eight hundred foot hill has provided an outlook and a bastion. For six hundred years, the Neill family ruled this area of Ireland with the Griann being the symbol of the Neills' power. Then, in the twelfth century, the Munster king, Murtagh O'Brien, destroyed the fort. In an act of final revenge, each Munster soldier was instructed to take one stone from the fort so that, in the end, the hill was leveled. In 1874, the fort was rebuilt, and it still stands as a beacon of unchangeability. The fort is visible for miles around.

As I stood on the top of the wall, I believed that I too had become part of the Griann. The weather was flipping over its displays while I read of the forts varied history. But, I was intent upon the contrasting truth. Weather, power and structures come and go, but God says, "I, the Lord, change not." How blessed I am to be part of his eternal security.

But who is this who cometh by the shore?
(Nay, love, look up and wonder!) who is this
Who cometh in dyed garments from the south?
It si thy new found Lord, and he shall kiss
The yet unravished roses of thy mouth,
And I shall weep and worship as before.

(The New Remorse- Oscar Wilde)

Each day we meet someone new, someone maybe even from another culture whom we cannot understand, whom we wish to question. That person can have profound influence upon us if we but respect him or her, if we allow some emotional attachment to take place. Be open today to a new relationship. The poem reminds me of a scripture verse about Jesus who also came to a new culture to offer a new way of life, and He was rejected.

June

Lakes of Killarney-Kerry

LondonderryDerry walls - never breached

It was a long but interesting three hours. I have sat in North American lounges and waiting rooms and been intrigued in my penchant for people-watching. (At times, it's even got me in hot water!) As I sat in the lobby of the Craigavon Hospital awaiting my sister-in-law, I observed features both common to humankind and dissimilar to my North American background. Similarities—casts on limbs, downcast looks, diligent care workers, confused patients, self-confident doctors and nurses, visitors buying fruit, cards and flowers, most accompanied by another. I saw a range of ages from ill infants to the elderly on stretchers, and a sense of quiet acceptance of physical weakness. Dissimilarities—simplicity – less technology/more personal engagement, a lack of hurrying, a gamut of dress ranging from the cosmic casual to the sedately Victorian (the over 65s in Northern Ireland still go out to every event in a collar and tie, or dress and pantyhose), distant aloofness and coldness sensed from the shop staff. I received the impression that I was not the sole person waiting. Everyone was waiting. For what I was not sure, but there was an air of expectancy. For healing? For support? For direction? For backup? I was waiting for relatives to return from an x-ray appointment. I am not known for patience, but that day, I learned that we are all waiting for someone or something.

Await the moment of truth today. It will come. And remember that someone is waiting for you too. Don't be thoughtless and don't keep them on tenterhooks long. Christ has said he's coming and won't keep us waiting.

Thou knowest all; I seek in vain
What lands to till or sow with seed –
The land is black with briar and weed,
Nor cares for falling tears or rain.

Thou knowest all; I sit and wait
With blinded eyes and hands that fail,
Till the last lifting of the veil
And the first opening of the gate.

Thou knowest all; I cannot see
I trust I shall not live in vain,
I know that we shall meet again
In some divine eternity.

(The True Knowledge – Oscar Wilde)

I like Wilde's last two lines and I see the potential in lines one and two in stanza three. It is a great motivator for me to know that my life is not in vain, and that I have an eternal future with God. And that I will meet my loved ones in Heaven. The mood of the first two stanzas is less positive. I know, unlike Wilde, that I can rise above weeds and failure and blindness. My hope is both in this world and in the next.

I spent thirty eight years teaching under the watchful eye of Blessed Edmund Ignatius Rice, the founder of the Christian Brothers of Ireland. These brothers have been responsible for educating thousands of boys worldwide. Rice was born in Callan, County Kilkenny amid times of great persecution of Roman Catholics by English Protestant landowners. The very symbol of their God, the crucifix, was a banned image for Catholics. In Callan, I entered Rice's family cottage to appreciate his roots. In my usual flurry of sightseeing movement, I did not notice an unusual crucifix on the wall, but my colleague did and asked as to why the horizontal cross member was almost non-existent. The guide's answer: "If British authorities were to arrive unannounced to check that laws were being adhered to, a family member could more easily hide the "offending" crucifix up a sleeve without the full crosspiece of the icon hindering movement."

Two lessons struck me. What cruelty has been imposed over history in the name of religious correctness and how thankful we should be of our current freedom to worship God! Then I picture the mutilated cross and realize that, without that full and awful cross, my Saviour could not have died for me. He and I needed that horrible upright pole and its bar too, from which Christ was suspended for our sins, between heaven and earth. He could not suspend any part of His suffering to obviate his goal.

Where dips the rocky highland
Of Sleuth Wood in the lake,
There lies a leafy island
Where flapping herons wake
The drowsy water-rats;
There we've hid our faery vats,
Full of berries
And of reddest stolen cherries.

Come away, O human child!
To the waters and the wild
With a faery hand in hand,
For the world's more full of weeping than you can understand

Where the wandering water gushes
From the hills above Glencar,
In the pools among the rushes
That scarce could bathe a star,
We seek for slumbering trout
And whispering in their ears
Give them unquiet dreams;
Leaning softly out
From ferns that drop their tears
Over the young streams.

(Refrain)

(W. B. Yeats)

I may wish to shield another from the woes and evils of this world. I may attempt this in subtle, languid ways or I may try to accomplish the barring of the way of the world by more harsh means. The desire is laudable, but the truth is that I cannot shield my child, nor anyone, from what the world really is. I can set up a little bower which may seem like a sanctuary of security. The world will still weep on me and him or her. That's the nub of reality. Today, we can let go somewhat, let go of our control over others and over our children. What's more, the child does not really wish us to steal his or her true life experiences.

In 1935, the Limited Editions Club decided that James Joyce's *Ulysses* needed modern illustrations—sketches of a caliber equal to Joyce and his novel. They chose Henri Matisse (1869-1954) as the artist. The celebrated French artist produced twenty drawings and ten etchings, all of which appear in the edition of *Ulysses* that can be found in the Martello Tower at Sandy Cove. Matisse did not use his unique, simplified yet stylized motifs to portray the Dublin that Joyce had sketched in the novel, but rather a return to Homer's *Odyssey*. Matisse used Homer's, not Joyce's, script to draw his scenes. The six episodes on which he focused, however, find their counterparts in Joyce's chapters. Columbia University has offered the original etched soft ground plate for these treasures at $2075 apiece. Scenes such as Odysseus blinding Polyphemus and his return home to Ithaca are evocative to say the least. Seeing both Matisse's signature and Joyce's manuscripts inspires. The most powerful aspect of this inspiration comes from the fact that both art and literature inspire a spectrum of emotion and reaction –from distaste and displeasure to praise and awe. Both Joyce and Matisse aroused this range, but all must admit to their talent.

That's what life is about: respect for diversity. Espouse multiculturalism today.

False Sphinx! False Sphinx! By reedy Styx of old
Charon leaning on his oar,
Waits for my coin. Go thou before, and leave
Me to my Crucifix.

Whose pallid burden, sick with pain watches the
World with worried eyes
And weeps for every soul that dies, and weeps for
Every soul in vain.

(The Sphinx – Oscar Wilde)

The first image comes from Greek mythology in which the boatman, Charon, has the job of ferrying the dead across the River Styx to the underworld (for a price!). The spiritless Sphinx can go that way if she wishes; she does not inspire me. She is false. In turn, that dark picture is dismissed in favour of one eternal image of death and resurrection at the crucifixion of Christ.

Wilde's picture is not the one I want. Wilde's portrayal of Christ, while correct in its burden, is not in its failure. Wilde, you had it wrong. Every day, millions use the crucifix and the one who hung on the cross as the stimulation of faith. I don't need to worry about crossing to the other side, nor is the cross of Christ a failure. I believe!

Most literary people are familiar with Yeats' desire to be buried in Drumcliff, County Sligo. However, long before W. B., another character used Drumcliff as a center. Away back in 514, St. Columba (Colmcille, in Gaelic) founded an internationally famous monastery in the town. Many sought out its halls of learning, only to see it plundered by the Vikings in 807. St. Columba had to leave Drumcliff for Iona, Scotland because he had instigated a war. Since he had disputed a copyright law (yes, true, he had copied a psalter from St Finian without permission) and the king ruled "to every cow its calf and every book its copy". In 561, Columba clashed with Finian and in the ensuing war, 3000 died. As penance, the saint had to convert an equal number of new Christians while he was in exile/banishment on Iona. Suffice it to say that the saint succeeded, but the motivation for his success was hardly positive, was it?

Today we are faced with choices: to fight or support, to learn or to destroy, to innovate or to copy, to make amends or to take revenge. It seems that Colmcille was involved in all of these and to his credit, fostered the positive over the negative. Will we choose today to power ourselves past the mistakes of the hour and to overshadow our loss and destructive tendencies with a clear witness for God?

Serenades

The Irish nightingale
Is a sedge-warbler,
A little bird with a big voice
Kicking up a racket all night.

Not what you'd expect
From the musical nation,
I haven't heard one-
Nor an owl, for that matter.

My serenades have been
The broken voice of a crow
In the draught of a dream,
The whiz of bats

Or the ack-ack
Of the ramp corncrake
Lost in no-man's-land
Between combines and chemicals.

So fill the bottles, love,
Leave them inside their cots,
And if they do wake us, well,
So would the sedge-warbler.

(Seamus Heaney)

How unusual to invoke a series of amusical birds for a serenade – the rackets of the nightingale, the crow, the corncrake; the non-music of the owl, the bat. At this moment, Heaney serenades his love away from the reality of children. It is his voice which attracts his love. For a brief second only, she will hear the dulcet tones of her lover of the "musical nation". Heaney has heard his own serenades (raucous ones) and is now to transcend all serenades with his own poetry. He is to take his lover away from the duties of family and into the bliss of romance.

Your voice has power to inspire, to serenade. It is music in the ears of someone, no matter how unattractive by standards set by others. Use your voice to inspire. It can lack form or tone, but it must inspire.

Castle Coole is an ornate neoclassical mansion, begun in 1790 and not completed until the 1820s. The Earl of Belmore lavished such money on its architecture, construction, decoration and furnishing that he died deeply in debt. His son took over the building of the castle. The Portland stone for building the façade was shipped from Dorset in England to Ballyshannon, Donegal, then hauled overland. In 1821, King George IV was to visit Ireland, so the Earl had made orders for a State bedroom and bed specially appointed for the king. In the end, the royal personage never slept in the bed. A visitor can view it and the rest of the ostentation that composes Castle Coole. The oval ballroom is breath-taking. Do you want to rent it for a reception to transport you and your guests into a dream world? It's available! Luxuriate in the gilded Regency furniture and dance on the dark oak floor! You can find it near Enniskillen just an hour and a half from Belfast.

The "Lifestyles of the Rich and Famous" always intrigue and inspire us. Do we want to be like them? Hardly, maybe, but they inspire us to try harder, to succeed to raise the bar, to do better. Just maybe one day we can become a little more like the wealthy. We know we will never lie in that bed, but the dream is enough! Dream big today.

It was a pleasant drive in the very cool spring air, with the scent of ubiquitous Irish rain squalls in the nose. The road to Carrowmore Megalithic Cemetery was well posted. The car park was just off the main road and the visitor's center was a trove of information. Ireland's and Europe's significant grave site was excavated in 1977 and archaeologists found the monuments set in an oval cluster around a central cairn and they say that the tombs have been here for six thousand years. The reasons for their existence vary–prestigious burial places for high society or sacred ground for a tribe's worship services. Each mound has a central chamber and outside and around it are strategically placed boulders (one has thirty one rocks surrounding the cairn). In the vault are cremated human bones, antler pins and a stone ball beside unopened sea shells. There is clear evidence that the tombs have been reused over and over. We strolled over the grass to stoop and peer and read the plaques. Soon the sun came out, but an eerie feeling pervaded the mist hanging in the air. I half expected a banshee to keen across my path and overpower the noise of passing lorries. I was in the place of the dead.

It boggles the mind to imagine how such structures were built, but they stand as mute reminders of the human desire to memorialize death, to continue past it and to worship. Don't concern yourself with a tombstone today, but set up something by which others will remember your good deeds. Provide an act of kindness and what's in the grave won't matter. Jesus left his tomb empty and it was just a borrowed one too. What He did before His body was laid there provides you with your impetus today to go out and find someone to love.

When Belfast was granted the royal rank of a City by Queen Victoria, plans were made and effected to build a cathedral on the site of the old Ste. Anne's church. So, in 1899, the Cathedral Church of Ste. Anne was begun. Because Belfast soil is so water-logged, the foundations had to have pilings sunk to a depth of fifty feet – that's fifty feet closer to the burning earth's core. In the cathedral, I came across the tomb of Lord Carson of Duncan who had been a QC (a lawyer) for Lord Queensbury whom Oscar Wilde sued for libel. You may remember that Wilde was infamously tried and served the hell of prison for being a homosexual (a crime in those days). In Saint Anne's, however, is a more symbolic version of a journey to a fiery centre then to hellish persecution in prison. The floor at the cathedral front door is a maze of marble slabs. There are two destinations to this maze. Follow the white marble pieces and you move inexorably to the holy sanctuary of the church. Follow the black marble inlays and you hit a dead end. The white is said to be the path to eternal life; the black will end you up in hell, presumably.

Today is one marble slab in your journey. Are you on a white or a black slab?

And to be mere Fortune's lackeyed groom,–I swear
I love it not! These things are less to me
Than the thin foam that frets upon the sea,
Less than the thistle down of summer air
Which hath no seed; better to stand aloof
Far from these slanderous fools who mock my life
Knowing me not, better then the lowliest roof
Fit for the meanest hind to sojourn in,
Than go back to that hoarse cave of strife
Where my white soul first kissed the mouth of sin.

(Taedium Vitae – Oscar Wilde)

Wilde is clearly not enamoured with his present condition as he writes; yet, he has made the first step toward freedom. He has verbalized his state – "a lackey" in a "cave of strife", kissing the mouth of sin" – "I love it not." Nor would I love it, Oscar. Next, he distances himself from the mockers and the slanderers. He vows that any lifestyle, no matter how lowly, is an improvement upon where he is now. Despite Wilde's doleful words, he gives us inspiration to take steps to move away from a life of addiction to someone, some habit, some object. Today is the day to act. Don't "go back to that hoarse cave."

To a Friend whose Work has come to Nothing

(W. B. Yeats)

Now all the truth is out,
Be secret and take defeat
From any brazen throat,
For how can you compete,
Being honour bred, with one
Who, were it proved he lies,
Were neither shamed in his own
Nor in the neighbour's eyes?
Bred to a harder thing
Than Triumph, turn away
And like the laughing string
Whereon mad fingers play
Amid a stone,
Be secret and exult,
Because of all things known
That is most difficult.

Few nations/peoples have tasted defeat as much as the Irish. They can teach the rest of us a lesson in war. It is a hard insult to the loser, especially when a victor has been declared in flaunting pride, even if it can be "proved he lies". When one knows that right is on his/her side, yet might still prevails, it is difficult to turn away, to exult in the purity of our heart, to move on.

Have you suffered humiliation today? Has the truth been buried? Has the statement been made that you have lost? I can personally vouch for the fact that silence wins the day.

Ireland has become synonymous with lace. Some of the best known lace comes from Clones and Carrickmacross in County Monaghan. In the 1850s, there were one thousand five hundred lace makers in Clones alone and families wove their own motifs (harp, shamrock, fern) into their fine artwork. As for Carrickmacross , the lace industry began there in the 1820s through the efforts of a Rector's wife and was revived later by a spinster, Ms. Reed. Her attempts at maintaining the industry in town failed until a Mr. Kennedy opened a lace making school in the early twentieth century. That too died out. Finally, the Sisters of St. Louis revived a lace cottage industry when they opened a convent in town. It carries on today. If these people had not fanned into flame this fine art each time it was about to sputter out, Diana, Princess of Wales would never have been able to adorn her wedding dress with yards and yards of Carrickmacross lace. It was gorgeous that June day, was it not, all you millions who watched the wedding on TV?

Patience is not one of my fortes and I need to be inspired to act and think more patiently, like the men and women who would never let the lace industry die out. A lace-maker can inspire me to slow down and exercise patience. I promise I'll do that today. And you?

Templedouglas church in Donegal in 521 AD heard the cries of a baby named Crimthann. This little lad was to become a leading light in the early Christian church in Ireland and Britain. His baptismal name means "fox" in Gaelic, but we do not know if his parents had some connotative goal in christening their son this way. The boy, however, had none of the qualities we might associate with a fox—he became known as Colm or Columba, meaning Dove. We presume it was because of his peaceful and gentle nature that he received this new name. Over time, Colm acquired a "nickname"— Colmcille, meaning "dove of the church." Templedouglas church became a favourite haunt of Colm so that he could pray and serve as altar boy. He eventually became a saint, Saint Columba or Colmcille. From humble roots marked by a slab of rock in a field where Crimthann was born, he grew into a giant for God. A beautiful Celtic cross stands tall near the slab in the field to celebrate this life. The effort taken to travel and search down narrow laneways for church and cross was worthwhile for me. I meditated on who we really are and what our origins mean. Our name is of little importance; it is our character which reveals our true identities. It is not the highness of birth which opens doors to success, but it is our motivation to go out and touch others which makes us flourish and grow.

Take another laneway today and think about your origins and identity. You have a future which does not necessarily rely on the past or present.

Memory of my Father
(Patrick Kavanagh)

Every old man I see
Reminds me of my father
When he had fallen in love with death
One time when sheaves were gathered.

That man I saw in Gardner Street
Stumble on the kerb was one,
He stared at me half-eyed,
I might have been his son.

And I remember the musician
Faltering over his fiddle
In Bayswater, London,
He too set me the riddle.

Every old man I see
In October-coloured weather
Seems to say to me:
'I was once your father.'

Admittedly, we are all inter-related and not the human islands that we perceive ourselves to be, or even wish to be. The human race is one, originating from one. "I was once your father." I was once one with you, and can be again if you and I but connect. Even death does not negate or delete that reality. When you go out this June day or an October day, look into the eyes of others and feel as one with them. John Ball wrote in his famous novel, In the Heat of the Night, "You are a credit to your race, the human race." That's my inspiration today.

The Trout
(John Montague)

Flat on the bank I parted
Rushes to ease my hands
In the water without a ripple
And tilt them slowly downstream
To where he lay, tendril light,
In his fluid sensual dream.

Bodiless lord of creation
I hung briefly above him
Savouring my own absence
Senses expanding in the slow
Motion, the photographic calm
That grows before action.

As the curve of my hands
Swung under his body
He surged, with visible pleasure.
I was so preternaturally close
I could count every stipple
But still cast no shadow, until

The two palms crossed in a cage
Under the lightly pulsing gills.
Then (entering my own enlarged
Shape, which rode on the water)
I gripped. To this day I can
Taste his terror on my hands.

This moment frozen is time is an encapsulation of controlling power used on the defenceless, innocent and trusting. I note that there is no indication of the author's sentiments after he captures the trout. No expression of remorse, for his own admission that he could actually "taste the terror." After I read the poem, I hoped that the trout had been able to slither free from the grasp.

Don't bully or engage in power-tripping today. You may generate terror which you may not feel.

It is all too common now to buy a property in real estate that is not as it seems. I have personal experience. A scandal called the "leaky condo syndrome" caused losses of millions of dollars for homeowners in British Columbia. Builders followed a faulty code, and interior rot in walls developed. Two real estate incidents in Ireland reminded me of two concepts in the business world: 'buyer beware' and 'invest for the present and for the future'. In Ballymote is the Church of the Immaculate Conception. It was built in 1864 on lands donated by Gore-Booth family of Lissadell House. Builders could not find a solid foundation base and so used huge bales of wool as the foundation! That's an accident waiting to happen, yet the church still stands (something to do with faeries or Irish luck or the holy place!?). Also in Ballymote is its castle built by the Red Earl of Ulster in 1300. It is the strongest castle in Connacht, but it sold for just four hundred pounds ($1000.00) and three hundred cows to Red Hugh O'Donnell in 1598. Red Hugh got immediate value in his cows and in the property. He used it as base for further conquest. The property today can fetch millions in land value and heritage promotion.

Our advice for today is to be alert for the scam and deceit in people. And, look to how you invest, not just financially, but in character building and attributes deposited in the lives of others.

Along the shores of Lough Foyle in Donegal lies a fishing/tourist port, Greencastle. In 1783, Bishop Harvey (also Earl of Bristol) oversaw the operation of his diocese, literally. Harvey was known as the "wicked prelate" by George III and perhaps by his parishioners too. The bishop was in charge of St. Finian's Church in Greencastle and he lived in Dunhill Castle. Harvey was instrumental in building St. Finian's, so he designed it so that the entrance of the church was directly facing his room in his palace/castle. He had the reputation of 'spying on' his flock by watching the congregation going into the main entrance, via his telescope. As they entered Mass, he kept a tally of who mixed with whom and who was faithful. He thus knew when he could "hit up" for more tithes because the soul had been negligent at 'following the Lord's command' by absenting his/her body from the liturgy or because someone rubbed shoulders with the wealthy.

We sometimes comment that our governments impose and impinge on our privacy, or that Big Brother is watching. That may be a political reality, but it is so sad that one of God's pastors had to check up on the habits of "the elect" in a deceitful way. What are you doing today? Don't go to church just because someone is watching or because God sees (though He truly does). Worship today because you want to offer to God praises for His accomplishments in your life.

Mid-Term Break

I sat all morning in the college sick bay
Counting bells knelling classes to a close.
At two o'clock our neighbours drove me home.

In the porch I met my father crying –
He had always taken funerals in his stride-
And Big Jim Evans saying it was a hard blow.

The baby cooed and laughed and rocked the pram
When I came in, and I was embarrassed
By old men standing up to shake my hand.

And tell me they were "sorry for my trouble".
Whispers informed strangers I was the eldest,
Away at school, as my mother held my hand

In hers and coughed out angry tearless sighs.
At ten o'clock the ambulance arrived
With the corpse, stanched and bandaged by the nurses.

Next morning I went up into the room. Snowdrops
And candles soothes the bedside; I saw him
For the first time in six weeks. Paler now,

Wearing a poppy bruise on his left temple,
He lay in the four-foot box as in his cot.
No gaudy scars, the bumper knocked him clear.

A four-foot box, a foot for every year.

(Seamus Heaney)

Dealing with the death of a young child is heart-wrenching and incomprehensible. Here we see Heaney's anguish at his younger brother's passing, simply but upsettingly. The brutality of emotions at facing the strangers who arrived for the wake, his parents, the neighbours, and then images of the body are factual, yet deeply disturbing. "A four-foot box, a foot for every year." He measures his loss, but cannot fathom it. Those last words hit like a brick when the reader realizes just how young the lad was.

Empathize with someone who has had a young friend, sibling, child pass on. It inspires that person and you.

I have watched them fish everywhere in Ireland. The Irish (and Scottish) are crazy about recreational fishing. Easky in Sligo was no exception, and rightly so, because "easky" means "fish" in Gaelic (watch out fishers; Easky is a surfing paradise too). Towering over surfers or fishers is Roslee Castle at Easky. This castle was the base of the McDonnells, Scottish mercenaries for the O'Dowds. These paid foreign soldiers would do the dirty work for the ruling class. Once used and paid, they could become dispensable despite the place to which they had risen. The "gallowglasses" of the McDonnells , as they were known, were disenfranchised. The McDonnells' castle, Roslee, was handed over to the O'Dowd's (Daniel) by James I in 1618. And, the Irish just went right on fishing. There is a fascinating story about Roslee and a unique fishing yarn. The castle sits beside a river. The cook for the O'Dowds set a trap in the river and ran a line to a bell in his kitchen. Whenever a salmon entered the trap, the bell rang and the cook ran to fetch this fresh catch. Mr. and Mrs. O'Dowd would have the super fresh catch of the day for dinner.

"We can never be sure of the bite in our mouth ' (Irish) nor of our future. Life is uncertain, but we can plan and can rely on the will of God to know best. Carpe Diem. Act as if today is the last you have. Let the fish inspire you.

Just outside Drumcliffe in County Sligo is an imposing cold structure near Ballygilgan Strand on Sligo Bay – Lissadell House, the home of the Gore-Booth family from the seventeeth century. Today its past is only a shade, since it was last updated over one hundred years ago. But, in its history, Lissadell, despite its noble and class structured grandeur, echoed with a surge for equality. Sir Robert kept a large store for food for his tenants during the Great Famine. Next, Sir Josslyn was one proponent of the Cooperative concept. Eva was a suffragette and her sister, Constance, Countess Markiewicz born in 1868 [both best known and memorialized by Yeats in his poem, "In Memory of Eva" ("two sisters in silk kimonos, both beautiful, one a gazelle")] took part in the Easter Uprising of 1916 against British Rule and was sentenced to death for her nationalism. She was elected to both British House of Commons and to the Dail Eireann (twice). This potential socialite championed the cause of the politically and economically oppressed. The Gore-Booth family for generations believed in equality and used its influence to achieve what it could for the weaker segment of society.

Today is maybe a day when you can play your role, whatever your share of influence or wealth, to place the unequal one rung higher on the ladder of society. Offer a voice, hold a hand of practical help for the repressed. God made us all in one image.

On the western shore of Lough Neagh in Northern Ireland sits a three hundred year-old fisherman's cottage, very near the Ardboe Cross. It's pure white with a little row garden out front. Narrow windows are on either side of the emerald green half-door. Naturally, the roof is thatched, with durable local lough-shore reeds. Inside, one divided room and a fireplace large enough for cooking and heating fill the space. The roof beams are bog ash, maybe two thousand years old. It's called Coyle's Cottage, and the bearded, capped gentleman at the door could have been Mr. Coyle three hundred and fifty years ago, just home from his working sail on Lough Neagh with his catch of trout or eel. Several weeks after being there, I was in Cape Breton, Nova Scotia, Canada, touring Fort Louisbourg. The first site on the tour of the fort is an old fisherman's cottage. It is also low and small and thatched (not as nicely), though not whitewashed. Inside there are ancient beams, a divided one-room arrangement and a massive fireplace. The fisher would have headed out onto the Atlantic for cod or haddock and returned to his cottage outside the protection of the fortress walls. As you can imagine, there is a reason for the similarity of construction and function. Some immigrants to Cape Breton were Irish.

The world is truly a small place, where the inspiration to live and work is common around the globe. That drive goes with us wherever we go and whatever our nationality. Conspire today to maintain that drive. Work hard, live simply.

As a child in Brantford, Ontario, I knew of the importance of the Massey-Ferguson factory to the economy of our community. When it and the Cockshutt factory went under in the 1960s, the city suffered greatly. I never knew then of the connections of Harry Ferguson of Dromore, Co. Down to my home town. Ferguson was an inventive genius. He revolutionized farming by creating the integral tractor and hydraulic plough. He built and flew his own plane in 1909. He set up his own auto repair and sales business in Belfast and incorporated care safety mechanisms like seat belts into his business. Then in 1938 he teamed up with Henry Ford to produce the Ford-Ferguson tractor. Soon though, conflicts induced him to mass-produce over half a million of his 'wee grey Fergies' in the UK. Farm equipment manufacturing plants under the Ferguson name sprung up all over the world. I recall riding on a Ferguson as I worked a summer job on a farm outside Brantford in the 1950s. As I experienced the multimedia presentation in the Irish Linen Center and Lisburn museum, I was awed by this man who was, it seemed, born to succeed. The exhibition in the museum is called Harry Ferguson, Local Genius, Self-made Man, Visionary.

Such men and women make me feel both jealous and empowered at the same time. I want their genius, but know I will never gain that height. They do, however, give me the hope that I too can contribute my small bit to society. My own vision and genius inspire me today.

The stuff of legends is at Cave Hill, rising about four hundred meters above Belfast. Crannogs, cairns from four thousand years ago, and early Christian forts (McArt's fort still stands) are the settings and grist for the oddest tales of defence against humans and animals. The bills are volcanic lava cooled into basalt set on limestone, which was quarried in the 1800s. One pit is known for its shape (it looks like the Devil drinking at a trough) as the Devil's Punchbowl. I like the legendary imagery. The caves themselves are purportedly the remains of iron mines, but more fascinating and dire tales of the caves' inhabitants abound—wild cavemen, smugglers and criminals. The whole hill is referred to as Napoleon's Nose with McArt's Fort acting as the Emperor's three-sided hat. It takes imagination to see the little man, but that adds to the intrigue of being at Cave Hill. Finally, such a habitat is a natural home for peregrine falcons, kestrels, badgers, bats, skylarks and pipits—a setting for characters out of Tolkien's or Lewis's fantasies.

Cave Hill inspired me to rise above and beyond the dirty city. In travelling that short distance from Belfast, I entered a time machine and enjoyed the excitement of history. Find your own little piece of fantastical history today. Start with your own genealogy. Your own family has a past which can take you down a time line and inspire you.

Malone House, originally the site of the seventeeth century fort on Moses Hill, is set in acres of land in South Belfast. It is a grand late-Georgian Mansion in the parkland known as Barnett Demesne. William Barnett, its last owner, gave it to Belfast in 1946. He had bought it from William Legge who had the influence to have the main Belfast-Dublin road moved so he could have a more private view. The interior is a superb site for wedding receptions and art displays with musical accompaniment at high class lectures or presentations. The grand staircase off the central foyer is the centerpiece of the home. Even the snack and afternoon tearoom, the Malone Room, is palatial—marble surround fireplace, chandeliers, fresh-cut flowers and standard linen tablecloths. When one leaves the manor to take one of the hundreds of paths, the parkland is equally impressive—open meadows, old-growth forests, views over the Lagan River, valley farmland in the distance. One path leads you to Mary Peters Stadium—yes, an athletics track. It is named after the thirty-five year-old Irish pentathlete (MBE and CBE in 1990) who tried for many years to win gold at the Olympics. Finally, in the 1972 Munich games, she succeeded. She not only won, but she broke the world record with a personal best in the last event, the 200 meters. She had displayed grit after placing fourth in 1964 and ninth in 1968. Today Mary Peters administers campaigns in aid of the disabled and other charities. She has headed up the Association of UK Women Athletes.

Side by side in the same lands stand two antithetical structures—one symbolic of the grandeur and glory of human tradition, and the other dedicated to sweaty, steadfast determination. Both have a place in our lives today.

Donegall Square and Shaftesbury Square are two of the most famous names on the map of Belfast. Both names take us back to families who occupied Belfast Castle. The castle is an awe-inspiring sandstone structure set in woods and overlooking the city. Many marital knots have been celebrated here. But let's go back to the 110s when the Normans built the first castle on the site. In 1611 the Chichester family (English landlords) built a stone and timber castle which burned down. Finally, the Chichesters came to live at Ormeau in Belfast in the nineteenth century and the Marquis of Donegall (Chichester) planned a new home upon his remarriage, the current here in Scottish Baronial style. The poor man, however, ran over his 11,000 pound budget and it took his son-in-law (Lord Ashley, Earl of Shaftesbury) to step in and pay the bills. As I wandered the halls, I touched the oak paneling and thought of how privileged we were to have such preserved history. I descended to the cellar which has a Victorian atmosphere. There I savoured an afternoon cold drink after my hike at Cave Hill, and thanked God for true family support, by blood or by matrimony.

Without our families, our names and our hopes might die.

Ireland has produced more than its share of great authors, including four Nobel Literature giants. The most recent of these is Seamus Heaney in 1995. Born in 1939, Heaney displayed his talent early in school and then as a lecturer. In 1963 he received his break in life when mentored and promoted by an Englishman who saw his potential. From then on, his writing output and his rise in popularity were prolific and meteoric. Queens, Berkeley, Harvard, Oxford—quite a heady atmosphere for a boy from Castledawson and Bellaghy, Co. Derry, son of a farmer. Heaney has never forgotten or abandoned these roots, for it is in these beginnings that his inspiration as a poetic genius comes. "I'm very close to home. I have two homes, this house and the house where I was brought up. When I go back, I merge into it," he said in Dublin in 1979. Some of that background is painful. "Midterm Break" refers to his brother's death; there is a dedication to his mother in The Haw Lantern, and "Follower" deals with his father's legacy. Some of his poetry reveals a deep connection with his hometowns. I visited Castledawson and entered the "Door into the Dark" (his volume), a doorway into "The Forge" (his poem). The forge is a blacksmith's cottage set up as it might have been when Heaney, the little boy, stood in the door and watched the Devlin family at work. "All I knew is a door into the dark: Outside, old axles and iron hoops rusting." Yes, there are actually hoops and axles outside!

Heaney has forged inspiring and beautiful poetry. I stood in the museum in Bellaghy and touched his coat and cap and school desk. As I imagined sliding on his coat, I was inspired too, to hammer out something of "beauty and a joy forever" (Keats). Today, I will.

Along a wild road in the Sperrin Mountains in Co. Tyrone I am directed to the Sperrin Heritage Centre. In the carpark, the views across the Glenelly Valley are, without a lie, breathtaking. Glaciated monstrous mounds make up the backdrop which drops down in thousands of acres of purple heather. In the lowlands, dots of white move about—sheep. In the valley a silver river eats through and loose stone hedges cut off sections of a green quilt of farmer's fields. Homesteads spew wisps of smoke into the blue sky. I must find out about this gold in "them thar mountains." I enter the center and learn gold was discovered close by and I can still pan for it now. Another kind of gold was found in the Sperrins. The poteen (Irish whiskey) stills produced as much profit as gold. And an Irish story would not be complete without something supernatural. Finally, the ghost in Murphy's General store reveals itself to the delight of children. Out in this "back of beyond", I can sense the rich heritage of all of Ireland. That heritage consists of a geographic upheaval centuries ago and the creation thereby of a striking lead. It is economic failure and success. It is the love of social entertainment. It is superstition. It is faith.

In this one center, I appreciated that rich fabric of dear old Ireland. The Irish and Ireland inspire me to enjoy life and beauty, to work and play hard and to open my heart to the spiritual every day.

See, I have climbed the mountainside
Up to the holy will of God,
Where once that Angel-Painter trod
Who saw the heavens opened wide.

And throned upon the crescent moon
The Virginal white Queen of Grace,-
Mary! But could I see they face
Death could not come at all too soon.

O, crowned by God with thorns and pain!
Mother of Christ! O, mystic wife!
My heart is weary of this life
And over-sad to sing again.

O, crowned by God with love and flame!
O, crowned by Christ the Holy One
O, listen ere the searching sun
Show to the world my sin and shame.

(San Miniato – Oscar Wilde)

Going through a day with guilt or shame hanging on one's head and heart like a pendulum is draining, unproductive and unnecessary. Such feelings result in a "weariness of life." Who will listen? Where can I go to rid me of shame, to expunge my guilt? Wilde, like any Catholic, prays to Mary and pleads with her to listen. For me, I go directly to my God through the Spirit and forgiveness and a mind at peace are immediate. Anyone who can listen is a source of reprieve and release. Do you need someone to listen to today? Find him or her – there is someone out thee. Can you be a listener? Be open to that role and point the person to God.

Newgrange - site of winter solstice marker - Meath

Poulnabrune Dolmen - Clare

Along the A4 in Northern Ireland a simple sign diverted me to the "Ancestral Home of Ulysses S. Grant—US President." I turned up the twisting country lane, and after a few kilometers, out in the "back of beyond" (as all country places in Ireland seem to be), I visited a very small cottage set up as it would have been before Grant's great-grandparents left Ireland for America. Amazed at these Spartan living and arrangements, I traipsed from spot to spot reading the anecdotes on the plaques. One slowed me down. At the door to a shed was a stone with a central hole carved therein. The sign told me that Grant's ancestor pounded the branches of whin bushes in this stone and then fed them to his horse team so that the horses' mouths were tough for the bit. Indeed, that would toughen the mouth—touch a whin bush and you will feel how prickly and harsh it is. But, the farmer had to be certain to feed the whin to both horses in the team. If only one partook of the whin, its partner would shy away because of the bad breath of the whin-eater! I contrasted the life of Grant at the American White House with the lifestyle of his forebears and his horses in the little white house. I was sure that Ulysses heard accents of the hard life back in Ireland and that background provided him with some of his grit to be President.

Did Grant wend his way back to Ireland to appreciate those who had toughed it out and then sacrificed as emigrants to give him his new life? I want to learn today that every experience in my past and in the history of my family has worked toward making me who I am today.

Carrickfergus Castle just northwest of Belfast is steeped in eight hundred years of military history. The castle dominates the sky in the town and would have been a menacing sight to any naval attackers entering the harbour. It is huge. During my visit, I learned that sieges had been mounted on Carrickfergus by the Scots, Irish, English, and French and was even in action in WWII. Tall, blond John de Courcy of Somerset built the walls and keep in about 1178. The keep is thirty meters high and its walls are three to four meters thick. Amazing defenses to keep out invaders! Inside, a whole community functioned and one of those kept inside was Princess Affreca, wife to Courcy. In the current display there is a life-size figure of Affreca sitting in a window seat, lovingly looking out to sea. She would have loved to escape, maybe out the Postern Gate or Sally Gate, reserved for military emergencies. Here she was holed up far from her Norse family on the Isle of Man and her native Norway, a victim of a political alliance with an ambitious, chauvinist, marauding soldier, John de Courcy. She wanted to go home. De Courcy and Affreca had no offspring and she devoted her time in Ireland to founding a monastery at Greyabbey dedicated to Mary. Affreca's remains and effigy are at Greyabbey. Her features on the statue there are more peaceful and settled than those on the effigy at Carrickfergus.

I contrasted the two Affrecas and was inspired to direct my goals in life, not inspired by the dreams of others, but by my dedication to God and to others in need.

The great city known for its creation of the Titanic and more recently the Titanic museum (go see the latter; it is superb) has grown into a vibrant town now that the Troubles are past. It sports a perky image despite its years. And these years of existence also shine out every day as one appreciates the design and architecture of the city. Today, I want us to draw inspiration from two rather conflicting buildings: a bank and a church. Charles Lanyon was a famous Belfast architect who was assigned the task of re-inventing the image of banks in Ireland. In Lanyon's day and earlier, bankers had a cut-throat image with dark and dirty designs to fleece the poor common man. Part of that image came from the bank's façade—seedy, dirty, plain, 'grungy'. So, Lanyon set to work and today we have those open, soaring, ornate, bright facades which were designed to lend banks a trustworthy image. That's the bank; now let's move on to Sinclair Seaman's Church. This dockside church was designed to let sailors feel at home while in Belfast port. Its pulpit is a ship's bowsprit figurehead of Mizpah (Up to now the Lord has helped us) and the organ has port and starboard lights—red and green. I could even imagine the sailors rolling to the waves' motion as they sang! They were no longer on the dangerous sea but in heaven. Now each of these buildings was created to portray an image of surrealism and to lift the viewer beyond where he or she might have been.

These buildings inspired me to lift my head above the clouds today, to see beyond my petty analyses of the foibles of people or places. Will you follow my lead?

While in Belfast, I dropped by the Ulster Museum just up the street from Queen's University. Among all the archived treasures there, one small item which lifted my heart that day. Set alone in its case was a thin gold ring. It took me back to the Spanish Armada. During the Armada's tangle with Lord Nelson and its ultimate defeat, several galleons in the fleet's number fled along the coast. One such ship, the Girona, foundered off the Giant's Causeway. Among the people and things which went to the bottom was this golden ring. It is a lady's ring inscribed with this Spanish phrase, "No tengo mas que dorte." 'I have nothing more to give you.' Five words in the original which express an ineffable love for her soldier/partner. Its owner and its wearer have long ago disappeared, but years later her sacrificial love for him lives on. I again put my fertile imagination in gear – I pictured her offering the man her eternal circle as they parted at a raucous Spanish port – a poignant scene in a noisy pre-war zone. Then, I envisioned the sailor as his ship struck the basalt Irish rocks, and I heard his last breath as he sank clutching his lover's ring. He too had nothing more to give. His goal to fight for Spain, be a hero and return with money to settle down with her; all was gone. But, his and her feelings live on in the Ulster Museum to inspire us today.

Give until there is nothing more in reserve. Do it out of love. That's what Jesus Christ did for our salvation.

The Forge

(Seamus Heaney)

All I know is a door into the dark.
Outside, the old axles and iron hoops rusting;
Inside, the hammered anvil's short-pitched ring,
The unpredictable fantail of sparks
Or hiss when a new shoe toughens in water.
The anvil must be somewhere in the centre,
Horned as a unicorn, at one end square,
Set there immovable: an altar
Where he expends himself in shape and music.
Sometimes, leather-aproned, hairs in his nose,
He leans out on the jamb, recalls a clatter
Of hoofs where traffic is flashing in rows;
Then grunts and goes in, with a slam and flick
To beat iron out, to work the bellows.

Heaney's sensual imagery in this masterpiece is superb, is it not? The sights, the sounds, the feel, the smells. The central fulcrum of all this action is the anvil / the altar.

Just as the smithy has a pivot, so too does the poet and the person. The anvil and the Muse of inspiration sourcing out the creation of resonance and newness. Not only the brawn and brain of Heaney's life environment need a central engagement point. We all need it today. Mine is Christ and His Spirit: the Rock and the Breath of life. My anvil and my bellows, and, I hope, yours too.

Driving in Ireland can be a challenge. The main two lane roads can clog quickly once a spewing lorry or a farmer's tractor backs up traffic. The country lanes are my kind of driving, but one never knows what is around the next corner – sheep, a speeding driver in the center of the road, a farmer herding his cows across the lane to the milking parlour? Near Lough Key in Sligo, I opted for the lane and met no obstacles. I did, however, come across the "Red Earl's Road" built in 1300. On this road, I learned of the Battle of the Curlews. In 1497, O'Donnell and McDermott fought (the Fighting Irish). O'Donnell was supposedly invincible, but this time he lost and lost big. The family's book outlining its standards and written by St. Colmcille was taken by the McDermotts as a prize of war. The book, known as the "Cathach" or the 'Battler', meant so much to O'Donnell that he plotted for 2 years for its recovery. At the Battle of the Curlews (*Ragh* Mountain in Gaelic), O'Donnell won the book and it was restored to its owner. It now sits in the Royal Irish Academy.

Is a book worth fighting over? Indeed, it is. Many have fought and died to defend their beliefs as set down in any number of books. More than any have fought to defend the Bible. And the most definitive battle was undertaken and won on a mountain too. It's called Mount Calvary. At times, it looked like the Christian's book would be "taken" (burned, banned, denounced), but, it has stood the test. Today's a good day to pat your Bible, or the book in which your standards are defined, and be inspired by its existence.

With midnight always in one's heart
And twilight in one's cell
We turn the crank or tear the rope
Each in his separate hell
And the silence is more awful far
Than the sound of brazen bell.

And never a voice comes near
To speak a gentle word:
And the eye that watches through the door
Is pitiless and hard
And by all forgot, we rot and rot
With soul and body marred.

(Ballad of Reading Gaol – Oscar Wilde)

What a pity to think that no one cares, that I am alone and permanently marred, even if I am suffering alone as a criminal (as Wilde was labeled in those days).

Search out someone today who needs your attention, however brief, maybe only a word. Offer that person sunlight for a second, and the sound of beauty in a genuine warm hello. Go to a prison or an old people's home.

He gave the little wealth he had
To found a house for fools and mad
And showed by one satiric touch
No nation wanted it so much
(Jonathan Swift)

Erin, the tear and the smile in thine eyes
Blend like the rainbow that hangs in the skies
(Thomas Moore)

Out of Ireland have we come
Great hatred, little room,
Maimed us from the start
I carry from my mother's womb
A fanatic heart
(Yeats – Remorse for Intemperate Speech)

"In Ireland the inevitable never happens and the unexpected constantly occurs."

(Sir John Pentland Mahaffey)

"Do you know what Ireland is?" asked Stephen with all venom. "Ireland is the old sow that eats her farrow."

How much do you value your native land? As much as the Irish? Despite the self-deprecation, to the Irish, their country is one worth dying for. How about that as an inspiration for you?

Some of my first memories of school were learning of the 'lake-dwellers', who created whole villages on stilts so as to provide a natural protective barrier. I could not believe it when the images in an ancient school text became a reality in the three dimensional. On numerous loughs (there are three hundred on Lough Gara in Sligo alone), I found "crannogs". They are lake dwellings from the Bronze Age and were used until the 1700s. The Irish enlarged on the concept of stilted houses when they actually created small islands from heaps of stones thrown into the lake. Once the surface was reached, the locals covered the rocks with oaken planks and then a foundation of more stones was laid for the homes. Finally, a palisade enclosed the community or home. Sometimes the crannog was used only as a hunting or fishing blind. Such setups preserved not only present generations, but also a museum of artifacts from the lake bed. The dwellers would create a rubbish heap by tossing garbage "overboard" and the water preserved a treasure trove of material for archaeologists – material which exactly details the lifestyle and dates of the peoples. Today, these crannogs resemble actual islands complete with vegetation or small fishing huts.

Humans will go to almost any end to provide for themselves safe shelter and they also leave behind evidence of who they have been. We not only want to leave our mark on the world, but also we do so without thinking. We are a testament. What an inspiration that can be for parents to shelter children and pass on the torch of an inheritance, to a stranger, to a friend, to a relative, to a shut-in, to the dispossessed, to a child. Inspire someone by giving part of you to him or her.

Marble Arch Caves is a popular tourist attraction in County Fermanagh on the Lough Erne circuit. The caves were cut by three rivers coursing down Slieve Cuilcagh. The three streams unite underground and emerge as the Cladagh River. Where the river gushes from the caves is the Marble Arch, a thirty-foot high rock archway formed by years of water powering its way through. The Arch has given its name to the cave system, where a tour of seventy-five minutes (walking and a boat ride) takes you past dank walls, limestone stalagmites and cascading stalactites. In a typical Irish rainsquall, the river rises so high that the caves are closed. We were lucky enough to be able to take the tour, following Declan our guide. He called out in the darkness to my wife, "Esther, are you bringing up the rear?" in a broad Irish brogue. When we turned out our flashlight, we experienced what true inkiness is. The darkness was frightening. Nothing was more inspiring to me than to flick the switch to see where I was. My teeth chattered from fear as well as from the bitter, damp cold—even in July! I never wanted to be so far underground again. I was so appreciative of light.

Turn on a light today—go outside—be thankful for the light of day. Some don't have the luxury – living in the closets and caves of fear, isolation and imprisonment. Work to free them.

Not far from a cairn at Tobernalt is Tobernalt Well, hid in a grove. It is a pilgrim's destination on the last Sunday of July. The rock served as liturgical altar during the Penal laws when the Protestants outlawed the Catholics' attending mass. Masses were held in secret outdoor venues instead. This was one such site, at a well. The rock and well have gained significance because the Irish say Saint Patrick prayed at the rock and hence the water from the well is holy. It provides cures for backaches, blindness and headaches. Pilgrims insert their fingers into indents Patrick was supposed to have made and they leave petitions on rags on the Rag Tree, a holly bush. Saint Patrick is said to have come here because the well had been the site of pagan rituals. He wanted another focus. The habit at Tobernalt continues today – the procession is decked out in garlands to mark the beginning of Lughrasa, a Celtic festival for the god of harvest, Lugh.

The question arises why the Christian must rely on the physical symbol – a rock, a tree, a statue, an altar, whatever. Instead of the spiritual inner sense of strength from the Spirit of God, we garner strength from items and people around us. It is the fruit of lips which we use to praise God that supplies our power for and from God. Our harvest, our rock, our well-spring is Jesus Christ and his tree was at Golgotha. We need only Him for our cures. His garland of holiness has become our possession of praise.

The sin was mine; I did not understand.
So now is music prisoned in her cave,
Save where some ebbing desultory wave
Frets with its restless whirls this meagre strand.

(The New Remorse- Oscar Wilde)

The sin which Wilde alludes to here is unknown – large or small? But he committed it without a full sense of its consequences. As a result, he has stopped the music in someone's heart, or in his own. Not entirely so, Oscar; somewhere there is a flicker of a note of music in a wave, on a beach. Just go to an Irish beach **again**, Oscar. Irish beaches are not meagre; the strands are endless. The Irish hope for change is as endless as their beaches.

I am inspired today that there is always a hope for reconciliation after the wrong is done in a sin, no matter how grave it may have been

You've got to search for these stones. It's a casual walk just outside of Sligo City, overlooking Lough Gill. One which a couple would enjoy on a pleasant summer afternoon, just a kilometer's saunter through an Irish glade. Unless you've been pre-informed you won't search through the overgrowth at the top of the hill – two cairns of stones, most likely entrances to passage tombs, the burial spots of two Irish fighters, Remra and Omra. Remra's gorgeous daughter, Gile, was bathing outdoors at Taberralt Well and Omra spied her. Omra chose to linger and enjoy ogling her beauty. As happens, one thing led to another. They met and loved – and were caught by Remra. Inevitably in things of the heart, conflict ensued and Remra declared war on Omra. After the battle, Gile came upon both father and lover dead on the field of fray. Legend has it that Gile's tears flowed in such quantity that Lough Gill was formed. Hence its name, meaning Bright Lake. How could any brightness derive from such an ill-fated story? Well, it's the lake itself: a gem among any lakes. It is an unlikely event that such beauty flowed from such tragedy, but we can take comfort in the fact that the Irish wish good to come from evil in almost any circumstance. It's a principle of being Irish.

The tale reminds me of David and Bathsheba, a story in the Bible. He stopped to watch her bathe. He sinned. Bathsheba's husband died and David was forbidden his most ardent wish. Yet, from David and Bathsheba's union came Solomon – a gem of wisdom, the creator of the beautiful temple. Yes, beauty does flow out of conflict, pain and suffering. It's God's principle, as well as an Irish blessing.

Windharp
For Patrick Collins

(John Montague)

The sounds of Ireland,
that restless whispering
you never get away
from, seeping out of
low bushes and grass
heatherbells and fern,
wrinkling bog pools,
scraping the tree branches,
light hunting cloud,
sound hunting sight,
a hand ceaselessly
combing and stroking
the landscape, till
the valley gleams
like the pile upon
a mountain pony's coat.

Sounds do affect the human soul and psyche. These poetic forceful images of the sounds of Ireland have touched not only the Irish at home, but those true Irish around the globe. That windharp has circled the world and, "combing and stroking the landscape", it has inspired us until our personal valley "gleams like the mountain pony's coat."

The harp is one of the symbols of Ireland. Latch on to a sound today which inspires you and becomes the symbol of your existence. Or, create your own windharp to motivate others.

The harp that once thro' Tara's halls
The soul of music shed
Now hangs as mute on Tara's walls
As if that soul were fled.

No! My harp is not dead.

I am not usually naïve nor easily manipulated. However, I was taken in rather badly by the charm of an Irishman upon my second visit to Eire. Picture, please, the narrow twisting high banked lanes of Ireland. The banks are topped irregularly by hedgerows or loose stone walls. We were meandering slowly through the countryside when the road straightened into a cut through a wide plain in County Roscommon. I could now view the road for more than a hundred yards ahead! A male figure stood waving his arms in my lane. A tiny van was parked in a lay-by. I geared down and, after stopping, rolled down my window. "Will youse have some petrol youse can spare me. The wains is in yon vayical and I be's wantin' to get home." Little heads bobbed and waved in the back window of the van and the man's cap was off in abject begging. I gave in to my feelings of sympathy. Better stated, the man sprang into action at my delay as if it was a denial to his request. The siphon hose was out of the passenger seat in a jiffy. From long practice of his art, he had relieved me of half my tank of fuel in a blink. I was unaware of the magnitude of his take. He grinned a dutiful thank you and I went stupidly on my way. What a "mark" I had been! Only when I realized that I needed to refill my tank 100 miles in advance did I curse my idiocy. I am certain that, if I had retraced my route in a week or so, the same man would have been working his artful thievery, his satirical grin fixed once more on his victim.

What a parallel to the Great Deceiver who takes from us more than petrol – he takes our purity, our innocence, our joy, our time. Today, be on the watch for his guile.

It's Orangemen's day, and what a celebration it is! Parades, drums, pipes, flutes, accordions, banners, top-hatted men flaunt the victory of the Battle of the Boyne, July 12 1690. (actually, July 11 on our modern calendar.) The site of the battle near Drogheda has been preserved, and there is a walking tour to help one envisage the bloody skirmish between King William III of Orange (Protestant) and his own father-in-law, King James II, England's Catholic king. The battle was more than just two armies in strategic conflict. At stake were the power of the British throne, religious dominance in Ireland, and French influence of Louis XIV in Europe. The walking-tour takes one to large murals depicting the events of the battle at any given hour. William personally led his thirty six thousand men to victory over twenty-five thousand English and French soldiers (the largest number of deployed troops ever in Ireland.) James was present too, and was sent home in retreat and defeat. Part of the site hosts the setup for a mock reenactment of the battle, staged every year, complete with cannons, and seating for the audience.

I did not see the retro battle, but I was able to stand in the field and picture the noise and blood. I envisioned how Ireland would be different today if the outcome of the battle had turned the other way. I would not have been party to my first Orange parade on July 12, 1969. Is today a turning point in your life? Be inspired to fight your battle and, in victory or in defeat, you will be stronger.

If an Irish person was to repeat that old poem, he or she would be expecting the impossible. Ireland's Atlantic situation enforces a wet climate. Indeed, if it is not raining, the Irish call it "a Great Day." The rain can come at any minute. The downpour soaks and then subsides until the next black cloud is pushed overland from the Atlantic. One rainstorm predominates in my memory. We were enjoying an informative and engaging stroll along the Liffey and into the streets of Dublin. It was July, and the sun warmed the city to an unusual 19 degrees Celsius. Without warning, the torrent struck and we were drenched even before we could get the umbrellas from our backpacks. We dove for cover into a café and the proprietor happily served us food and drink until the cloud had passed over in fifteen or twenty minutes (such business people may be the only ones who love the rain). He bid us a merry "Cheerio!" as we recommenced our sightseeing.

I am one of the few who love the rain, and I am inspired by its fresh cleansing of the environment. If you happen to be one who detests rain, take a change of heart today. If it's raining now, or might rain soon, try enjoying it. Maybe even go out and run in it. "Singin' in the Rain!" It will do you a power of good and will actually inspire you to look at the rainstorms in your life from a positive perspective.

Penal Rock: Altamuskin

(John Montague)

To learn the massrock's lesson, leave your car,
Descend frost gripped steps to where
A humid moss overlaps the valley floor.
Crisp as a pistol-shot, the winter air
Recalls poor Tagues, folding the nap of their frieze
Under one knee, long suffering as beasts,
But parched for that surviving sign of grace,
The bog-Latin murmur of their priest.
A crude stone oratory, carved by a cousin,
Commemorates the place. For two hundred years
People of our name have sheltered in this glen
But now all have left. A few flowers
Wither on the altar, so I melt a ball of snow
From the hedge into their rusty tin before I go.

This poem recalls the Penal Laws when Catholics were denied their religion and civil rights. Crying out for spiritual blessing, they (the Tague family here) huddled at mass rocks like this one and received the "water of the Word" from a fearful priest. Montague takes us, in words, to one such "oratory" which is now deserted. He places on it the simplest of sacrifices, water, as a commemoration of those once present. Why is the glen empty? Because of a reversal of priorities (self-imposed or externally imposed). The Irish have "left the glen." Some died; some emigrated. Others left rural life for the big city.

It is tempting to be diverted from our foundation or goal. Don't let that happen today. If you've got roots, stay there.

They were euphemistically known as the "Troubles", and began in 1968. Northern Ireland was held captive and ransom because of bombings and murders initiated by both sides, Loyalists and Republicans. The atrocities still surface periodically, even now in the twenty first century. I landed in Ireland for the first time in 1969 at the height of the escalation of terrorism after the 1968 Londonderry Massacre. British soldiers and SAS troops were a common sight, even on the residential greens. I recall my mother-in-law offering one platoon of soldiers a cup of tea as they passed. Such patrols were in sixes, three on either side of the road. The last man walked backwards, scouring rooftops for IRA snipers. Helicopters chattered overhead. Barricades and checkpoints had been raised in every village. British snipers sat in blockaded and razor-wired forts as cars passed the checkpoints. One incident stands out. It was midnight, and we were returning from a friend's home. The narrow road was blocked ahead. Heavily armed infantry scoured every car for explosives. I inched forward near to the head of the line. To my right, I noticed a glint. Prone in the tall grass, in the inky blackness, lay a gunner eyeing our every move concerned that I might have opened my trunk/boot. It was eerie. We were at war, at yet we were not! In all the havoc, the citizenry carried on as usual, fearless of the maelstrom around them. When I was asked in Canada how I could go to Northern Ireland without fear, I laughed. I really was not afraid.

Fear is such a powerful, sometimes degrading emotion. There is a higher emotion, which allows one to proceed, protected, not by soldiers, but by spiritual faith and power. This day may present a fearful image for you, but don't succumb to needless threats. There is more to life than fear of the unknown.

But strange that I was not told
That the brain can hold
In a tiny ivory cell
God's heaven and hell.

(Roses and Rue – Oscar Wilde)

Nay, let us walk from fire unto fire,
From passionate pain to deadlier delight,-
I am too young to live without desire,
Too young art thou to waste this summer night.

(Pantheon – Oscar Wilde)

The mentality of our current society is "gratification at all costs." The brain and the body push for material heaven at the risk of hell. Walking on fire is readily accepted as the route to happiness. I am most struck with Wilde's antithetical juxtaposition of "passionate pain to deadlier delight." Switch the adjectives around, and one has a truer bead on reality. I will not waste my strengths on a consuming drive for fleeting pleasure. Today, I will make my words and actions count for more than a minute's or an hour's delight.

Every July 12, the Orangemen march in force throughout Ulster (and around the world) to remember the victorious Protestant king, William of Orange who overcame the Catholic King James at the Battle of the Boyne. From the date of that battle in 1690, the Protestant faith has remained predominant in Ulster. From then until 1795, sectarian feuds raged between Ulster Scots (the Peep 'O Day Boys) and Irish Catholics. On September 21, 1795 in a sleepy field, the Battle of the Diamond, one such feud, took place. The site is near the village of Loughall, County Tyrone. The "Prods" won and the soldiers resorted to Dan Winters' Cottage across the road. There, they formed the charter order of Orangemen to ensure a unified front from then on. In 2002, a friend who lives in the area, drove me down to the field; it is marked by one granite stone. Then we crossed the road (actually at a crossroads – hence, the term "Diamond") to Winters'cottage standing as it was in 1795, complete with lead shot from the battle lodged in the roof. One "Twelfth" in 1969 at Loughall, I watched the black-clad and orange-sashed men carry their banners bedecked with Biblical scenes. I'm sure many did not realize that their existence commenced at a site so nearby.

Affiliation is an inspiration. Join up today – a club, a band, a team, a church – just don't fight over dominance.

At the conclusion of my guided tour at Mountstewart in County Down, home of the Londonderry family, we entered the kitchen. The room was of considerable difference in décor from the rest of the gorgeous home. It was plain and utilitarian. One of the intriguing items on display was a round wheel containing four slots, in one a bone-handled knife (no stainless steel in those days). On the side of the wheel was a small brush. This was the knifeboy's equipment. A typical meal, we were told, had ten courses, each requiring a knife. If forty guests were present, the knife boy had eight hundred twenty knives to clean, four at a time! His job was to clean off excess food with the exterior brush and then insert the knives into the wheel, turn it so that other brushes inside cleaned the blades well, finally rinse the knives in water. If he began his chore when course number one was done, at say 8:15 PM, he might still be hard at it at 1 AM. In the end, he had to account for each knife, in a tally presented to the head butler. Such a chore was an endless tunnel ad infinitum and the knifeboy was often an elderly gent who had been in the employ of the Londonderrys for years.

I marvel at such dedication to a menial, mind-deadening task. He inspired me to revisit my attitude to my job. He might have complained about his lot, but more likely he treated it as an honour to serve the noble family. We each have a chore today, our attitude to how we engage in our task, however much a drudge, should inspire others and ourselves. Because we work "as unto a higher power."

William Carlton wrote that "faeries are fallen angels who are not good enough to be saved, nor bad enough to be lost." Would you really want someone that ambivalent to be looking after you? A rath was a ring-fort, a commonplace discovery by archaeologists and farmers as they search and till the Irish soil. As far back as 300 AD, Celtic and pre-Celtic tribes and families would build safe enclosures for humans and livestock. These earthen or wooden forts are found everywhere. Such physical protection however, was not thought adequate. Outside the rath, the tribe planted a ring of thorn trees and shrubs, so that the faeries who lived there could offer their brand of protection. Anyone who cut these faery forts or even disturbed them, ran the risk of death or bad luck.

What would you do today to assure your safety? I've got a guardian angel, for I am certain that unseen angels surround us. I've also got a fort in my Saviour Jesus. That's my inspiration to step our fearlessly today.

I confess that I love visiting cemeteries and reading tombstone inscriptions, so I had to go to the Clifton cemetery in Belfast. In the late 1700s, the cemetery of St. George Church was flooded once more at high tide, and the Marquis of Donegall donated ground near the poorhouse for the Clifton Street burial ground. Once readied, plots were put up for sale for eight guineas for the rich, and a wall was constructed around the cemetery to offer protection on the investment. This was the era of body-snatchers who sold corpses to anatomists. Alas, the wall was insufficient protection so relatives often stood guard at fresh graves until the body was no longer of value. Or, an iron cage called a coffin-guard, was set over the grave. The cemetery holds at least two characters of interest. Dr. Drewman, the first to call Ireland "the Emerald Isle," lies here, as does Mary Anne McCracken, sister of Henry Joy McCracken who was hanged on July 17, 1778 for his role in the Uprisings. One man had a picture of his pet dog mounted atop his memorial to keep watch. The cemetery has known several periods of deterioration, but since 1990 has been restored as one of Belfast's links with the past.

We humans are a strange breed. We fear death immensely, yet are obsessed with it. I am inspired by the devotion of the living for the dead in Clifton Burial ground. They give me heart that we respect each other and that we wish to harbour memories. We should never live only for the present or for the future.

No, that's not an oxymoron! The Irish are, to be sure, the butt of some cruel jokes. Nor is this phrase the Irish equivalent of the CIA. The Irish monastery was renowned as a superior seat of learning. The Irish monks read Hebrew, Greek and Latin and other current languages beyond their own. The Pope recognized their skills and sent these monks throughout Europe to educate the people. During the twelfth century, however, King Henry II of England took over Ireland and ruled that no Irishman could attend seminaries. He withdrew all Irish monasteries from all over Europe. Such was the effect of this action that Europe fell into a state of illiteracy which prevailed until the Renaissance. From 1600 onwards, the Irish were denied access to learning. Over the centuries, in spite of these edicts, Ireland has produced more than its share of deep thinkers and authors (Shaw, Joyce, Wilde, Synge, O'Casey, Heaney, MacNeice).

It is an accomplishment to press the mind to its potential and to push and educated others to rise to our level. Education is indeed the key to fulfillment. Learn or teach a new fact today.

The entry to Stormont Castle is majestic—a long, straight dip, then a rising avenue to a Neoclassical mansion. The original home was built in 1830, by Reverend John Cleland. It was a plain, Georgian rectangle, modest to reflect a Reverend's lifestyle. But twenty-eight years later, the same Cleland family commissioned the current Baronial structure with battlements, turrets, and iron cresting. What caused this flashy change? Did the Clelands adapt their goals in life from the spiritual to the material? In 1921, a second shift occurred. Stormont was put on the auction block, and was designated a political home—"the demesne shall be...the seat of the government of Northern Ireland." It was opened in 1932 and has become the symbol of Northern Irish parliament, and the Secretary of State for Northern Ireland calls it home.

What do we "home in" on? Where do our priorities lie? In the material? In the spiritual? In the political? My motivation and inspiration comes from the spiritual. I can never eliminate the material world, or political influence (and by that I mean a broad spectrum of ideas, not just governmental bureaucracy) from my life. I encourage you to place the spiritual as the major force of inspiration through today.

Northern Ireland has two celebrated jails. In 1843, architect Charles Lanyon designed the Crumlin Road Gaol in Belfast. It was closed in 1996, but in its hundred and fifty-year existence, has seen a multitude of faces—women, children, and political prisoners. Another prison, the Maze at Long Kesh, was constructed in the 1900s as an RAF airfield, and then converted to house one thousand seven hundred detainees held without charge, accused of involvement in the Troubles of the 60s, 70s and 80s. Unionist and Republican radicals alike made the place a seething Hell. I recall driving down the M1 and enquiring what the highly fortified and austere set of H-blocks to the north was. Barbed wire, armed towers, helicopters and patrols encircled the Maze. Once a political prisoner entered, there was little chance of exit, except by escape or death. Indeed, one of Long Kesh's black marks is the Hunger Strike in 1981, and subsequent death, of Bobby Sands. Sands and his fellow inmates were protesting an inability to get "special category status"— acknowledgement as political prisoners rather than merely terrorists.

Incarceration is meant to serve as a deterrent to criminals. I'm not so sure it does. The inspiration of a cause transcends the vile prospect of languishing in a cell. Some of our greatest religious and political leaders have gone to jail for the right to worship or speak freely. Those men and women inspire me to stand tall, even in a jail, as long as I am not committing a crime in support of my cause.

Come in, my son, and lie on the bed,
And let the dead folk bury their dead.

Nay, go not thou to the red-faced dawn,
Lest the hooves of the warhorse tread thee down.

(Ballade de Marguerite – Oscar Wilde)

We need not be callous or cavalier about death, but we must live in the acknowledgement of its inevitability. A fear of or obsession with death overpowers the thoughts of some. Such a fear is unhealthy and unworthy of faith. A fear of the causes of death is salutary, however – causes such as war, drugs, alcohol, hatred, anger, poverty, speed. Shun those vices today and death is more distant. Inspire yourself to gain control or seek those who can help you grasp the power of the Devil by the throat.

So began Saint Patrick's confession on his deathbed. He continued, "the least of all the faithful, and utterly despised by many." When Patrick, reputedly born in Scotland in 387, was sixteen, his town, Bannavem Taburnicue (either in the UK or Brittany, France), was attacked. His father, Colphurnius, of High Roman family and a church deacon and his sister, disappeared. We have no word of the fate of his mother, Conchessa of Gallic descent. The boy was put into slavery by the Irish pirates, sold to Milchu of Antrim, a Druid high priest. Young Patrick tended sheep near Ballymena on Mount Slemish for six years. There he prayed until an angel told him to run away. He fled to the coast, but realized that he was abandoning his master who needed a ransom of gold the size of his head. The angel told him to follow a boar, which rooted up a good treasure that Patrick later used as his redemption. He ended up in France, both in Tours and off the south coast on Lerins where he worked for God. For eighteen years he laboured and learned until Celestine the Pope gave him the name Patricius (Father of the People) and commissioned him to Ireland to combat the teachings of Palagius. Patrick landed near Wicklow Head in the summer of 433, and never looked back. The only ones who considered him evil were the Druids; for thousands, he was the Holy Bearer of God's Good News. His start as a slave gave him the learning he needed to take the message to the people—he had learned their culture and language.

So, was he a sinner, unlearned? Hardly. What is your self-perception today? Is it valid? Or would someone else think more highly of you. Today hold yourself in high esteem.

Claddagh is a small fishing village on the Corrib River in Galway. Its sailors developed the Claddagh symbol as a "sigil" to be painted on the sails and ships of the town to confirm an alliance. This symbol of two hands around a heart with a crown above has gained world renown in the ring of the same name. Friendship, love and loyalty meet in the ring. Many are family heirlooms (though large numbers were given up by women leaving Ireland in the Famine – they were melted down). Be careful how you wear a Claddagh ring if you have one. On the right hand, heart outwards, you are fancy free. Heart inwards – you are "taken". On the left hand, heart inward, you are happily married. The earliest rings bore the initials RI, supposedly the originator, Roland Joyce of Galway. He was captured by pirates and sold to an Algerian Moor goldsmith who trained Joyce in jewelry craft. Joyce formed the Claddagh ring for his love and, once freed, returned to the town. There he set up his own goldsmith shop to begin further production. It is said he resisted an attractive offer to marry his boss' daughter so he could stay in Algeria. There are other legends as to the ring's origin, but this one inspires me the most. It's about love at all costs.

I feel honoured that someone would wear the Claddagh for me, despite who and where I am. It's not just for lovers – I bought one for my daughter, at her request. Will someone wear a Claddagh for you? I hope so, to inspire you.

Any good American history buff might well tell you that he was Woodrow Wilson, the self-righteous and irritable president at a turbulent time in our world. Wilson's roots are in Ireland, for there his grandfather was born just outside of Strabane, County Derry. From there, he moved to the U.S. Old man Wilson owned another white house, but so much less palatial than Pennsylvania Ave. The Irish home is partly thatched, partly slated, a simple farmer's cottage. From this background, Wilson put his stamp on the world. First a teacher/professor, he became President of Princeton and began the concept of core studies followed by concentration in a specialty. Once into politics and then in the White House, Woodrow Wilson dealt with woman's suffrage and then WW I. Despite his attempts at American neutrality, the U.S. entered the war, but Wilson worked for peace. He introduced the idea of the League of Nations, ultimately incorporated into the 1919 Paris Treaty and the Treaty of Versailles. In 1919, he won the Nobel Peace Prize, though he never saw America become a major player in world peace. From the hearth fire in Derrygalt, Strabane came the spark to make Woodrow Wilson a large historical figure. He died in 1924 but his wife lived on until 1961.

Each one of us can work for peace; we may not become a renowned president or win awards for our strivings. Anywhere, however humble, is a place to light or stoke the fire of peace. And, anyone can do it. Start today.

(bonus!)

1997 marked the 150th anniversary of a dark time in Ireland's history, the Great Famine. Sligo City has three moving memorials erected in 1997. First, there is a statue of a family of three. They huddle in despair on the dock. The parents particularly show signs of sorrow and physical deprivation. They are thin, having handed over any food they have to the little girl. She is tenderly touching her mom's arm and pointing out to sea, hopefully expecting a new life in the New World. Then there is the Famine Graveyard on the site of the old workhouse which took in over 30,000 in a nine year period. Deaths here totaled about 2530 and the bodies were buried behind gates (new ones were erected on July 27, 1997). The gate's top section is a network of two dimensional skulls and the base consists of sparse and feeble tendrils of growth (perhaps signifying the lost potato crops which brought death to so many?) Behind the gates is the third memorial: a bronze sculpture of a hawthorn tree. Its title is *"Faoin Sceach",* the Lone Bush, representing a tree under which victims lay down to die and be buried as nameless losers in Fate's lottery. The Hawthorn Tree was viewed as the sacred protector of unknown dead.

As I stood with my face pressed against the cold iron bars, surrounded by the massive abandoned buildings of the old almshouse, I wept at the loss through no fault of the people of Ireland. Three structures were erected to honour and memorialize the fact that God sends hounds of oppression and banshees of fear into our lives to strengthen us. The Irish are a better people today and the world is a better place because of this sad part of Irish history. "When I will have tried you, as by fire, you will come forth as pure gold."

(bonus!)

Inniskeen Road: July Evening
(Patrick Kavanagh)

The bicycles go by in twos and threes –
There's a dance in Billy Brennan's barn tonight,
And there's a half-talk code of mysteries
And the wink-and-elbow language of delight.
Half-past eight and there is not a spot
Upon a mile of road, no shadow thrown
That might turn out a man or woman, not
A footfall tapping secrecies of stone.

I have what every poet hates in spite
Of all the solemn talk of contemplation.
Oh, Alexander Selkirk knew the plight
Of being king and government and nation.
A road, a mile of kingdom, I am king
Of banks and stones and every blooming thing.

I adore Kavanagh's unique, maybe skewered look at being a poet. No Muse or contemplative reflection or withdrawal into serious mood. He is the king of the social road and social whirl. His joy is the "language of delight", the coded naughty chat and the shared secret.

Break out of your world today. Fly into a social life if you are used to seclusion and retreat from the crowd if you normally are a social butterfly.

Powerscourt - Wicklow - burned castle, now a 5 star hotel

Queen's University - Belfast

I had booked the hotel room by phone from Canada in 1981. The black and white photo of the inn on the shores of Lough Corrib was an idyllic sight. The write-up in the hotel guide promised exquisite natural foods (today it would be called organic cuisine): vegetables and herbs from the garden, trout freshly hooked from the lake and grilled in newly churned Irish butter. The room was described as "charming", "rustic". I should have been suspicious when I asked for a "crib" for my eighteen-month-old daughter. The innkeeper breathed a long silence until my Irish wife alerted me that a "crib" in Ireland is a stall in a barn. I wanted a cot, she whispered. I went ahead and booked and we were turning off the N59 at Oughterard down a dark rutted track a few weeks later. We bounced for two miles to the inn. The food was passable. The "cot" was Spartan. The facilities were turn of the century. The room was dark and dismal. The welcome was not stereotypically Irish. The next morning the Irish fog and mist did little to alleviate my depression at what I had reserved for a pleasant family reunion with my brother-in-law's family. I wolfed down my full Irish breakfast and my eagerness to sightsee soon brightened my spirits. My Connemara marble bookends and the watercolor I bought at Maam Cross still grace my family room to remind me of the real beauty of Ireland. Kylemore Abbey, the refuge of Benedictine monks during WW 1, was my retreat that morning to purge me of my disappointment. I strolled through the grounds decorated by God with fuchsias and St. Daboec's heather.

This was not deceptive advertising. Like Eve, I had been blinded by vain descriptions and had turned away from what God had to offer.

Someone began a rumour in Monaghan City one day in the nineteenth century. Maybe a faery or a leprechaun whispered in someone's ear – a man stumbling home from a pub or a devout lady on her way back from Mass at Macartan's Cathedral. Wherever it began, the superstition fuelled itself and solidified in Monaghan – that Monaghan would be destroyed by an earthquake whenever Saint Patrick's Day fell on a Monday. What's more, in the quake, the town would be inundated by the two lakes on either side of town – Peter's and Convent Lakes. During the 1900s, the more superstitious country folk rarely came to market day in Monaghan (held on Mondays, wouldn't you know) for fear of not getting home. They had expanded the rumour to an exaggerated level to include every Monday. There is the last record of a March 17, 1862 on which there was no produce for sale in town. Thereafter, it seems that people realized that nothing evil ever happened on a Monday, March 17, so life went on.

Can I be inspired by a rumour? Yes, as long as it takes shape. The rumour went out one day in 1858 in Monaghan that Bishop McNally had spent eight hundred pounds to buy land to build a cathedral. Finally in 1892, the cathedral to Saint Macartan was dedicated. Its majestic spire rises two hundred and fifty feet to heaven. I know its architect, McCarthy, did not live to see that dedication, but the rumour from MacNally that McCarthy brought to life still inspires today.

I've driven and walked the lanes and paths around Dungannon, Caledon, Benburb, Moy, Charlemont, Knocknacloy, Tullygiven, the Blackwater, the Oone scores of times. I know them all well. Yet, some Irish have never heard of such place names. These were, however, all featured sites in the Battle of Benburb in 1646. The Irish, led by Eoghan 'Red' O'Neill administered a crushing blow to the Scots-English army under Monroe who was trying to invade southward. Monroe held the Irish in despised disregard, but he did not count on O'Neill's strategical supremacy. The account of the battle includes an offensive move by O'Neill to Charlemont and Moy, a detour ploy by Monroe to Caledon, a pitched battle set at the Blackwater River, reinforcements coming from Dungannon. Then the final coup de grace by O'Neill came as he pushed Monroe's troops into a swing with their back to the Blackwater. The last rays of the setting sun of June 4 blinded the royalist army and the wind blew the smoke from their own cannons back into their eyes. The conclusion of the account states that "Scottish bodies created a bridge over the Oone and the Blackwater. Other fleeing soldiers were lost in marshes or drowned in Tullygiven Lake and other lakes around Knocknacloy."

As I walk the quiet roads around Tyrone four hundred and fifty years later, I consider the spoils and effects of war now buried under farmers' fields. And, I admire and am inspired by masterful strategy. I will plan and strategize today to maximize my opportunities for success.

Down a pleasant country road at Drumballyroney, south of Banbridge, I met the Bronte sisters, Emily and Charlotte and Anne, they of *Jane Eyre*, *Wuthering Heights,* and *Tenant of Wildfell Hall* fame. This wee townland is far from Haworth, Yorkshire, England with which most who know and love the Bronte works associate these great authors. Yet, this area in Northern Ireland is called the 'Bronte Homeland'. A little schoolhouse and church act as a museum and shrine dedicated to helping the tourist learn of the Bronte roots. Patrick Bronte (his actual name was Brunty and he changed it to Bronte on arrival in England for social status), father to the girls, was born in a one room thatched hut and grew up to become a teacher and preacher in the district of Drumballyroney and at Glascar School. Patirck's father, Hugh Brunty, was a master story teller, so little wonder that the grand-daughters had this skill. In the schoolroom in which Patrick taught are vestiges and life size dioramas of his life and writings. In the church, I stood in the pulpit where Bronte expounded the scriptures to his Irish flock. There I waited for a Muse to fall on me, a seed of literary life such as he implanted into his daughters. Perhaps a little inspiration lighted upon me. I returned to the schoolhouse and read of the move of the Bronte family, taking up residence in the remote but elaborate parish home in Haworth. It was there the Bronte sisters began the journey to the stardom they hold today.

I am inspired by humble beginnings and by great literature and I write on for others, just as the inspired writers of Scripture did, though I have not written material of that height.

The O'Neills were on their way to help the McQuillans in a raid and the chieftan came upon a cow caught in a thorn tree. Now, he ought to have known better, not to have cut a branch of a thorn tree, since this tree is sacred to the faeries – but O'Neill was so overtaken with compassion for the cow that he released her. As you expect, fate struck. On returning from the battle, O'Neill discovered his daughter, Kathleen, missing, carried off by the wee folk to the bottom of the lough. Wee Kathleen's shriek was heard from then on, whenever more ill was to befall the O'Neills. Ultimately, O'Neill's home, Shane's Castle was gutted by fire in 1816 – locals blamed the fire on the Banshee *Neiann Roe*, Kathleen's nemesis. Little is left of the castle near Antrim town – skeletons of there or four buildings and a magnificent one towered Tudor gateway. I stood mesmerized at the Camilla House; I was waiting to hear Kathleen's cry. Silence. Many would blame fate for the O'Neill's decline, or maybe they would blame the cow. But, let's point the finger at O"Neill himself. He knew the risk involved in the thorn tree and went ahead anyways.

Sounds a bit to me like the story of original sin – Adam and Eve knew better, yet chose to sin. We all know better, yet choose to commit wrong every day. I will be inspired by Shane's Castle to refrain, resist and desist. And seek forgiveness if I fall.

When I entered the main gate at Trinity College in Dublin, I was enveloped with a hushed reverence. The school was founded in 1592 by Queen Elizabeth I (Shakespeare's era) a Protestant college. The site had been an Augustinian monastery and the college did not begin to accept Catholic students until the 1970s. Yet, the chapel just to the left as one makes way along Parliament Square has overcome sectarianism by being the only inter-denominational chapel in Ireland. Apart from its religious significance, the College ranks high as a seat of learning. Samuel Beckett, Oliver Goldsmith and Edmund Burke were great writers who graced its halls. As I entered the Examination Hall with its gilded oak chandelier, I imagined Beckett's great mind there at work on an exam; he was already being infused with ideas for *Waiting for Godot* (originally written in French as *En Attendant Godot*). His lanky frame is draped over a table. Or, I wander into the Long Room of the Old Library, and the playwright is there too meditating in front of the busts of scholars lined down the stacks. The university has had a profound influence on its students. It evokes a special music that even the oldest surviving harp in Ireland (housed in the Library) cannot match. It has an aura which inspires a silent reverence for learning.

Today, can you find a spot which brings out a similar reverence? It does not have to be a school or a chapel, just someplace which makes you respectful and peaceful and creative.

Some quotations from Irish authors to brighten your day:

To love oneself is the beginning of a lifelong romance.
(Oscar Wilde – An Ideal Husband)

The Irish are a fair people – they never speak well of each other.
(Samuel Johnson)

She's the sort of woman who lives for others – you can always tell the others by their hunted expression. (C.S. Lewis – The Screwtape Letters)

Last week I saw a woman flayed, and you will hardly believe how much it altered her appearance for the worse. (Jonathan Swift)

Satire is a sort of glass wherein beholders do generally discover everyone's face but their own. (Jonathan Swift)

Self-esteem or low esteem!? I'd rather have the first. But, it is always healthy to have a sense of humour too about the impression you hold about yourself.

from the Closing Album
II
Cushendun
(Louis MacNeice)

Fuschia and ragweed and the distant hills
Made as it were out of clouds and sea:
All night the bay is splashing and the moon
Marks out the break of waves.

Limestone and basalt and a whitewashed house
With passages of great stone flags
And a walled garden with plums on the wall
And a bird piping in the night.

Forgetfulness: brass lamps and copper jugs
And home-made bread and the smell of turf or flax
And the air a glove and the water lathering easily
And convolvulus in the hedge.

Only in the dark green room beside the fire
With the curtains drawn against the winds and waves
There is a little box with a well-bred voice:
What a place to talk of War.

MacNeice's imagistic words paint the same picture as the scenic photo of Cushendun, a model of a Cornish village. In fact, they go beyond the photo. They are superior to a thousand photos. Cushendun is a gloriously picture postcard village on Northern Ireland's Antrim coast. Inside one small cottage, I can envision one Irish family huddled around their radio. They perhaps are listening to Churchill announcing to the U.K. that they are a war. "Churchill, he, our almost neighbour, who owns the home just a few miles up the road at Carnlough. His town and ours, Cushendun, are changed forever." Both Cushendun and Carnlough have war memorials naming a handful of villagers who left their scenic beauty, never to return. Drink it in, and relish this morning before you leave. It may or may not be your last look.

This was the eighteenth century in Dublin, the era when Dubliners built terraced town houses, Georgian style. These homes were an attempt to match English grandeur and the Irish succeeded. Merrion and Fitzwilliam Squares boast the best of the townhouses preserved from modernistic development. Let me fill you in on features of a Georgian town home in Dublin – a high brightly coloured door with a glassed separated fanlight above it and a heavy brass knocker. The kitchen and pantry were in the basement, the dining room on the ground floor and the drawing room on the floor above that. The latter's ceiling was adorned with lavish stuccowork. The next two floors above contained the main bedrooms and finally the children's and servants quarters were below the slated roof. Would you like to have been kitchen servants climbing four or five flights of stairs many times a day?

A vast switch from the homes which we enjoy now. Both styles of residences offer chances for domestic havens to inspire a family to share love and support and to spend time together away from the bustle outside. Let your home be a site of inspirational peace today and every day.

My guide told me that I was looking straight down from Harmony Hill to the Garavogue River. I didn't have to ask the origin of the name of the hill; she explained all. I heard, to my surprise, that the local families fought over who could get down the fastest to get the best place at the river on laundry washing days. Where is the harmony here? Isn't this classic "fightin' Irish"? I had to listen on. The authorities put in a road down the hill so that families could come down to wash their clothes in an orderly fashion. In this way, harmony in Sligo City was restored. The street was originally called Waste Water Lane; then, it became Waste Gardens and now it is a narrow road to the river named West Gardens. I don't know if the current inhabitants of West Gardens with its attractive name are aware that Waste Gardens or Waste Water Lane used to be used as the city dump and the sluiceway for human waste!! What is in a name? Shakespeare, through Juliet, would have us believe that "a rose by any other name would smell as sweet." He's right. We can "dickey up" anything with a reclassification or with a new label. But, it still is what it was.

There is only harmony and peace if it generates from God. Under the influence of sin, people will continue to fight over minor issues, even if we patch it up and call it peace. The filth of sin is still sin, even if we change and delete a letter or two and call it a garden instead of a lane. God knows the truth of the heart.

The Celtic cross has become a universal symbol of Ireland—the high cross with the central circle and molded/indented arms and upright. They inspire jewelry and religiosity. These crosses, carved in between the eight and twelfth centuries, are associated with medieval monasteries and artists. It has two tenons at each end for a base and a capstone. The distinctive ring served functionally for support, and decoratively to distinguish this cross from its more generic brand. Muiredach's Cross at Monasterboice, eighteen feet tall, is one of the finest. This cross and others told the biblical story in sandstone—St. Paul's journey, the Last Judgment, the Adoration of the Magi, Moses smiting the rock, David struggling with Goliath and at the bottom, Adam and Eve eating the forbidden apple, and Cain slaying Abel—veritable "sermons in stone" (as monks coined the term) for illiterate parishioners. The crosses served the same function as stained glass windows in Europe.

Education, in any form, inspires me, not only because I am a teacher, but also because education broadens, enlightens, and promotes tolerance. Today, learn a new fact, I'd strongly suggest basing your education on spiritual and moral values, much like the monks of Ireland promoted, from the Bible. This book educates and inspires!

She is too fair for any man
To see or hold his heart's delight,
Fairer than Queen or courtesan
Or moonlight water in the night.

As a pomegranate cut in twain,
White seeded is her crimson mouth,
Her cheeks are as the fading stain
Where peach reddens to the south.

Oh, twining hands! Oh delicate
White body made for love or pain!
O house of love! O desolate
Pale flower beaten by the rain.

(La Bella Donna Della Mia Mente – Oscar Wilde)

So many have written or sung of the perfection of the human body. Wilde's description here reminds me of Solomon's Song in which he praises the beauties of his lover, and she his glories. We all idolize a lover or a role model and might wish to write poetry as touching and as laudatory as Solomon's or Wilde's. At times, nonetheless, reality sets in; the perfection pales, storms come and pain is found in love. Even in this I find inspiration – that I can continue to love. Love today, beyond the imperfections.

It's not hard to find a pub in Ireland; some villages have as many as five or six for a population of three hundred. It used to be, however, a challenge to get a drop of the hard stuff during prohibition days. The Irish became industrious and adaptive in the production and sale of poteen (from the Gaelic *poitín*— little pot). The region around the Sperrins was no exception. Distillers became adept at making this clear spirit in secret places from fermented potatoes. They've been at it since the potato was first introduced into Ireland in the 16th century. In a short time, production of poteen became illegal, and the stills went underground. So that an Irishman could have his nightly drink, criminals were created out of decent citizens. Such men perfected the art of brewing small batches in pots. They became folklore heroes. As far as the Glenelly valley relates to the brew, there is a tale of skill on the other side of the law. In the nineteenth century, a constable at Cranagh Barracks was able, because of his large nose, to smell out a still.

I'll find a way to overcome obstacles or to circumvent protocol. I won't be a criminal, nor will I be a hysterical witch-hunter, but I will find a way to motivate myself and others.

I am a sucker for glossy advertising. I wanted an historical experience during my stay on the Antrim coast, so when I read that Sir Winston Churchill had once owned the Londonderry Arms, in Carnlough, I bit. The photo of an ivy-walled mansion did its part to entice me to book a room. Well, the reduced price of $125.00 played its role too. In reality, the hotel sat one meter from the main highway through Carnlough, the room was hardly luxurious, and the town had few facilities. Only the view was inspiring. That scene across the sea to mainland UK was no doubt one reason Churchill acquired Londonderry Arms. As I sat in my room in the hotel, I pictured "the bulldog's" inimitable force, and heard his unique accent in the hotel's corridors. I was caused to remember Seamus Heaney's poem "The Spirit Level," in which the child hears this "foreign" English speaker say, "'Here is the news...'/ A great gulf was fixed where pronunciation reigned tyrannically." Was the Irish child in WWII times listening to Churchill's famous call-to-arms as well as to a BBC announcer? Could that same child, perhaps in Carnlough, have heard and seen the embodiment of an Englishman in Churchill at the main entrance to Londonderrry Arms? A contrast, I would say.

We can either live in a fantasy of interpretation or see the Real Thing. I tend to believe that experiencing the true flesh is more inspiring.

For they starve the little frightened child
Till it weeps both night and day
And they scourge the weak and flog the fool
And gibe the old and grey
And some grow mad and all grow bad
And none a word may say.

(Ballad of Reading Gaol – Oscar Wilde)

I don't know if Oscar Wilde stood up for the repressed, the marginalized, the disenfranchised, the minorities, the children or women of his day. I do know that he was persecuted. Is he acting here as a spokesperson on behalf of the abused child, the hungry and homeless, the mentally challenged and the elderly? We see about us strong evidence that such groups and more cower in fear, suffer grievously, endure mental anguish and are driven to crime because of individual or societal bullies. Step up this day and assist these people in a practical way.

Three lakes are a magnet which draws tourists to Killarney. Upper lake, Muckross, and Lough Leane comprise this enchanted spot in Ireland. Above them, the Gap of Dunloe, strewn with boulders and covered by ancient glaciers sits watch. The three lakes meet at Dins Island, where kayakers shoot the rapids. The region emits an atmosphere of peaceful resplendency. I could imagine Queen Victoria's ladies-in-waiting putting fluttering hands together in delight at their scenic stop in 1861—the spot is now called Ladies' View. Killarney would warm anyone's heart. There is, however, a dark side to every paradise—Ross Castle was the last Irish stronghold to be seized by Cromwell in 1653 and that same tyrannical leader of the Roundheads burned down Muckross Abbey in the same year. As well, in the heather-covered hills above the lake is Kate Kearney's cottage. She was a local fair damsel who ran an illegal tavern for travelers in the 1800s. I dismissed those negative images as I made my way into Killarney Town to take a jaunting car ride, all the time amused by the Irish humour of the jarvey who guided us around. As I stood at the window of my Hotel Europe I reveled in the views across Lough Leane and on, upwards to the Purple Mountains.

This little bit of heaven in Ireland inspired me to praise God for his scenic handiwork. I had met the waters of joy that night.

There are two expressions which have come to us from Irish history. When the English forced their influence and dominance on Ireland from Norman to Tudor times, they had varying degrees of control. Any area outside the borders of English "civilized society" was Beyond the Pale. The Pale was at first only Dublin, but spread north, then south and finally west. Any Gaelic chieftain outside the pale was allowed to keep his land with the proviso that his offspring were raised within the pale. This situation ensured the fact that the English could mould the thinking of the "barbarians" their way. There actually were fortifications in places which marked the boundary between Palesmen and the Gaelic majority. Some of the animosity stemming from this division came to a head in 1880. The Irish became so incensed at the English landlords who continued to evict tenants that they began to boycott the farming businesses of the heartless English lords. It was a Captain Boycott whose products were shunned first. Hence the word 'boycott' passed into common English usage.

We strive today for inclusiveness. That's honourable and inspiring.

C ounties Meath and Westmeath made me green with envy. Near Trim Castle, there is a horse race called the "Nun Run"—yes, nuns can be jockeys too. I wanted to participate, but was barred. I wanted to be in the movies at Trim Castle (site of Braveheart), built by the Norman Hugh de Lacey in 1173, but was turned down. What was more serious to me was the Jealous Wall at Belvedere House near Mullingar. Richard Castle built the villa in 1740, but began to distrust his brother, whom he accused of having an affair with his wife. Castle imprisoned her for thirty-one years in a house nearby, and then in 1755 built a gothic folly (the Jealous Wall) to block his view of his brother's statelier home. The second brother had become more successful than Richard. As I stood before the crumbling three or four story wall with its gothic arches and windows in ruins, I realized how strong jealousy is. It eats away and leaves one embittered.

No longer did I want to run with the nuns, or act with Mel Gibson. I was satisfied with who I am.

Could we dig up this land buried treasure
Were it worth the pleasure
We never could learn love's song,
We are parted far too along.

'You have early wasted your life'
(Ah, that was the knife!)
When I rushed through the garden gate
It was too late.

Could we live it over again,
Were it worth the pain,
Could the passionate past that is fled
Call back its dead.

(Roses and Rue – To L.L. – Oscar Wilde)

The regrets of things undone, things said, things done haunt us often. We want to remake the past and reposition the stars. Nostalgia brings on pain at times, so it does. Wilde's statement implies that any digging up or calling back could be fruitless, useless. Today, blot out any regret or pain that cannot be mended or reconciled, and move on.

What's the top-rated Irish meal? A bottle of Guinness and a spud? That may be humorous, but the Irish have been masters at making more than a pound or two out of the Guinness brew. In 1759, Arthur Guinness signed a nine hundred year lease at forty-five pounds a year to take over St. James Brewery in Dublin, at a time when sales of beer were not going well. He adapted the black porter then popular in England, and, presto, got his start. "Guinness is good for you." And so, in ten years, Arthur was exporting his stout. And the water is not pumped from the Liffey; it comes from the Wicklow Mountains. Another provider of alcohol, this time a distiller of whiskey, Locke's of Kilbeggan, did not fare as well up against Scotch whisky (the Scottish spelling has no "e"). However, the aroma of the whiskey in the distillery hung on, and connoisseurs would visit the warehouse just to sense "the angels' share." Our third brewery/distillery takes us to Northern Ireland, Bushmills, a true single malt, single grain whiskey. The Old Bushmills Plant began officially in 1608, but probably two hundred years earlier, when illegal stills were at it, serving up the "powerful" stuff.

Uisce beatha—the water of life. It was introduced to Ireland by monks from Asia about one thousand years ago. Irish whiskey might be the ultimate smooth for some, but I'd rather have the eternal water of life from heaven—the Spirit of Christ in my heart. That inspires me more and beats out a temporary burst of excitement which comes from "a wee dram."

The name Wexford comes from the Norse, Waesfjord (estuary of the mudflats). Its street system follows the Viking fishbone pattern of alleys fanning diagonally off a main backbone thoroughfare. Everything ends up at the old Norse waterfront. Its unique "Yola" dialect has a Norse linguistic base. It even has a bull ring used for bull-baiting in Norman times. There are supposedly ancestral links between the Norse and the Normans. One purely English trace is significant. Selskar Abbey was the site where supposedly King Henry II did his penance after cruelly murdering Thomas a Beckett in 1170. Beckett had condemned Henry's attempt to diminish the power of the Church and increase his own state power. When Archbishop Beckett would not leave his church at Canterbury Cathedral, a gang of soldiers spilled his brains out on the stone floor. I have written elsewhere of my opposite experience in Wexford. I witnessed the true human spirit of kindness (Norse, Norman, Irish or English) when I was lost in Wexford. A motorcyclist took time out to escort me personally from his residential area straight to my hotel parking lot. And he would accept no payment.

No race has a lock on kindness. It's not Irish, nor any –ish, nor any -an, nor even an –ese. Love and kindness that inspire us come straight from God's heart. Be kind today.

I see a connection between the advertising motto of the school at which I teach and the town of Cobh in Cork. From my school have emerged men of every ilk and career path, the whole spectrum. From Cobh too set forth men and women and ships all destined to potential despair or to an almost insurmountable mountaintop. Cobh has one of the world's largest natural harbours, and so two and a half million emigrants sailed from here in the Famine Years. Earlier, and concurrently, forty thousand convicts set out from Cobh for penal colonies in Australia in other "coffin ships." Some floating jails sat in the harbour for weeks until departure date. More glamorous ships set out across the Atlantic from Cobh: the first transatlantic steam ship, the Sirius; the Lusitania, which has its memorial on Cobh's promenade—torpedoed by a German U-boat off nearby Kinsale in 1915; and, three years earlier, the last land which the Titanic saw was Cobh.

The departures from Cobh inspire me because, despite the potential for failure, many made the most out of this departure point and embarked upon political or entrepreneurial paths. The will to survive is strong. My colleagues and my students have also survived. Some have gotten further than others. And like the Titanic, some of the latter have been holed and sunk. Those who rose above the storm clouds are men of inspiration.

The Glenveagh Pass is almost moonscape in nature if it was not for the bogs and heather. The highest peak in the Derryveagh Mountains is Errigal, at 2466 feet. It is a quartzite cone, sand white cascading down shiny stone. The pass itself is forlorn and bleak – rock strewn, red, black and silver stones. As I descended to the valley, I was headed for a wild treat at Glenveagh National park – 25,000 acres of cliffs and boggy valleys. The park hosts the largest red deer herd in Ireland. Its gem, though, is set miles 'in the back of beyond', as the Irish say, on the southern shores of Lough Veagh. It is a castle built in 1870 by John Adair (he who created Tabasco Sauce). Mr. Adair was a brutal landlord who evicted families for miles around his estate, even after the Famine. Some say that he got payback when his wife died. The castle is now a much more amenable, welcoming place. A minibus took us to the castle from the carpark. We lunched in an ivy-bowered tearoom. We tossed pebbles into Lough Veagh from the pier at which a rowboat rocked. We ambled through the gardens carved out of the wild Irish countryside. We never were privileged to tour the interior, for the times of operation of minibus and castle did not coincide. We could, nonetheless, appreciate the generosity of the American art dealer who donated the castle to Ireland after he bought it years after Adair passed on.

One inspiration for many is to own their own plot of land, wild or landscaped. Even postage stamp sized. Even claiming a piece of soil as theirs for an hour. Value your land today.

The two words have a natural ring about them, and, indeed, that easy connotation has stood for over five thousand years, longer than the pyramids. At the Ceide Fields in Mayo, just west of Ballycastle, I came to possibly the oldest enclosed farm every found, covering ten square kilometers. In this spread-out community, all fields were enclosed within stone walls. Much has sunk below bogs, but there is evidence that farmers had huts and cared for two strips of land on either side. On his fields, the farmer grew barley or wheat and grazed cattle. Excavators have dug up pottery and a primitive plough. The bleak exterior landscape set atop three-hundred-foot cliffs stands in contrast to the pyramid-shaped (a gentle Irish poke at other cultures, maybe?) interpretive center. I paid my almost four dollars and had no difficulty in taking myself back almost five thousand years. I was impressed with the detail of dioramas of Stone Age calves and workmen levering stones. Perhaps the most impressive was the centerpiece—a carving of a gigantic fifteen or twenty-foot high bogwood fire. The flame was lit golden, but was in reality wood too.

It was a bigger-than-life symbol of the inspiring warmth inside an Irish farmhouse, in 3500 BCE or in the twenty first century. In my times, I have been inspired as I have sat in the kitchen/parlour of many Irish farmhouses sipping at tea, eating wheaten bread and being almost smoked out by the turf fire.

Oh, Helen! Helen! Helen. Yet a while.
Yet for a little while. O tarry thee,
Til the dawn cometh and the shadows flee!
For in gladsome sunlight of thy smile
Of heaven or hell I have no thought or fear,
Seeing I know no other god but thee:
No other god save him, before whose feet
In nets of gold the tired planets' nave,
The incarnate spirit of spiritual love
Who in thy body holds his joyous seat.

(The New Helen – Oscar Wilde)

Isn't it gratifying to know that you have someone to look up to? Someone to help you drive away worries and fears. Someone to wish for to share a permanent stay. Better still, that someone who also has the Spirit of God within. Supported by a spiritual partner, we can face any crisis. Search out someone like that upon whom you can rely. The ultimate partner is God's Son and Spirit to be the beautiful supporter today.

As I drove through the towns of Gweedore, Dobhair, Crolly, in West Donegal, I sensed I was in a unique area in Ireland. Donegal is one of the heartlands of *Gaeltacht* in Ireland, and these towns are seedbeds of a population in Ireland which prides itself in speaking Gaelic as a first language. Being a linguist, I was overjoyed to hear so much of a second or first language, and I tried some out myself, but was soon left behind in the flurry of foreign words. Crolly has another claim to fame, the Crolly Stone. The Glenveagh landscape has been subject to the sculpting of ancient nature. An Ice Age, scientists say, thirteen thousand years ago, was slowly beaten back. In its retreat the glacier dropped off a sizeable granite boulder which in turn prompted the Irish to put their own legendary spin on the rock's existence. Enter Finn McCool again. During a domestic dispute, Finn's mood degenerated into a temper tantrum. To his credit, he did not abuse his wife or children, or even go on a drinking binge. He picked up a rock, the Crolly Stone, and threw it across the fields until it landed where it now rests, precariously ready to topple over. The legend goes on: the stone will fall over when the first truly honest person passes by it.

I want to be inspired today by truthful transparency, set in comprehensible and calm language. I will attempt to hold my temper and deal with my colleagues and family in open dialogue without threat of subterfuge.

Ireland is a geologist's playground, specifically Narin and Rossbeg in Donegal set on a peninsular below Gweebara Bay. Along the R261, and onto a further secondary road, I reached a section running along the edge of a granite mass created by a slow cooling after an eruption of magma. The extreme heat at first caused new minerals to form in the rock, and there is evidence of these minerals in prisms on the beach at Carrickfadden; this material is more resistant to erosion than the original rock. Close by, at Rossbeg, I observed another force of nature. At Rossbeg, there are folded rocks, contorted stone formed after continents collided four hundred and seventy million years ago. At one point the crash forced up mountain ranges higher than the Himalayas. Rock was also pushed deep under the Earth's crust, heated to five hundred degrees Celsius, then driven back to the surface—the folded rocks at Rossbeg.

We humans believe we have such power and influence, don't we? It inspires and humbles me, this morning, to see the power beyond me which can be generated by all humans combined. An even greater power is generated by my God who lives in me.

I presume that you've heard of an Irish temper and of the Fightin' Irish? It's a hot August day and the car has over-heated. Maybe in Ireland, in Sligo, my temper will flare? Just inland from the Atlantic is a simple but gigantic boulder dropped off by a glacier in the last Ice Age. Typical of the Irish, they have spun a geographical and geological phenomenon into a wild tale only an Irishman could tell. Fionn MacCuhaill (Finn Mc Cool is a more recognizable name) has become the hero of this glacial rock. Here's how the legend goes: Fionn made a bet he could throw the rock from Ox Mountains into the Atlantic, at least one hundred kilometers!). He lost the bet and, in a fit of temper slashed his sword into the rock, splitting it in two. It stands this way now. He must have put a curse on it after that, for the locals warn you that if you walk three times through the cleft Finn made, the rock will close shut on you before you are able to get through the third try. Fortunately, Finn's anger has not harmed anyone and, as far as I know, no one has been caught in the crush of the rock.

We've all experienced the receiving end of a child's or an adult's temper tantrum; it can be fearsome. Or, hard to admit at times, our own temper has flowed with dire consequences. Only one person ever got angry and did not sin, ever. That was Jesus Christ. The encouragement for this day is to minimize temper loss. We have all been inspired and heartened by an even-tempered soul who stays calm when the world is crashing around him/her. You'll find someone like that today. Take a page from his/her book. Don't split the rock!

Clearances

in *memoriam M.K.H., 1911-1984*

She taught me what her uncle once taught her:
How easily the biggest coal block split
If you got the grain and hammer angled right.

The sound of that relaxed alluring blow,
Its co-opted and obliterated echo,
Taught me to hit, taught me to loosen,

Taught me between the hammer and the block,
To face the music. Teach me now to listen,
To strike it rich behind the linear black.

(Seamus Heaney)

The simplest of tasks taught by a dear mother or father can end up becoming a turning point in life. Heaney evidently learned four key lessons from a daily chore performed with his mom. The splitting of the coal block gave him parameters in life: 1) when to act and when to let go ("when to do and when forbear") ; 2) to accept the blows of life ; 3) to be a sounding board for someone in distress ; 4) to look for the silvery gold in the darkest night. Let Heaney (passed away on August 30, 2013) inspire you as he did me; learn at least one of these lessons today.

Out of his mouth a red, red rose!
Out of his heart a white!
For what can say by what strange way
Christ brings his will to light.
Since the barren staff the pilgrim bore
Bloomed in the Pope's great sight.

(Ballade de Marguerite – Oscar Wilde)

Some call it Fate, some Providence, some Destiny, some Luck. Many call it the will of the Divine. An acceptance of the higher will is one way of cultivating a peaceful soul for today. We may be dealt a white rose or a red one. Each has the beauty of a rose, and the thorns of one too. We may be the pilgrim (the faithful and the follower) or the Pope (the honoured one or the Leader). Each has a pivotal role to play; each has his or her burdens and weaknesses/drawbacks. Bow to the higher will, the will higher than the pilgrim's or the Pope's. Be content.

The highway wound down to the bog in spectacular twists as we neared our destination, Dunfanaghy, Co. Donegal. It was a gorgeous spring morning and life was at its peak. The town was a classic, gentle Irish village. When we found the tourist site we had been looking for, the Dunfanaghy workhouse, we were struck by the reality of life in this same idyllic space in the 1840s. The most heart-wrenching scene was a life-size diorama and accompanying audio account of an old lady, named Hannah, who had endured the rigours of the poverty, abuse and oppression of the Famine era. She was both mistreated by employers and disgraced by authorities, all the while suffering appalling hunger. She had to undergo the disgrace and ignominy of being assigned to the Workhouse, where death reigned and aid was often far away. Yet, she told her story, complete with lilting Irish wit to a lady of the higher classes who set Hannah up in a wee house. The author of Hannah's biography recounts the old lady's death as if it was a singing victory. Hannah was her inspiration; she inspired me too that day as I stood in the workhouse, moved by her strength and positivity.

I need a motivation like that each day, though, for all too soon I forgot wee Hannah's suffering as I became caught up again in my own good fortune, touring Ireland on one of its rare spring sunny days. No matter our enjoyment, we must try and remember the real suffering, and abiding patience and positivity, of which people like wee Hannah remind us.

September

Slea Head, Kerry

Valentia Island Lighthouse – west coast

Follower

My father worked with a horse-plough,
His shoulders globed like a full sail strung
Between the shafts and the furrow.
The horses strained at his clicking tongue.

An expert. He would set the wing
And fit the bright steel-pointed sock.
The sod rolled over without breaking.
At the headrig, with a single pluck

Of reins, the sweating team turned round
And back into the land. His eye
Narrowed and angled the ground,
Mapping the furrow exactly.

I stumbled in his hobnailed wake,
Fell sometimes on the polished sod;
Sometimes he rode me on his back
Dipping and rising to his plod.

I wanted to grow up and plough,
To close one eye, stiffen my arm.
All I ever did was follow
In his broad shadow round the farm.

I was a nuisance, tripping, falling,
Yapping always. But today
It is my father who keeps stumbling
Behind me, and will not go away.

(Seamus Heaney)

What's wrong with following? It can be all we ever do. It can imply naivete or it can be blind tradition. It can be annoying and bothersome and disconcerting. It can be drudgery. But it can be inspiring because the leader provides a mentorship and the follower gains a lesson. Heaney here seems to be saying that it is the latter of these two possibilities which is needed but he admits that he has fallen into the temptation of annoyance at his senile father. Watch out why and who you follow today.

The Children of Danu, the Celtic deities actually had their own family doctor, Dianecht. He and his daughter were responsible for keeping the gods alive and well. They guarded a magic spring into which killed or wounded gods were dipped in order to revive them. Dianecht is reputed to have saved not only gods, but all of Ireland. One goddess, Morrigan, bore an evil child whose heart contained three serpents. If left alive, these serpents would consume Ireland. Dianecht oversaw the child's destruction, and after, the serpents were burned and their ashes spread on a river. True to their vicious power, the snakes maintained their influence. The river boiled dry, but Ireland was saved. This odd doctor had a vengeful tendency too. His daughter planted three hundred sixty-five herbs on the grave of a chieftain whom Dianecht had killed. She arranged the herbs according to their properties, presumably so that her lover, the chieftain, could take from them one a day. In his jealous anger, her father overturned the little plot.

I'm sure that my doctor is not like Dianecht. She doesn't use magic or kill babies or fly into jealous fits. She follows the Hippocratic Oath, and uses conventional and natural medicines and procedures to care for me. I thank God today for our advancement in medicine. It makes the world a safe and healthy place to live.

And for your mouth it would never smile,
For a long long while
Then it rippled all over with laughter
Five minutes after.

You were always afraid of the shower,
Just like the flower
I remember you started and ran
When the rain began.

I remember I could never catch you,
For no one could match you,
You had wonderful luminous, fleet,
Little wings to your feet.

(Roses and Rue – To L.L. – Oscar Wilde)

It is a joy to observe someone who loves life and displays that verve with a smile, a run, a skip or a dance. That joy is especially heart-warming when the person has overcome past pain or rain in his/her life. Today put "luminous, fleet little wings" on your feet and come and fly with me.

Have you ever tried writing a limerick? The results can be hilarious. I enjoy the creative activity, as do my English classes. Limerick? The city of Limerick is much like any other European city. In my mind, though, it stands out because the poem bears its name and because, when I visited, my daughter was dastardly ill, and we had to leave her alone in the hotel while we toured the town. As for the poetic genre, the story goes that a brigade of Irish dragoons marching home from duty in France created the bawdy and often irreverent verse form as an outlet to while away the time en route to home fires, and as a way of mocking their French enemies. Another tale has it that a gentleman made up the verses to amuse his host's children. I trust they were not as risqué as the soldiers' limericks, or like some one reads today. Inspire yourself today with your authorship skills. Here are the criteria for a limerick: five lines, 8-8-6-6-8 syllables per line and rhyming as a-a-b-b-a, and funny enough to poke fun gently at someone's weakness. Many begin this way:

"There was a _____ from _____."

There was a young man from Ireland,
Who to limericks put his hand.
He deemed self a fail,
But others gave hail,
For old Ireland bring out the band.

See it's easy. You can do better, no doubt. Be inspired!

Upon seeking approval from the landowner, I trudged across his field to view the Bronze Age standing stone called the Holestone. It is in Antrim near Parkgate and is hard to miss. Standing 1.5 meters high, it is shaped somewhat like a shark's fin. Almost in the middle is a hole, not quite circular. No one really knows why the hole is there, but you can be sure that the Irish have created a tale about its significance. Since the eighteenth century, the Irish have bandied about the story that if a couple who undertakes a ceremony here, eternal love and happiness will follow. The woman reaches through the hole with her hand; the partner takes it on the other side. Presto! Eternal love. If only it was that easy, you say, and I agree.

That standing stone on the rise of land in Antrim is not the site where one finds everlasting bliss. I found lasting love at a cross with holes in it. Christ was nailed to that cross to expiate my sin, and yours. Therein I find love and by that I am inspired to pass it on to you, and to all who wish it.

I would have loved to have been present at Cranfield Church and Holy Well in early June to watch a pilgrimage. I could have heard the chants and prayers waft over Lough Neagh at Churchtown Point, but only in my head. When I was there, it was just before dusk in September, and the roofless stone ruins of the thirteenth century Churchtown Church and Saint Olcan's Shrine became somber in the rays of the setting sun. The leaning grave stones lent a deeper sense of past eeriness. But, I had come to see the Holy Well, just a few yards to the east. The well produces spring water and amber coloured pebbled crystals. Saint Olcan bestowed healing powers on these stones – plus protection in childbirth, from drowning in the Lough, from fire and burglary. Even emigrants to America swallowed pebbles to ensure a safe crossing of the Atlantic. Does the superstition prevail today? Yes. Saint Olcan taught that if a diseased one bathed the infected part with a rag dipped in the well, then hung the cloth on a tree or bush overhanging the well, the affliction was healed as the rag rotted. It's hard to believe, but I saw decaying rags hanging from branches. Someone must still believe in the power of the water of the well.

As I stood there, I thought of Jesus standing at another well offering "living water welling up to eternal life", and then I recalled the man at the pool who could not get into the "magical" waters fast enough to be healed. That kind of "holy well" inspires me to faith that Jesus will offer me healing in mind, soul and body. I'll take it.

almost believed I was strolling through the water gardens and parterres of Versailles as I toured Antrim Castle gardens. The long canal was reminiscent too and the wooded demesne reminded me of my walk from the main castle at Versailles to Marie Antoinette's farm house where she escaped from the life at court. The castle does not itself bear any resemblance to Versailles, but the legend about it does outstrip anything I've heard about the castle of the Louis of France, at least in tragic romanticism. On the night of October 28, 1922, a grand ball was in progress at Antrim castle. A fire broke out and halted the air of celebration. Fire brigades were unable to extinguish the blaze and the whole castle became an inferno. The citizenry could only watch, and as they did, a figure appeared in an upper window. It was a twenty two year old servant girl, Ethel Gilligan, who had been trapped in her room. One brave hero scaled the burning parapets to bring her down. Unfortunately, she died on the lawn below. Local lovers strolling in the park have spotted her ghost, they say, dressed in white floating through the trees.

I am inspired by the rescuer. Does the ghost live on in honour of his bravery? Did he have a romantic motive in rescuing her? Purely suggestion, even if you believe in ghosts. But, to have any motive to engage in a death-defying rescue is the height of romanticism. Rescue someone or something today – a dying plant, a trapped animal, a friend who feels enclosed, an old lady trying to cross the street....

The exterior appearance of facilities and students and staff makes for anything but a royal image. There are no sweeping manicured lawns or gardens or fountains. Instead only an iron fence separates the school from the street. Trucks and buses fume by, feet from the main gateway. The array of architectural styles of the wings and out buildings does not lend any signification as to period, not for that mater, beauty. The original building dating from the inception of this Royal School in the 1600s is sooty and grimy. As are the post war wings. The latest addition is overly modern and clashes. Even the sports facilities lack an attention to planning and care since the un-mown football and cricket pitches are jammed between two sections of the school. Inside, one can expect the wear and tear that comes with hundreds of teens on the move every day. However, the corridors, offices and classrooms and assembly hall do not even have serenity and dignity of age that an Eton or a Harvard has. Downright 'tatty'/ugly. Peeling paint, drooping draperies, banners askew, lifting floor tiles, broken hardwood – a starkness which indicates an institution, not a school. Yet, what a record the Royal School has! Its pupils, though on the surface sloppy, untidy and unattractive have provided the Royal School with reputation of excellence and honour. One would never know that a boy or girl standing on the pavement, cigarette in hand, hair unkempt, shirt tail out, tie stained, ugly brown jacket torn, gray trousers or skirt un-pressed and shoes untied will become a Rhodes Scholar, an MP, a renowned barrister, a world class cricketer, a proud mom or dad.

Ah, yes, it's just as well that God sees the heart and the end rather than the exterior façade. We are children of the King, not for what we are but for what we have become. Dress the part, inside today.

hat used to be a playground belonging to the privileged few is now in the public domain: Dungannon Park, County Tyrone. This vast acreage which was once the sprawling demesnes of the executives of the linen industry now rings with the joyous laughs of the leisured of all strata of society. When I amble in peace or stride out in vigorous exercise in this park, I get inspiration from the range of activities people are engaged in here. The expansive lake attracts lovers in rowboats, fishers on the banks or in other boats. A wee Irish lady wanders on a walk from the home for the aged on the hill above – she stands and feeds the ducks despite prohibition signs. The park attracts joggers and walkers on the maze of trails; frisbee throwing campers from the caravan site in the park; league soccer players in match play or practice on the four or five pitches; kite flyers; a cricket match in its lengthy process....; children screaming and hooting on the adventure playground. As I looked across the lake and fields, I saw the mansions of the executives in the distance, but felt privileged too because I was at ease here. It is a sublime and manicured park, a tribute to Dungannon Town Council. One year, during my visit to Ireland, the Council sponsored a Wild West day picnic. I did not attend but I imagined a frenzied bustle which would outstrip anything I had ever seen at the park. The same atmosphere of fun and joviality would be present though.

Go for a walk in a park today and you will feel different.

"I first set my eyes on Molly Malone" "in Dublin's fair city" at the corner of Grafton and Suffolk Streets. Just the statue, you must realize. The legend of this fair lady of the folk song goes back three hundred years: June 12, 1699 sees a figure expired on the pavement of a narrow winding alley. The ogling crowd quickly disperses when a doctor announces that the vapours of her typhoid fever may infect the onlookers. Molly Malone was a familiar figure pushing her barrow of seafood from Fishamble Street to cry out her wares in town. She now has only one voice, dead as she is: the minister at her funeral who likens her to Christ's fishermen. She has now been silenced, laid to rest in Saint John's graveyard. Yet, Molly speaks yet. Some say the ghost of Molly Malone still wanders cobbled lanes singing; you can even hear her handcart rumble along. Rumour had it that Molly plied another trade at night, entertaining clients, students at Trinity; she wore fishnet stockings and stiletto heels then. Controversy and confusion and fantasy reign as to dates, the origin of the folk song, her actual existence, the place of her burial. So, I stand at the statue and look into Molly's sad eyes and at her revealing attire, so unlike that of a fishmonger. If Molly was truly a simple hardworking girl earning pennies, she must be aghast at the reputation she has taken on, "supplanted by a misdated, misplaced, sexually crude image" (Sean Murphy – Mystery of Molly Malone).

I am inspired by a man or a woman prepared to do an honest day's work in manual labour, and ask nothing more than the love of those for whom they toil. Hat's off to you, Molly Malone!

Years back, we were staying at Lough Eske in Donegal at a luxury hotel, twenty or thirty minutes from Donegal City. The local tourist brochure mentioned Lough Eske Castle just down the road from the hotel; that was all. I had to find it. It was twilight and, in some fear, we traversed a long bowered but overgrown track. It was muddy and disconcerting. Then I spotted a tower and pressed on. Past rambling twentieth century but derelict sheds and outbuildings until we turned a corner to behold an eerie sight in the orange dusk. A massive structure in total ruins – walls crumbling, windows broken, wings collapsed, roofs fallen to the floor. We tiptoed through the front entrance. Beasts scuttled away. I was truly frightened. Our exploration over stones and beams was hurried and fitful. We were on a path to go down to the lake until we ran across a ten foot Celtic cross grave marker among the trees. An owl hooted. We turned back after this as it was becoming dark. Retracing our steps gingerly past the ruined castle once more, we hastened by twenty foot high rhododendron bushes to the main road. Now, three years later, I was looking at a 1930 photo of the full castle in all its glory when it was a guest house of the White family. The photo's owner's grandfather had been the gardener and gate lodge keeper at Lough Eske Castle in the 1920s and beyond. What had been a grand Tudor baronial castle built in 1866 and later lovingly tended by Mr. Robert Johnston, lay in a state almost but not beyond repair. How are the mighty fallen! The gate lodge, however, was renovated in 1997 to become a glorious holiday home on the shores of Lough Eske. Postscript: The same castle is now a five star hotel and our stay there some years after our initial foray was gloriously luxurious.

Those ruins of fallen glory of baronial life, set in contrast to an ordinary new twenty first century home of a servant inspired me. Then, the castle was restored, and that was a further inspiration. I want to renew all in my life; I do not wish ruination.

To a Child Dancing in the Wind

(W. B. Yeats)

Dance there upon the shore;
What need have you to care
For wind or water's roar?
And tumble out your hair
That the salt drops have wet;
Being young you have not known
The fools triumph, nor yet
Love lost as soon as won,
Nor the best labourer dead
And all the sheaves to bind.
What need have you to dread
The monstrous crying of the wind?

As I walked the strand at Benone near Portstewart, along the Antrim Coast, I enjoyed the sight of little ones dancing upon the shore and twirling like the seagulls. I then noticed a couple, obviously man and wife, sitting on the dried sand with drawn up knees, tense. They were arguing loudly about some domestic turmoil – all while the children danced 100 meters out on the tidal flats. The young were oblivious, did not know, did not care of the love clearly lost. Maybe they did and chose not to react – too painful. The wind and the youngsters were a symphony at play, not a mourning dirge.

It would be beneficial to be realistic today, yet also to regain some of the innocence of youth. "Cast care aside." Dance on the wind. Be a child.

In 1974 a blaze broke out at Powerscourt, a Palladian mansion built for the Wingfield family on the site of a Norman castle. Over thirty years later, the gutted, windowless home stands stark (now renovated). But, the gardens are a gem. The whole garden complex was commissioned in the 1730s, and finally reached its present glory in 1875. Central in the gardens is Triton Lake, approached by The Perron, an Italianate stairway laid into a mosaic in millions of beach pebbles. Two statues of Pegasus (the winged horse of Greek mythology), emblem of the Wingfield's First Viscount of Powerscourt, guard the stairs and terraced gardens. It took one hundred men twelve years to build the staircase. Three unusual features of Powerscourt Gardens drew my attention – a Japanese Garden built on reclaimed bog land – Pepper Pot Tower modeled after the Viscount's dining room pepper mill – the Pet Cemetery, last resting place for Wingfield pets: cats, dogs, and horses. My hour's tour ended at the sundial which reads, "I only mark the sunny hours." Hmmm. In Ireland, time must go very slowly on that timepiece.

As I exited the Viennese Bamberg Gate, I reflected on what an inspiring sunny hour my visit had been. Even without a home, this garden had given me a lift and an appreciation to value: diversity, order, creativity and respect for animals. Walk through a garden today and find an inspiration.

Down by the salley gardens my love and I did meet,
She passed the salley gardens with little snow white feet.
She bid me take life easy as the leaves grew on the tree,
But I was young and foolish, with her could not agree.
(W.B. Yeats)

Yes, I know I used this verse already in another inspiration, but I wish to use it again. Humour me. W.B. wrote this poem presumably about Ballysadare where he spent years of his childhood at Avea House with his great-uncle. The Ballysadare River falls over huge rock formations in a tumultuous cataract before it empties into the Atlantic Ocean. Dara's Cataract is "the most gentle place in the whole of County Sligo" as Yeats said. It augurs a gentle soul and lifestyle, particularly as one watches the fishers standing in the shallows below the falls. The whites and tans and the patient waiting inject one with peace and quiet. Everyone, however, including Yeats, is not so imbued. This sweet love of the gentle was a learned behaviour and it came from the secret of Ballysadare Falls. Yeats, as many of us, was headstrong and driven, so he resorted to Ballysadare to use a cataract to calm him.

All around us today we have sights and sounds designed to slow us down and to ask us to take life easy. Some of those prompts are unforeseen and unexpected. God bids this and yet most of us will still stay in the fast lane. Perhaps, though, you will come across a cataract in which you will hear the call of God to come apart and rest awhile, if not at Ballysadare, at another gentle waterfall of your choosing.

Lady Maria, wife of Hugh Chatworthy of Antrim castle would walk her Irish wolfhound in the gardens in the fifteenth century. One day, along the lough, a wolf emerged from the woods and Maria fainted. Upon recovery of consciousness, she found the wolf dead and her wolfhound covered in the wolf's blood. The dog became the privileged one in the castle – spoiled as the defending hero of the mistress of the house. However, one day the dog vanished. One night, later, amid the scream of a storm, the guards of the castle were awakened by the howl of the hound. They set beacon fires and spotted an enemy force below the walls. Because of the hound's alarm, the day and the castle were saved from falling into marauders' hands. When light came, a new statue stood on the castle highest turret – the wolfhound had been transformed into stone. Grateful family members commissioned another statue in 1612, this one containing the legend on a plaque beneath.

The images of pre-Christian Ireland have been the impetus for some of our motivators to inspiration; the wolfhound is one of those. This hound is number one and an inspiration to all who have devoted pets who on other occasions have risked their lives to warn and rescue. If you have a dog, give him/her an extra treat today. Its devotedness may some day save you. But, be sure to also gain spiritual salvation in Christ.

What would possess parents to name their son Baptist? Well, here he is, Sir Baptist Jones who built Bellaghy Bawn in Northern Ireland (better known for housing a museum to the acclaimed Seamus Heaney). In 1610, the Plantation of Ulster took place in which Scottish farming immigrants settled in Northern Ireland. Jones built Bellaghy on behalf of the London Vintners Company, one of the Plantation enterprises. He had been a soldier at Carrickfergus, then employed by another company who fired him for inefficiency and dishonesty. Jones got his own back, for Bellaghy was the only bawn (fort) on high and dry ground. Hence, it became one of the best seats of the plantations in Ulster. Jones had chosen this site because it was an early Christian ring fort, one thousand years old. He saw its value in protection, arability and water provision for a corn mill. In time, Jones' bawn was burned during the 1641 rebellion and the present bawn dates from the eitghteenth century. I pictured two men standing outside Bellaghy Bawn. One was Baptist Jones, proud of his entrepreneurial skills and achievements. Although experiencing a baptism of fire initially in Northern Ireland, he was now master of his ring fort. The other man I saw was Seamus Heaney, a man engrossed in the arts and letters. He stands at Bellaghy Bawn, proud of his contributions to Irish literature which have conquered the world. The pen is mightier than the sword, or the dollar.

Sit down today and do your regular business. Fair and well, but, don't forget to write someone a word of encouragement or to send a card. You'll baptize the receiver in an ocean of love. You'll become the "Baptist".

Digging

Between my finger and my thumb
The squat pen rests; snug as a gun.

Under my window, a clean
rasping sound
When the spade sinks into grav-
elly ground:
My father, digging. I look down

Till his straining rump among the
flowerbeds
Bends low, comes up twenty years away
Stooping in rhythm through
potato drills
Where he was digging.

The coarse boot nestled on the
lug, the shaft
Against the inside knee was
levered firmly.
He rooted out tall tops , buried the
bright edge deep
To scatter new potatoes that we picked,
Loving their cool hardness in
our hands.

By God, the old man could
handle a spade.
Just like his old man.

My grandfather cut more turf in a day
Than any other man on Toner's bog.
Once I carried him milk in a bottle
Corked sloppily with paper. He
straightened up
To drink it, then fell to right away
Nicking and slicing neatly, heaving sods
Over his shoulder, going
down and down
For the good turf. Digging.

The cold smell of potato mould, the
squelch and slap
Of soggy peat, the curt cuts of an edge
Through living roots awaken
in my head.
But I've no spade to follow men
like them.

Between my finger and my thumb
The squat pen rests.
I'll dig with it.

(Seamus Heaney)

Although Heaney cannot see his way clear to become a "digger" as his predecessors, he still reveals a strong admiration for the skill of his father and grandfather. From them he acquires his own motivation to dig, albeit in other ways, with his pen. The source of the end product, plain potatoes or finely turned poems, is the same: the soil of Ireland. Another inference gathers my attention, the four words, "snug as a gun." Others have taken the option to use variant instruments to show their love for Ireland – the terrorists' guns and gelignite. Heaney abandons that option in the last stanza.

What will I dig with today? I want to use a tool that inspires others: a shovel, a pen, a wand, a bow, a keyboard, a chisel, a brush...... But not a gun!!!!

Rising out the Tipperary Plain is a rocky stronghold, the Rock of Cashel. Saint Patrick came here in 450. The Kings of Munster ruled here. The church took it over and fostered it as a religious centre until Cromwell massacred its three thousand adherents. Despite the rock's formidable site of power, it fell and was abandoned. I began my tour through the dormitory block and saw the original Saint Patrick's cross. The chapel, the crossing (fortress), the roofless cathedral choir and finally the round tower, ninety two feet high left me with breathless awe. One fact made me smile – in the choir is the tomb of seventeenth century Miller MaGrath. He raised eyebrows by serving as archbishop of both Protestant and Catholic churches, at the same time. Now, that was politically dangerous, and no doubt required considerable public relations skills! The humour evaporated, however, when I thought of another Mount Cashel, in Newfoundland, Canada, now demolished. It was the site of an infamous orphanage/school where unspeakable abuse was committed by so-called religious men.

Two rocks of Cashel, each with a different image. One of strength and panache, the other of weakness and humiliation, both with burdens of the past. I am inspired to pursue the former today. Be strong. Build bridges.

In September, 1588, three Spanish Armada galleons had the misfortune to be forced ashore in bad weather off the coast of Sligo. The captain recorded in his memoirs that "within an hour all three ships were broken in pieces so that there did not escape but 300 men and more than 600 were drowned." The Irish call the rock on Streedagh Strand, "*Carig–na–Spanaigh*", the Spanish Rock. Between the local Irish and the English cavalry, most if not all survivors were hunted and killed, some hung from the rafters of an abbey. Gawkers and important politicians (even the Lord Deputy) came to the beach to ogle at the sight of about six hundred dead bodies on the shore and at the enormity of the ships. The obsession with the wreck even carried over to 1985 when divers located the wrecks and recovered booty items. And in the twenty first century, tourists, like me, came to see the timbers in the sea at very low tides.

What a penchant human nature has for an attention to the rises and downfalls of others, such as rubbernecking at accidents on the road. Today would be a good day to focus, not on the troubles and foibles of those around us, but on their good points and dilemmas. When I consider Christ, I ponder his accomplishments for his creatures, not his humiliation and his murder. The hateful Pharisees, Romans and Jewish peasants did enough of that as they sent Jesus to the cross and mocked him there. "I don't want to be a Pharisee" are the words of a children's song. Amen!

The morning wind began to moan
But still the night went on
Through the giant loom the web of gloom
Crept till each thread was spun.

(Ballad of Reading Gaol – Oscar Wilde)

Picture Wilde's image here: an endless night spilling into dawn, brisk with wind. The gloaming morning wind now incorporates a weaving image. It is, as if in this darkness the whole cloth of the day's dire events has been woven before the sun can rise. The mood can be dark – Wilde's fate is darkly set. The poet might have had this bitter emotion because he spent some time in Reading Gaol, indicted and incarcerated for his lifestyle.

Or, my feeling can be upbeat: my goals are to be created and plans must be made before the light of morning can bless the day's events. I'll take the positive mood – it's more inspiring. There is great encouragement for the day when we know that we are organized and set.

(from Oscar Wilde's pen)

I can resist anything except temptation.

Work is the curse of the working class.

Anybody can be good, in the country.

To lose one parent may be regarded as a misfortune; to lose both looks like carelessness.

The truth is rarely pure, and never simple.

I have nothing to declare, except my genius.

To love oneself is the beginning of a lifelong romance.

Smile!!! It inspires.

No, I did not write the "Sport of Kings"— although Ireland is famous for its horse-breeding and racing, this title is a different image. In Toomour in Sligo is a derelict church and yard with praying stones and a stone-slab cross. On the altar slab is a design which some say deems this place a royal mausoleum. The design takes the viewer to a nearby well, Kings-town, which gets its name for the dead who lie buried at Toomour. There are, however, nay-sayers to the "royal grave" theory. They attribute the name of the Kings-town well to a misreading, and mistranslation, of the ancient Gaelic. *Cloich Righ* means king's-stone, but some read the title as *Cluiche Righ*, Game of Kings. This phrase was the euphemism given throughout Europe to the Black Death of medieval times. It seems that this well was supposed to be the panacea, the holy cure for the dreaded smallpox which decimated the population of Europe.

Throughout time, humankind has wanted to cheat death with some sort of elixir. But the great Leveler or Horseman (as both Emily Dickinson and Yeats himself called Death) gets all in the ends, both kings and paupers. But there is a "cure" for death; it's eternal life in Christ. If you've got that, you've got reason to feel inspired this day and always.

Into the Twilight

Out-worn heart, in a time out-worn,
Come clear of the nets of wrong and right;
Laugh, heart, again in the grey twilight,
Sigh, heart, again in the dew of morn.

Your mother, Eire is always young,
Dew ever shining and twilight grey;
Though hope fall from you and love decay,
Burning in fires of slanderous tongue.

And God stands winding His lonely horn,
And time and the world are ever in flight;
And love is less kind than the grey twilight,
And hope is less dear than the dew of morn.
(W.B. Yeats)

Another of Ireland's revolutionary laments edged and tinged with a brooding, goal-oriented hope that the heart will laugh once more. Some seem to always have a cause. In this case, it is Irish patriotism/nationalism, but all hearts need a cause of some kind – any cause. Find a worthy cause and support it today.

There is nothing like an Irish yarn. The Irish are masters at spinning the mystical with the natural and thereby creating the stuff for great Irish authors. Let's go back to W.B. Yeats. He notes in "The Dreaming of the Sidhe" that "the Hag [of Beare] sought the deepest water in the world to drown her fairy nature of which she had become dissatisfied." We have to go to Lough Gill (another of Yeats' famous sites) to get the story. Slieve Daene (Mountain of the Two Birds) and Slieve Dargan are two mountains to the north and west of the lake. On Slieve Daene is another lake, Lough Dagee (Lake of the Two Geese). On Slieve Dargan is a cairn of stones to the memory of Cailleach, the Hag. This unhappy fairy challenged Mad MacSweeney (who believed he was a bird and lived in trees) to a jumping contest, then a diving contest. Cailleach could not best MacSweeney, so at last she turned herself into a goose and dove into Lough Dagee never to be seen again. Because, so it goes, Lough Dagee's depths reach the limits of Hell. MacSweeney continued to live the life of a bird. What a fanciful, intriguing and complex tale of disappointment in state and conflict in forces.

It takes me to Romans chapter 8 in the Bible where Paul expresses the concern at two great forces in conflict, the old and the new man and his disappointment that the old man triumphs so often. The solution is in a sin offering. One option an ancient Jew had was to bring two pigeons or doves which were to die for the forgiveness of the sinner. No madness or dissatisfaction or conflict after these birds die. The Jew enjoyed God's forgiveness. I am inspired that today we can too under Christ's sacrifice.

A Drink of Water

(Seamus Heaney)

She came every morning to draw water
Like an old bat staggering up the field:
The pump's whooping cough, the bucket's clatter
And slow diminuendo as it filled,
Announced her. I recall
Her grey apron, the pocked white enamel
Of the brimming bucket, and the treble
Creak of her voice like the pump's handle.
Nights when a full moon lifted past her gable
It fell back through her window and would lie
Into the water set out on the table.
Where I have dipped to drink again, to be
Faithful to the admonishment on her cup,
Remember the Giver, fading off the lip.

I am struck by the images of the woman and her bucket – overused, maybe even abused. Yet, she and it did yeoman's work. The significance of the two emerges in the last half of the poem. When she is fast asleep from fatigue and the bucket sits idle and available on the table, Heaney draws on the strength still in the two, emanating from the daily chore of drawing water. He is not allowed to forget "the Giver", that irrepressible, supernatural force: God.

Can you take time out today to give? Someone will remember you, the giver. And remember the true Giver, God. Praise Him.

While I was in Keadue, I was intrigued by the guide's instructions to visit the "sweat houses". I don't mean workhouses or sweatshops. So, I approached the small stone (some are shale or earthen) building whose door was only eighteen inches high and twelve wide. I struggled inside, imagining the white hot stones on the sill burning my bare buttocks if this had been years ago in a real sweat house. The fire had been lit inside and the stones heated. The fire was then raked out and the chimney sealed. Here I was inside, I imagined, with some green rushes to sit on and a pail of water to douse the stones. I endured the heat for about fifteen minutes and then plunged into a mountain stream. Ah, the sauna is complete and my arthritic joints feel fine. How did the Scandinavians get the sauna from the Irish? Norsemen raided many other lands and Ireland was not spared, particularly the upper reaches of the Shannon River. They thought the idea of the sweat house had merit so carried the concept home. But, did the Irish get their idea from the Greeks or the Phoenicians?

It is said that imitation is the highest form of flattery and this is one idea that spread world-wide, from which origin, who knows? Our societies are predicated upon following examples/role models. Some are laudable; some are not. At one point or other today, you will not only set an example, but also consciously or unconsciously be a follower. Let me encourage you to control what you do and whom you look up to. Do you know who the supreme image is? Christ.

Why do we like being Irish? Partly because
It gives us a hold on the sentimental English
As members of a world that never was,
Baptized with fairy water;
And partly because Ireland is small enough
To be still thought of with a family feeling,
And because the waves are rough
That split her from a more commercial culture;
And because one feels that here at least one can
Do local work which is not at the world's mercy
And that on this tiny stage with luck a man
Might see the end of one particular action.
It is self-deception of course;
There is no humanity in this island either; (extract)
(Louis MacNeice)

Despite MacNeice's last two lines of this excerpt which plummet him back to reality, I believe that the sentiments of the true Irish "spirit" belong in every soul. That, I acknowledge, is improbable since the Irish are sublime and unique – inspirational. Nonetheless, try today to harvest some of the riches of the Irish mind – a "family feeling", an indomitable superiority over adversity, a singular and immediate goal, a non-materialism and a citizenship beyond this world. That's the Irish inspiration.

Ireland 1972

(Paul Durcan)

Next to the fresh grave of my beloved grandmother
The grave of my firstlove murdered by my brother.

I was in Ireland in 1972 and saw and heard first hand the effects of "the Troubles". None of my relatives were victims. The closest I came was my brother-in-law's brother who was gunned down at home because he served in the UDR. Wider battles which became internecine murders and wars became reprehensible.

From where does such hatred generate?

It is almost inconceivable that someone's brother would murder the partner of the sibling. Family love should remain true, above all. "Love your enemy," Christ said. "Let love of the brothers continue," said the apostle. Good advice today.

"Without which none is genuine." Such are the words under the logo on Belleek China to indicate that the logo confirms the genuine nature of the craft. At the end of the spectrum from rock hard crystal is the fragile beauty of another of Ireland's exports taken from the soil: Belleek Parian China. In 1849, to provide employment after the Great Famine, Bloomfield discovered that his land had the right mix of feldspar, flint, shale and kaolin in order to open a pottery factory. The little town of Belleek sits on the border between Eire and Northern Ireland and is testament to the fact that arts break down barriers. Tourists of all races flock every day to the gorgeous old stone factory and showroom which is located on the River Erne. The china made inside is almost transparent in its fine nature, and, with its soft original beige and green or in a more modern beige and pink, it sets a gentle mood. All Belleek china bears Irish symbols: an Irish wolfhound, head turned to Devenish Round Tower, a harp and two sprigs of shamrock. Each piece must be turned out without flaw or it is destroyed. Other local artisans craft works from local clay too. We stopped by at a home based pottery about five miles outside Belleek to watch a man deftly cut strips of clay and interlace them to be painted and then fired into a vase. It was not Belleek, but it was beautiful. The vase had gone from a mass of grey clay to my sideboard.

The potters here in Ireland reminded me of another potter spoken of in the Bible. God is a potter who moulds me into an admirable masterpiece. I am inspired today to ask God to continue His moulding and making until I begin to resemble Christ.

The sole residents of Skellig Michael, an island off the coast of the Ring of Kerry, are thousands of seabirds, particularly gannets. Between 600 and 1200, however, the island was home to monks who wished solitude. They were self-supporting. To accomplish this aim, they gathered eggs and feathers and hunted seals. They then would trade their surplus to passing boats for tools, cereals and animal skins. The latter items were needed to produce vellum in order to continue their work of copying manuscripts. I managed to convince a local fisherman to set me on the pier at Skellig Michael where I climbed the thousand year old stairway, up seven hundred feet to the monastery perched on a ledge. I was very much alone for six hours. What a sublime, inspiring experience to have no companions but the wind, the rain, the sea and black tipped gannets! Below me, in one hundred and sixty five foot waters, roamed basking sharks, dolphins and sea turtles. I looked east to Ballyskelligs Bay and wondered why the monks left to reside in the Augustinian Priory on the "mainland".

I don't think I have ever been closer to God than on that day. Get alone today and commune with nature. You will be with God.

Surfing at Louisbourg – Clare

The ubiquitous thatched cottage

I was told to be sure to visit Easkey Lough in Sligo to appreciate the vastness and almost lunar-like qualities of the Irish table top mountains. On my way, though, I passed through a fetching glen (isn't the Irish word "glen" so much more full of imagery than "woods"?). A sign post diverted me from my goal at Easkey Lough, and I was pleased by my diversion. Surrounded by dry escarpments is a green meadow dotted with whitish rocks, benches, a cross and a statue of Christ. It's called Mass Hill. I was almost going to call it a god-forsaken place until I realized the irony of my words. This spot was where persecuted Catholics came to hear Mass during the Penal Laws. The Protestants, after William of Orange's victory in the 17th century, repressed Catholic freedom. Catholic church possessions were confiscated and the priests had to turn to saying Mass in these remote spots, using a rock as the altar. Parishioners faced a year in jail if they revealed where the Mass was said.

As I stood at the cross here in Sligo, I could sense a palpable fear and reverence combined – fear that the mass site would be raided at that moment by Roundheads and reverence that Catholics made such sacrifice to worship (whether I agree with their format or not). I was inspired to be thankful for our constitution which grants us freedom to worship as we see fit. Offer an inspired prayer of thanks now for all our rights enshrined in the Bill of Rights (American, or Canadian, or British or the land of your origin)

For lo, what changes time can bring!
The cycles of revolving years
May free my heart from all its fears
And teach my lips a song to sing.

Before yon field of trembling gold
Is garnered into dusty sheaves
Or 'ere the autumn's scarlet leaves
Flutter as birds adown the wold.

I may have run the glorious race
And caught the torch while yet aflame,
And called upon the holy name
Of Him who now doth hide His face.

(Rome Unvisited – Oscar Wilde)

There are few greater agonies than depression and lack of self-esteem. The heart longs to sing, but cannot. The face looks up, but sees only darkness. The desire to succeed is present, but lacks completeness. The Eternal City is always beyond the stretch of the hand. It's devastating; I have been there, you see, so I know how it feels. If you see or sense someone today who needs lifting, affirm him or her. You will be unveiling a hidden face. You will be setting a fire and unleashing a song.

My first exposure to Killymoon Castle on the Balinderry River near Cookstown, County Tyrone came in 1969. My church had rented a site for a summer kids' camp on the opposite side of the river. In the sight of the great round towers, we sang and learned of God. I knew nothing then of Killymoon's history. The original castle built in 1671 for the Stewarts who settled here from Scotland, burned in 1802 and Stewart employed John Nash to design his new castle (if you walk up Regents Street in London, you'll see Nash's architecture too). For those six generations, the Stewarts inhabited Killymoon, but the new castle was soon lost to the Stewarts through the hard times of the Famine. Killymoon was sold for $50,000.00 above its cost. From then, the castle saw several owners, through to 1922 when the owner experienced financial problems and sold Killymoon for $250.00! The current owner at time of wriitng, Coulter, has opened a golf course on the site, the reason why we no longer can enjoy the camping site under the shadows of the castle. Many years later, I have been able to view the castle through the kindness of the Coulter family.

As I learned what I had not known or appreciated in 1969, I was impressed by how and why Killymoon changed hands. It inspired me not to place my trust in real estate, for times change. For all the gorgeous Gothic chapel, the double return staircases, the octagonal drawing room and oval dining room and the ten foot high wall around almost sixty acres, this too shall pass.

The Irish countryside is a wild place, particularly in winter, and Moneydarragh Bog near Gleneely in Donegal is no exception. The bogs of all Ireland provide winter fuel and at Gleneely, the inhabitants make a social event out of cutting stacking and taking home the "turf". Even visitors are invited or pressed to learn the art of cutting the peat and enjoying the fellowship in gathering winter warmth. Many archaeological finds occur during cutting. For thousands of years, the oak trees formerly covering Ireland have been preserved in the bogs where they fell. Turf diggers find these hardened logs and save them for craftsmen to carve into artwork. Even fully preserved bodies have been uncovered in the moist, swampy bogs. One can see the blackened earth for miles, dug up, piled. Chances are it is not a human digger today, but a mechanical one. Off in the distance, undisturbed yet, are acres of dark purple bog heather. They hide more fortunes and finds.

What will you dig for today? Or find today? Don't do it alone; make it a social event and stack up joys and sorrows, successes and failures for future use, be it practical or creative. Don't forget to enjoy the scenery in today's dig too; you are certain to come across a gem or a relic of past spiritual men or women or doctrine. Go dig some fuel today. Inspire by a fire.

Around, around they waltzed and wound
Some wheeled in smirking pairs;
With the mincing step of a demirep
Some sidled up the stairs:
And the subtle sneer, and fawning leer,
Each helped us at our prayers...

And as we prayed, we grew afraid
Of the Justice of the Sun.

(Ballad of Reading Gaol – Oscar Wilde)

This section of Wilde's masterpiece of penal experience strikes me as an indictment of the excesses, the snobbery, the shallowness, the hypocrisy of certain elements of our society. Some respect and even fear true and social justice, but, alas, not all. I will work for justice today. Join me.

There once was another men tell us,
The Giver and Taker of life
A lovingless God and a jealous
Whose joy was in weeping and strife.
He is gone: his temple 'tis sunken
In ashes and fallen in dirt,
With dreams of the Lady of Lust.

(Ye Shall be Gods – Oscar Wilde)

Sorry, Oscar, there is a God and there is only one God, with one character. God is blamed for so many events and ills in the world. "How can a loving God allow such happenings?" we hear. Our answer to the cause of the ills of men, women and children is found in Wilde's last three words. The force of lust is ultimately responsible for degradation in the world. The Originator of Sin created Lady Lust and all her confreres. And, the Devil is not a dream at all. Just as God allows you free will to choose or reject His love, so he allows Satan his free will, for a time. I will not blame God today, but give Him the glory for who I am.

The dunes have changed shape a thousand times over in the last one hundred and fifty years. Sands have shifted due to erosion and wind. And society has changed, but little. It has donned a mask of respectability, but prejudice and denial of rights are just below the surface now, instead of glaringly vicious as they were in the 1800s and 1900s in Ireland. Just beyond the Doagh Visitor's Centre lies another of Ireland's countless gorgeous strands. At this one, high cliffs guard the southern end. They stand mute, yet having overseen the atrocities of the Famine on Doagh Island. That morning in March, there was not a living soul on the mile long beach except me. Was it the same in 1846 or in 1880 as the persecuted tried to flee hunger or the tormentor? How many weak souls plunged from the cliffs in despair or just walked into the sea until the tide sucked them under forever? Or did the waves see others less desolate who came to the beach in the hope of gathering seaweed to boil and eat, only to die from the plague in the kelp? I ambled on, deep in lonely and sympathetic heart until I came to the narrow bays and inlets. The tidal power was awesome. A breaker would crash into an inlet and the water level would rise ten feet, swishing kelp and spume into hideous shapes in and above the dark waters. Systematically, synchronized by the moon, other waves smacked their heads on outcroppings, sending fountains fifty feet into the air. The din could have been the guns of an evicting party or of falling bodies or of dying souls. No one saw or heard the strand that hour but me and God.

I could not have helped the victims of the Famine, but God heard and saw and remembers. In the end, in any loss or injustice, God will right all wrong. He will speak the final word, not the hills, nor the sands, nor the waters. Remember that today.

Most have heard of the Boyne and Shannon Rivers and know that Ireland's name is actually Eire. I wonder if many know of the derivation of the names. *Boann* (Boyne) was the Goddess of bounty and fertility. Her logo was the sacred white cow. *Boann* had a husband, but he was unfaithful and fathered a son to the great god Dagda. To hide their union Boann and Dagda caused the sun to stand still for nine months, such that the son was conceived and born on the same day. As for Shannon, the name comes from the goddess *Sinend*. She came near the well of knowledge, curious as to its contents, but her action flouted the rules. The well waters mounted from below and drowned her. Hence, the Shannon River flowed. The third goddess is one of a triple goddess government over Ireland during the time of the Gaels. (*Eiru, Bamba and Fodhla*). *Eiru* could change forms from a beautiful queen to a sharp-beaked crow. From her name came Eire. These three names have something in common; they bring the supernatural, magical, divine, miraculous realm into the everyday world of common people—rivers, mountains, loughs, bogs, fields.

Behind each of our names is the potential for a miracle, a divine nature. We don't get it from mythical gods or goddesses but from the one True God and from his Spirit.

My department head at the school at which I teach comes from Birr in County Offaly. I never knew of the significance of the Birr Castle Demesne, simply because she never thought to mention it. A visit to the castle filled me in on an inspiration. The Birr Castle goes back to 1620 when it was built by the Parsons family. One of these Parsons, the third Earl of Rosse, in the 1840s constructed at Birr what was the world's largest telescope for over seventy years. And it still works! His drawings of galaxies compare with modern photographs. This Parsons has world fame because he invented the steam turbine engine which powered the Queen Elizabeth I. The fourth Earl, also an astronomer, measured the moon's surface temperature—confirmed by Neill Armstrong! The female Parsonses created the gardens, the largest in Ireland and whose box hedges hold the Guinness Record for the highest in the world. There is a waterfall, a suspension bridge, a birds-of-prey zoo/center and a theme garden. The parterre contains box hedges which form romantic crossed Rs and a cloister walk.

The Parsons men and women put Birr on the map and inspired others like me with their inventiveness and artistry. I left with a deeper motivation to have my family develop their artistic and scientific skills.

One of the features I have noticed about various cultures is their disparate attitude toward personal cleanliness. Some of those attitudes have been dictated by extenuating circumstances. For example, when I was a child, at a time when my parents' thinking was still tinged with experiences in the Depression, we had a bath once a week. It was necessary to conserve energy, so I was told. Another conundrum I have never understood is the tendency of certain cultures to bathe daily before they go to bed, and not in the morning. There is surely a perfectly good reason for this habit. In Belfast, I found a third puzzle which most would find bizarre today, but had total practicality in the late 1800s. In 1888 the Ormeau Baths, a community bath house, were built. I admired the brick building with its curved roof and chuckled at the thought of whole families traipsing down the Lisburn Road in an Irish squall so that they could take a bath. Local homes were built without baths—Ormeau was a luxury. I also chuckled at the present use of the Ormeau building—the baths are now an art gallery!

I do not understand the reasons why some do what they do. It puzzles me. Yet, they have perfect rationale for their behaviour. I think I'll go and have a long, luxurious bath as I contemplate life today. It will help me to be less judgmental.

'Curse God and die: what better hope than this?
He hath forgotten thee in all the bliss
Of his gold city, and eternal day' –
Nay, peace: behind my prison's blinded bars
I do possess what none can take away.
My love, and all the glory of the stars.

(At Verona – Oscar Wilde)

Wilde initially takes up the words of old Job who endured depressing, even suicidal, moods when he flew in God's face and when the Devil scourged him. A conscious stop to these ravings is effected in "peace". Wilde reminds himself that he possesses two qualities: love and vision. I wish to transcend Wilde's mode of defeat of the repressive mind. Today, I will acknowledge that love and vision come from God, not from my own will.

The Giant's Causeway in County Antrim is a must-see tourist site despite what cynics tell you. I've been there three times and each has given me a fresh inspiration. It is Finn (Fionn) McCool who generated the name. According to legend, the makings of a "bridge" were a result of his attempt to reach Scotland and his true love by throwing rocks into the sea. The true story is much more scientific, just cooled lava turned into basalt hexagons and heptagons. Since my first visit in 1969 access to the causeway and cliffs has been limited. But there are still unparalleled thrills to be had along the coast paths. Part of the thrill is in the danger of slippery or falling rocks, cliff edges and rogue waves. The actual thrills are in the gigantic rock formations: a granny, a wishing chair, and boot, chimney tops and a "musical organ." You can easily spot each image carved in the basalt, fit for a giant. The organ is my favourite, for I could go right up and touch the organ "pipes" and imagine McCool sitting down to play his wedding march! There was one more giant feature; the torturous climb to the top of the cliff gave me a raging hunger. Along the precipice under a full spring gale, I made way back to the carpark to have a "giant" lunch in the Causeway Hotel.

That day I was transported into a giant's world where I could dream giant visions. I'm doing that today too.

One of Dublin's jewels is Phoenix Park, Europe's largest enclosed park; the wall runs eleven kilometers around it. In fact, it is five times the size of Hyde Park in London. Numerous sports fields form just a part of its facilities. The question arises as to how the park's name originated. A spring rises from the pond in the park. The Gaelic for "clear water" is "*fionn uisce*" (a loose English pronunciation of which is feen-iskie). Near the spring is Phoenix Column, topped with—you guessed it—a statue of the mythical bird. Take your pick, but I like the first interpretation. Two other "columns" rise in Phoenix Park. At the park gate is the Wellington Testimonial obelisk, sixty-three meters high, and made from captured French armor. Finally, there is a twenty-seven meter steel cross at the site where Pope John Paul II celebrated mass before one million people in 1979. That's four features which raise their heads at Phoenix Park. A fifth is one we've all no doubt seen. The Park has a zoo, famous for breeding lions. One king of the jungle bred at Phoenix was the MGM lion which raises its head and roars as each MGM movie or cartoon begins.

Be proud and inspired today. Raise your head in self-respect, in prayer, in victory, in a new beginning, or even just to let the rain fall on your face so you can drink from God's spring from heaven. That would be enough to inspire me.

Some pursue peace, others war. Some try for peace in war. In Parnell Square in Dublin is the Garden of Remembrance dedicated to men and women who have died fighting for Irish freedom. A cruciform pool is laid with a mosaic of broken swords and shields, representing peace. Where is national peace? There is a statue of the Children of Lir who were changed into swans by a wicked stepmother. Where is domestic peace? The Garden saw the Irish Volunteers fight in 1913. It also heard the anger of the leaders of the 1916 Easter Rising as they were arrested and held here overnight before being taken to Kilmainham Gaol. A group of 2500 insurgents occupied the Post Office for five days. What was supposed to be a nationwide revolution against British rule ended with its leaders court-martialed and brutally shot before a firing-squad. The Germans, at war with the United Kingdom, had delivered arms to the Irish nationalists, but they still lost. A German ship, the Asgard, stands in the courtyard of the Gaol. Men whose names are famous in Ireland, Plunkett, Connolly, Parnell and de Valera, were herded from the Garden to Kilmainham. As I stood back and contemplated Eamon de Valera's portrait, I wondered if he thought the fight for freedom and peace in Ireland was all worth-while. De Valera finally served as Ireland's President until 1973. Fighting was still rampant.

Does peace inspire? Yes it does. Fight for peace today, but avoid bloodshed in the battle.

By that I mean a theater, not a chapel church in a monastery, but it could just as well be a place of worship. W. B. Yeats and Lady Gregory founded this theater in Dublin in 1898 and it staged its first play in 1904. Its logo has an Irish wolfhound in the foreground, held at bay by a legendary Irish youth, lithe and handsome. It's hardly an image classic to drama, but then the Irish breed their own brand of literary stars. Controversy and non-conformity have often been hallmarks of the Irish. One such event was during the staging of Sean O'Casey's "The Plough and the Stars" at the Abbey in 1926. Nationalism was a key and sensitive issue then and the Irish Free State had barely been born (in 1922) after a civil war. In the play, the flag of the Free State appeared in a pub frequented by prostitutes. Some saw such a display as demeaning to the nationalist cause. Even earlier, Irish sensitivities were alarmed when "The Playboy of the Western World" by J.M. Synge was staged at the Abbey in 1907. Moral conservatives protested in the street. Irish literature persevered, nonetheless, and continues to blossom. It is the longest running arts and letters form in the world, from Cuchulainn to Heaney.

The stage inspires me. We all love to play the part and to applaud someone who can do it well. Be inspired to put on your best thespian image, but don't fake it.

I stood in the Shankhill Graveyard in Belfast and closed by eyes. I had just been across Cambrai Street to St. Matthew's Church to view the Ballaun Stone, found in 1855. Now I pictured it here as the altar for a Druidic sacrifice 1500 years ago. Around 'Old Church' *(Sean Cill)* area in those times was a ring fort to stave off death from wolves, wild boar or marauders as the Trade Route through here to Antrim. I fast-forwarded to see the Ballaun Stone now serving as a baptismal font (baptism is also a symbol of death). Once more, years pass. Royal Irish Rangers are decimated in the Battle of the Somme in 1916. Only seventy six of seven hundred return to the Shankill to live out their life. World War II now. A fourteen year old RAF pilot is buried in the Shankill. The final images of this documentary flashing in my brain are during the Troubles. Shankill's poor population falls by 40,000 as the area becomes a war zone, and innocent families flee to live in safer environments. Some did not make it, for the last picture is the fish and chip shop on October 23, 1993 at which a sectarian attack killed ten. As I turn to leave the Shankill, it has grown dark. I walk down Shankill Road and the eternal flame of the Belfast Street Lamp has come on to honour the ten who died. I pass the Memorial Garden, tribute to the war dead, and I at last reach the intersection of Shankill and Northumberland. I spot a brass sign – "Shankill Road Mission." Its founder, Reverend Henry Montgomery, signed the petition in his blood to protect Home Rule. But, perhaps the fifteenth President of the United States said it best. On a wall mural on the Shankill are his words, "My Ulster blood is my most priceless heritage."

Sacrifice, the right kind, inspires. Give something up today.

The National Gallery in Dublin is an eclectic composite of inspirational art. Its importance was enhanced when George Bernard Shaw left one-third of his estate to the gallery. Among the works on display is an international mix of styles. A Renaissance work of Andrea Montegna shows the decapitation of an Assyrian chief. The female holds the long blade in her right hand as she helps deposit the head of Holofernes in a bag. Another painting of Caravaggio (1602) was found only in 1990 in the Dublin Jesuit House of Study. It is a poignant dark scene of the Taking of the Christ. Then, central on the ground floor is "The Sick Call," of 1863. Lawless has painted a suffering woman escorting priests and doctor by boat to a home where the years after the Famine have taken a toll. Another image of the Famine is in a Foley sculpture—The Houseless Wanderer. Finally, Jack B. Yeats has a whole room to himself. His "For the Road" is a mottled mystery—a free-wheeling horse in the foreground canters down a forest lane toward what appears to be figures in the sunlight beyond.

All the pieces inspired me—yes, even the "dark" ones—to look at life from another's perspective. Dark can become light. In the darkest moments of disease, death, capture, we must see beyond to resurrection and hope.

Ireland is renowned for producing the best of horses. The Irish Derby is an internationally renowned equine event held at Curragh in Kildare. The race course is actually a two thousand-acre grassed plain. The Irish love their horses. Thousands flock to a show; my brother-in-law has been to the animal show at Ballinasloe in October. It's evidently an event attracting crowds in the tens of thousands, rain or shine. I'm sure one or two horses on sale there came from the National Stud at Tully (actually owned by the British Crown). This breeding center was opened in 1900 by an Anglo-Irishman who eccentrically had strategic skylights set in stables to allow foals and mares to be "touched" by faery sunlight or moonbeams. He sold the foals based on their astrological charts! The Stud is a five-star horse hotel. There is a secluded foaling unit where mare and foal can enjoy quality time after birth. The stallions wait in well-appointed sheds to be taken out at least fifty times per season to "service" the mares who enjoy their own lush paddocks. I didn't see it, but I was told that one special "teaser" stallion is introduced to the mares so breeders can know when the time is right for mating. I'm sure that he gets an extra sugar cube or two! As I tried to look "horsy" leaning on the rails watching some racers get exercised, I was inspired by their equine power, led by a comparatively weak human with only a bit, bridle, and crop.

In the Bible, James speaks of our passions which need to be bridled the same way. That day, I controlled my temper and hope to every day, though I fail! When I succeed, I feel like a "stud"!

Lord Wavertree (he who founded the National Stud as William Walker), like any good Edwardian elite, leaned to Orientalism. Hence, on the same grounds as the Stud, the Lord (who received the title only because he bequeathed the farm to the Royals) commissioned a Japanese Garden. He called in Tassa Eida, his son Minoru, and forty Japanese assistants to spend four years laying out and planting. I really believed I was back in Japan; the native maples, mulberries, cherries, magnolias, not to mention sacred bamboo groves and bonsai reminded me of strolling in gardens in Kyoto or Hiroshima. The rock gardens, lanterns, wooden bridges and *toori* arches helped me relive my times learning Japanese right in Japan. I was most impressed with the deeper message of the garden, for it is an allegory. I began the walk at a dark cave, the Cave of Oblivion, and ended it at a Zen, raked stone garden, the Gateway to Eternity. The garden, you see, is the journey from the cradle to the grave. I wondered if there was some contrasting connection between the entrance to life of the foal and a human baby. If so, it is a sad parody.

The inspiration lies in the conclusion. We have an eternal hope, a life after death.

Between Temple Bar in Dublin and Liffey Street is a high-arched foot-bridge. John Windsor, an English iron worker, built this gorgeous photo-op spot in 1816. I am sure that more than one drunken Irishman (or tourist, for that matter) has stumbled across the bridge on his way home from a pub in "The Bar." Temple Bar was once a notorious red light zone and then became the Bohemian Montmartre of Dublin, known for its artists and writers. Ha'penny Bridge could tell some tales! It is officially known as the Liffey Bridge, but was christened the "Wellington", then the "Ha'penny." So whence its nickname? Well, I'm not convinced every non-salubrious soul used the bridge because, up until 1919, there was a half-penny toll to use it. Half a penny was about 1 cent, even then a small price to pay for a shortcut. It's not the users of the bridge who inspire me, but rather its symbolic image. It's an attractive mode of access. Even when it cost to cross, this bridge provided a quick link between two walks of life.

The little bridge inspired me to appreciate my link from earth to heaven, by crossing the bridge of Christ, effected at a far greater cost than a half-penny.

Saint Michan's Church in Dublin is a nondescript building from its exterior. Come inside with me now to see the ghoulish! We must descend to the vaults. Careful now, the steps are worn smooth. If you reach out your hand to steady yourself at the bottom, you just might latch onto strands of hair or skin from mummified bodies over two hundred years old! Now, I'd not be joking around, would I, begorrah? Yes, the church's magnesia limestone walls provide a climate which staves off decomposition. So, yes, there are preserved bodies visible after the wooden caskets have been cracked open. Two of these bodies are said to be the brothers Sheares, leaders of the 1798 rebellion, later executed. As I return you to the upper world, please still take care. In the church, the organ may begin to play a requiem and Handel may still be at the keyboard (he was supposed to have practiced the Messiah at this bench). Even outside you are not immune. United Irishman, Robert Emmet's remains could be in an unmarked grave in the churchyard. Emmet was publicly hanged in 1803 for his abortive plan to effect Irish liberty by taking Dublin Castle. In the graveyard at Saint Michan's, you may still hear his last defiant patriotic words as he choked to death at the noose.

It's all very inspiring—it inspires me that our voices and our influences never pass away. I can still promote good or evil from beyond the grave.

The Dunluce Center in Portrush does just what today's title says. It consists of a three-part Dunluce Center: Finn McCool Adventure Playground, The Treasure Fortress and Turbo Tours. The last is an action ride synchronized with some of Hollywood's most action-packed movies. The Fortress is a high-tech treasure hunt set in a real castle. Two of us were out to collect enough "magic" on a quiz trail so we could free a spellbound princess and her Spanish treasure dowry. We failed! One secret portal we could not find or open. The third site was for the kids. There are three floors; the variety ranged from benign touch screen games to full-blown action in an obstacle course or a climbing wall. All three are under the watchful eye of the giant Finn standing at the entrance. The whole of Dunluce center is pure and clean fun.

If you can't go to a playground today, have fun somewhere else! Laugh, squeal, twirl and fly. Today is a fun day. That inspires me.

This great author was a native of Belfast. Near the intersection of Holywood Road and Newtonards Road in Belfast is a life-size statue of Lewis opening a wardrobe, the gateway to Narnia. The author is holding onto a chair back and stepping forward. What suspense captured by sculptor Ross Wilson in 1888, but only unveiled in 1998! Further along is St. Mark's Church, the Lewis family church where C.S. was baptized. There is even a "Lewis Window" in the church donated by Christian apologist Clive Staples. Finally, one takes a right turn into Circular Road and finds Belmont Park in "Bernagh," where C.S. Lewis wrote his Pilgrim's Progress while on holiday in 1932. The treasures of Narnia have been enjoyed world-wide by children and adults alike. Whether interpreted as a spiritual allegory or simply a tale of fantasy, the works of Lewis (himself an unapologetic, born-again believer), have motivated readers for decades.

As are most readers, I am inspired by Aslan, the lion, who fights for right and love, even to death. I want to be an "Aslan" today! – thanks to the literary genius of C.S. Lewis.

On Glendalough lived a young saint
In odour of sanctity dwelling
An old-fashioned odour, which now,
We seldom or never are smelling.
(Samuel Lover – on St. Kevin)

And since the whole thing's imagined anyhow,
Imagine being Kevin. Which is he?
Self forgetful or in agony all the time…?
'To labour and not to seek reward,' he prays
A prayer his body makes entirely
For he has forgotten self, forgotten bird
And on the riverbank forgotten the river's name.

(Seamus Heaney – St. Kevin and the Blackbird)

St. Kevin was purported to have stayed in one position in prayer so long that a blackbird came and made a nest in his palms. Kevin stayed steady through the nesting season until the chicks were hatched.

That's purity and there is nothing wrong with emanating an odour of purity today in meditation and work. After all, it's a fragrance we rarely smell.

Belfast City Hall ranks up there as one of the most impressive city halls in the world (the only one I like better is Paris' Hotel de Ville). This building in Northern Ireland is a Grade 'A' Listed building of historic architecture and deserves its listing. Standing smack dab in the center of Belfast on Donegall Square, the Hall boasts a fifty-three meter dome. You just can't miss it. It has stood for almost a hundred years as a focal point as well as a rendezvous spot. Statuary and marble friezes are everywhere, but one statue caught my eye. Above the door is a figure of "Hibernia encouraging and promoting Commerce and Arts in the city." Hibernia is the goddess fostering winter (the derivation is from Latin – hiber = winter). The region of Scotland and part of Ireland was called Hibernia by the Romans, probably because of its northern bleakness, so foreign to Italy. In Belfast, the goddess' goal is to have the city flourish. Indeed, Ireland is a success story. Both the republic and Northern Ireland at one time topped the EU in economic growth. Thirty five years ago, when I first visited Ireland amid the fomenting Troubles, I would never have thought that Hibernia's encouragement would bear fruit. Then Belfast's core resembled a war zone. Now, it is a throbbing boom town. City Hall's Hibernia kept the faith and prevailed.

Keep on in persevering grace, and winter will fall away to spring and summer and harvest.

I could not believe it either. The guidebook pointed us to the wall of St. John's Cathedral in Sligo City and intriguingly attracted us to what the connection was between the Thornaby family burial plot and Dracula. Bram Stoker's mother was Charlotte Thornaby. Charlotte entertained her son with black tales about the cholera epidemic in Sligo in 1832. Charlotte was the daughter of an army lieutenant, so she saw close up the ravages of the disease. I am sure she told young Bram the story of the "Long Sergeant Callen". She must have, since she included it in her own memoirs. The tale goes like this: one aspect of cholera causes the victim to slide into unconsciousness and Sergeant Callen succumbed to cholera and this state. He was trundled off, at least his body was, to be measured for a coffin. Because of the Long Sergeant's size, the coffin makers could not fit him into any standard sized box. Rather than make a custom coffin, the carpenter took his hammer to break Callen's legs so that he would fit. Imagine the horror of the undertaking crew to have Callen leap up from his "death" in pain at the first hammer blow to his knees. By the way, Long John made a full recovery from his cholera. Bram Stoker's Dracula could have been inspired by Callen. Dracula has won the infamy of being the classic monster/villain who rises from his coffin to haunt his victims with his teeth.

My visit to the Thornaby plot reminded me that I have a more horrific adversaryinSatan and also that I have a blessed and eternal resurrection from death. They triedto break our Saviour's legs but it was prophecy not pain that prevented it too.

Postscript
(Seamus Heaney)

And some time make the time to drive out west
Into County Clare, along the Flaggy Shore,
In September or October, when the wind
And the light are working off each other
So that the ocean on one side is wild
With foam and glitter, and inland among stones
The surface of the slate-grey lake is lit
By the earthed lightning of a flock of swans,
Their feathers roughed and ruffling, white on white,
Their fully grown headstrong-looking heads
Tucked or cresting or busy underwater.
Useless to think you'll park and capture it
More thoroughly. You are neither here nor there,
A hurry through which known and strange things pass
As big soft buffetings come at the car sideways
And catch the heart off guard and blow it open.

Yes, I've done that, Seamus Heaney. The western coast of Ireland is wildly inspiring. I was "neither here nor there." It only takes a drive-by, but the Irish wind is less than gentle, rather a hurricane force. But, like the Spirit of God, it enters the heart and blows it open to make its home therein. You don't have to go to County Clare to be buffeted by God's wind today. His breath is everywhere.

Ireland has produced more than its fair share of great writers, but is not quite as well-known for its artists. If one knows the eighth century (come on now, admit it; you don't!), it was then that Irish art blossomed. The Book of Kells and various metalwork masterpieces date from that era (the Tara Brooch and the Ardagh Chalice). At this time in Irish history, monasteries made a point of producing relics in honour of holy men; thus, they commissioned works to be created by resident artisan monks. The art piece we are considering today was found in a bog at Moylough, Sligo in 1945 by a farmer digging four feet into the turf. His turf spade struck a hard object and he bent to carefully uncover a belt. The leather straps, four pieces hinged together by tinned bronze, are decorated with silver panels, glasswork and inlaid studs. It even has a false buckle. Instead of keeping his find, Mr. Towey passed the belt to the National Museum where it sits in the Treasury Room. Experts say this belt is a relic in honour of or from some saint. It boggles the mind to imagine how the Moylough belt ended up in the bog. Was the belt purely ornamental, or did it serve some purpose? Who was the artist who spent hours creating this gorgeous piece?

Today's a day for belt-tightening. The belt does fit, and it is the Belt of Truth. Be inspired today to tell the truth in love and forego the little white lies. Truth is a beautiful trait and can flourish anywhere, in the darkest of environments. Make a point of letting your truth and light shine all day.

Inishmurray Island, a small unimposing stretch off Sligo's coast is a microcosm of the potential ills of society we live in today. And, the island is today only a bird sanctuary. Actually, in the sixth century, St. Malaise founded a monastery here and an oval enclosure contains several buildings. 1) the Men's church – and by extension the inference that there was to be no women's church, 2) St. Malaise's church (the saint's statue now stands in Dublin) 3) the schoolhouse (inhabitants later reapportioned the use of an oval shelter. 4) the House of Fire (from medieval times), 5) three altars with upright slabs engraved with crosses (turn them anti-clockwise and you curse your enemies).

These five aspects of Inishmurray represent parts of today's society against which I must guard. There is no room in the modern world for sexism. There is no cause for hierarchical positions and power-brokering. There is no excuse for a lack of education. We need homes for peace today, not abuse nor a fire of ill-will. Let God house the fire of life and let him put his Spirit into us and into our homes. There is absolutely no place for vengeance in the name of religion. If we attempt to approach a day with the Spirit of God, we can hope to avoid the stark end of Inishmurray – abandonment and destruction.

O fair wind blowing from the sea
Who through the dark and mist dost guide
The ships that on the billow ride
Unto what land, oh, misery!
Shall I be borne, across what stormy wave
Or, to whose house a purchased slave?

(Ophenodia – Oscar Wilde)

I wonder if Wilde had Saint Patrick in mind when he penned these words? Yet, for Saint Patrick, slavery became a blessing. Without his capture, Ireland would not be today what it is–a land of spirituality and intrigue. Enslavement does have its gilded side.

This day, I want to be slave to the standards of heaven and of Christ – love, joy, peace, longsuffering, goodness, gentleness. It may be a sacrifice, but I and others will benefit. Be a bondslave of Christ.

The "twin towers" of East Belfast are visible from almost anywhere in the city. They are the Harland and Wolff cranes on Queen's Island Wharf. The two large letters H and W on the yellow/orange steel girders are testament to a legacy for Belfast. The legendary shipyard produced the Titanic and the Mauritania to name just two. Indeed, the cranes have legendary names – Samson and Delilah. I am sure that those cranes motivated many a man and his family, for Harland and Wolff was the city's livelihood for years, employing thousands of what the guidebook calls "artisans" in the construction of ships, giant floating masterpieces. Just a walk away is McMaster Street on whose cobbles the children of shipwrights played hopscotch or soccer in the light of gas lamps. They waited for dads to return from work so that they could go inside the rented "parlour row houses" to sup on "champ" (Irish mashed potatoes and green onions with large dollops of butter poured into a well in the centre of the dish – yum, delicious!). These families were proud of the heritage. If they had been walking the street today, the men would see the impressive Titanic Mural on Dee Street. One jarring feature in the area (to me anyway) is the Odyssey Centre – a modernistic exhibition/concert hall and ice rink. I'm not certain that the shipbuilders would have understood this kind of art, but they can and do talk in the new Titanic Museum.

Hard labour is an inspiration, in spite of any failure. I encourage you to get down and do some work which dirties the hands today.

(bonus!)

I spent some time at Slane's Castle. I have this odd penchant—I love walking in ruins and envisioning the former state of the building and events held there. The directions at Slane took me to the east side of the walls of the castle. On the wall is the "Black Face of Stone." As with so much of intriguing Ireland, there is a story. This black face is a woman's and the expression is consummate sadness. The tale (abbreviated by me here, but should you want to sit down with a pint, a local will embellish nicely) goes like this—the statue is more ancient than the castle. The O'Neills obtained it in Asia, and had it installed as an icon to their perpetuity. If the stone face falls, the O'Neill name will die out. Now just imagine how that could be! The O'Neill clan has proliferated throughout the world. I think they're safe no matter what happens to the Eastern Face.

As I pondered this face, I was inspired, not by its melancholy look, but by the fact that I have no threat against the perpetuity of my name—not because I have a son, but because my name is written in God's eternal book.

Eleven upright stones stand in a straight line, set north to south. This four thousand year-old structure, near Strabane in County Tyrone, is Goles Stone Row. The alignment covers only a distance of sixteen meters but it is always amazing to me how Stone Age men could accomplish such feats of precision and strength. When men are driven and inspired by a spirit beyond them, they can organize anything. Some say it was a desire to assess the rising moon's influence which drove the ancient tribe to set up Goles Stone Row. Also in the Sperrin Mountains, further east, near Cookstown is a circle, Beaghmore Stone Circle. It too is perfectly set, drawn as if by a compass or a modern geographer. Here ceremonies and rituals to bury the dead and to observe solar, lunar and stellar activities were held in the Bronze Age. Form and function are an anathema to some, but a foundation of faith to others. It is clear that men and women and children over a period of two or three thousand years valued the stability in life as seen in circles and alignments.

Thank God today for the seemingly stiff bureaucracy in your life (personal, governmental, religious), which nevertheless gives it form and function.

Titanic Museum - Belfast

Titanic Museum - Belfast

I stood in a ruined shell of two churches, back to back. Killevy Churches is a unique site. In the fifth century a nunnery was set up on the site. From this holy setting came the inspiration to build not one, but two places of worship. The west church was constituted in the eleventh century, the east one in the fifteenth. The motivation to have two churches on one spot is admirable. "*Cill*" is Gaelic for Church. "*Shleibhe*"—kill-levy—means mountain (*Slieve*). So theses churches were the "churches on the mountain", or a place to go to God. I read how *"cill"* became "kirk" in Scottish Gaelic and I remembered how my Scottish parents spoke regularly of the "kirk." I learned too that *"donagh"* (Donaghmore, etc) were churches founded by St. Patrick, and that *"bann"* and *"lawn"* (Bangor and Lawnkeg) were areas fenced off for church use. I've been through Eglish a hundred times, but just learned that Eglish means church—there are at least three in a town of a few hundred. Finally, there is "temple" (Templepatrick), the English influence. As I kicked through the long grass in the cemetery and jumped over fallen stones of church walls, I realized I was in the presence of God, and I worshipped.

Whichever prefix is used to indicate a church matters little. What touches the heart is a reverent worship of God following the pattern of Scripture. Have you worshipped God today yet? Praise inspires.

An Irish wake is, in essence, an oxymoron—a time of joyful mourning. At the Ulster American Folk Park near Omagh, one Saint Patrick's Day, I gathered to attend the "American Wake" or "Living Wake." This event was held often in the eighteenth and nineteenth centuries in the hours before family members departed for the "New World," perhaps never to return. Actually, the day before, I had attended the "Emigrant's Return," a reenactment of Thomas Mellon returning home after making a good life for himself in America. The Irish and American connection goes on. In May at the Park, they celebrate a rural Ulster and American frontier wedding with something old, new, borrowed and blue. Then, on July the Fourth, one can celebrate Independence Day in Ireland by watching a scene from a battle. In September there is a Bluegrass and Folk Music festival and finally on October 31st, you can sample barnbrack and pumpkin and shoofly pies—an Irish-American Halloween.

Celebrations are good for the soul— stomping ones or serious ones. They inspire me. Enjoy today! It's a celebration of you, and maybe of wider cultural bonding.

(by Saint Brendan)

A map of the sixth century showed a shipload of monks leaving Scotland, stopping in England, Wales and Ireland, bound ultimately for the Land of Promise. They traveled via Iceland through vicious groups of "sirens" and ended up in.... Newfoundland, Canada. Columbus even had a map which included "Saint Brendan's Isle" in the western Atlantic. This information came from a Latin text from the early 500s – Navigatio Santo Brendani. This Saint Brendan was an Irish monk born in Tralee. He built a *curragh* from wood, leather, tar and animal fat and embarked on the currents and winds which took him to the Faroe Islands, Iceland and Greenland, and finally to Newfoundland, the Promised Land of the Saints. Sound implausible? Hold onto your seats. In 1976, Tim Severin left the Dingle Peninsula in a similar boat and indeed reached Newfoundland (Saint Brendan's Isle) after one year. It took Saint Brendan and his monks seven years. They met sea monsters (whales), encountered crystals that rose to the skies (icebergs) and were pelted by flaming rocks (the volcanoes on Iceland. The story reaches another peak when we learn that stone carvings written in Old Irish dated from between 500 and 1000 were found in West Virginia. They contain Christian symbols. Did Brendan get home – well, being buried in Clonfert Cathedral settles that, they say.

So, my friend, the Irish have upstaged even Leif Erickson and Chris Columbus (by nine hundred years). All men inspire us to search for a New World. Let's build a boat?

Crom Cruich – *"Dar Crom"* (in Gaelic) / "By Jove" (in translated English mythology) – He is the horned god, the "crooked mound" or "bloody crescent". Those are truly images of All Hallows Eve, Irish style. The main idol of Eirin stood in Mag Sleacht plain in County Cavan and around it were 12 smaller idols to whom pagan Irish bands sacrificed one third of their healthy children on Samain (November 1). The worship of stone idols has been documented elsewhere in Ireland too, in County Fermanagh (The Hunched Man, the Eater of Worlds). Crom Cruich was, however, the greatest and most evil. He demanded those sacrifices and slavery in return for milk and corn and the fertility of cattle. It was dangerous to even worship him since his worshippers often perished in the act by pouring their blood around the base of his altar. Saint Patrick is said to have destroyed Crom Cruich and to have forced the golden idol back into the earth. Nonetheless, such fascination with evil persists. Slaine, one of Galaxy comic books most popular characters, a futuristic science fiction work, is a take off of Crom Cruich. Slaine becomes High King of Ireland and one of five brothers who divided Ireland into five equal portions. He was ritually sacrificed himself.

What's to worship today? Is your idol justified in your mind because it is not inherently evil? Anything that diverts the energy of soul and mind away from the high ideals of life and God is an idol. Beware it and subdue it.

The man had killed the thing he loved
And so he had to die.
Yet, each man kills the thing he loves
By each let this be heard.
Some do it with a bitter look,
Some with a flattering word.
The coward does it with a kiss,
The brave man with a sword.

(Ballad of Reading Gaol – Oscar Wilde)

Most say, "I am **not** a killer and would **never** kill!" Thus they would decry any punishment for such a sin which might fall upon them.

Yet, think; today, you kill enthusiasm, ambition, love, care, joy by a dismissive look or word. Or, you may kill a friendship by a betrayal or an attack. Beware of figurative murder.

It's Gaelic, *boirean*, meaning rocky land and it is barren. Oliver Cromwell's surveyor said, "It is a savage land, yielding neither water enough to drown a man, nor tree to hang him, nor soil enough to bury him." That sounds like Cromwell's men – hard and vicious. The Burren, below the Shannon Estuary, produces both Mediterranean and Alpine plants, and in summer it is a splash of colours covering the layers of limestone. In winter, the hills are at warmer temperatures than the valleys, would you believe, such that the Irish cattle graze on high ground in winter. Wild animals, birds and insects abound – rare butterflies, Irish hares, whooper swans and cuckoos. The Burren in the west at the Cliffs of Moher drop six hundred and fifty feet into the Atlantic. Over its vast plateau is a warren of thousands of caves; one of particular note is Bear Haven where one can see hibernation pits of brown bears which used to roam the Burren. Dotting the wilderness are stone forts, wedge tombs, dolmens and castles. I ended up on the southern fringe of the Burren at Kilfenara which is an unusual Catholic Diocese; its Bishop is the Pope.

The Burren was one of my favourite spots in Ireland because it inspired me to see beauty in the wild and the unusual. I felt quite at home in the Burren. You too can be inspired in finding your own unusual atmosphere, your own "burren". That might even be the "rocky land" of Jesus Christ.

On the "Island of Doagh" we visited two large stones. One is called the Mass Stone. It has carved onto it some unusual markings which are unclear as to their complete meaning. What archaeologists have discovered is that the stone commemorates a battle fought by tribal chieftains at one point in Celtic history. We don't know the winner or the loser, just the fact that a battle was engaged and, most likely, the bones of the warriors lie beneath the sands near Trawbreaga Bay. Why is it called Mass Stone? Not because a mass was said here, but because of its mass – a wide heavy slab telling a heavy story which had wide implications. Land was lost; families were deprived of fathers and mothers – all in the name of the power lust of a chieftain. The next stone was the Penal Altar where mass was said by Father O'Docherty in the 1770s to remember the intentions of the sufferers of the prohibition of rights as a result of the Penal Laws – the right to live the Irish culture, the right to speak the Irish language and the right to worship as the Irish saw fit. The masses were outlawed and on this wind-swept forsaken hill, the faithful would gather at the Penal Altar to celebrate the Eucharist and commemorate the loss of the rights of deity.

Israel in the Bible piled up stones of remembrance at the Jordan River to celebrate their arrival at the Promised Land – at the loss of a whole generation. Israeli leaders raised these altars where offerings to God were burned. What stones of our memories do we raise? All, positive and negative recollections, need to be engraved somewhere so we do not forget. 'Lest we Forget.'

High in the Bricklieve Mountains, I met again with death. This is Carrowkeel and even more eerie than Carrowmore. The challenge is first to reach the site, snaking up an unpaved, pot-holed one lane path which threatens to send your car rolling into the valley. The danger zone is worth the risk, for at the top the views are worth it alone. Then, the fourteen passage tombs spread widely over the mountain top strike at the heart. They date from the Bronze Age and their construction in this remote region defies imagination. Some say that a series of about eighty huts to the west was the village of the builders. How did they survive here and from where did their supplies come? At one of the limestone domes about five meters high and one hundred and fifty meters in diameter, I hunched down and crawled inside. In this one I saw none of what archaeologists have found – cremated human remains, beads, pins, pendants and pottery. I am glad I did not find such items. In respectful fear, I did not venture to the two cairns with cruciform chambers. Whoever went to such great labour to lay to rest their dead strikes respect and awe into me. I was moved at Carrowkeel, but not as much as at another vastly simpler resting-place signposted on the road down to the highway and Castlebaldwin. It is a rest home for retired donkeys! The poor sad-eyed droopy eared beasts of burden are well cared for in their stable until they pass on (I guess there's a donkey heaven?). The donkeys are not ensconced in enormous passage tombs, but most likely are buried and forgotten.

There is a "retirement home" and resting place for all of us, donkeys and kings. On earth it may be simple or ornate. Consider your end today, but don't be too intent on what it looks like here. The place of which I speak is in heaven, where our Christian treasure is. I would not want either Carrowkeel or the Donkey's home after reading my Bible.

Hero or Traitor? November 9

There is a statue of Bartholomew Teeling at Carricknagat in County Sligo. Teeling allowed the landing in Ireland at Killala Bay of a French invasion force in 1789 to help out the rebellion against the English. At Carricknagat, a British cannon made General Humbert's army hole up until Teeling rode forward and shot the British cannoneer. The English retreat was short-lived and the French met defeat in County Langford. Teeling was not as fortunate as the French soldiers who were sent home. He was hung as a traitor in Dublin still decked out in his tricolore, not the red white and blue of the British but the French blue white and red. To the Irish, Teeling is a hero and even in 1920 he aroused an incensed reaction when his statue's hand was shot off by the British Black and Tans. Each day we can be an inspiration or a hindrance to ourselves and to others. Even Jesus was considered a traitor by Judas because he had not lived up to the Zealot's impression of what a Messiah should be: a revolutionary. Then again, Judas was a hero to the Pharisees because he betrayed Jesus.

What a complex world we live in! We can, however, take our bearings from God's assessment of His Son. – a man who pleased Him , honourably, truly and purely. He's my hero today and every day. He won a battle for me fair and square without denying Himself, His Father or us.

This too I know – and wise it were
If each could know the same –
That every prison that men build
Is built with bricks of shame
And bound with bars lest Christ could see
How men their brothers maim.

With bars they blur the gracious moon,
And blind the godly sun.
And they do well to hide their Hell,
For in it things are done
That Son of God or son of Man
Eve should look upon!

(Ballad of Reading Gaol – Oscar Wilde)

Nothing is hidden from the eyes of God. He knows the very secrets of our hearts. He sees all the atrocities committed in every secret place. That can inspire me today, not to run and hide in fear or guilt; the knowledge of this truth, however, can motivate me to do good to all because He is watching – just as a child proudly acts out when he knows his parents are watching.

Out on a wind swept hill in County Tyrone near Coagh sits the Ardboe High Cross. This type of Celtic cross has no known parallels in Europe, with its tall narrow shaft and a colleen which joins it to the small head. This sandstone relic dates back to the ninth century, part of a sixth century monastery. It was a centre for prayer, preaching, confession and sealing secular agreements. The cross is very weather worn and damaged since emigrants would chip away a small piece of the cross to take overseas (in fact, one emigrant's farewell hymn ends, "My plenty blown... and shamrocks grow green round ... the Old Cross at Ardboe"). The real purpose of the cross was a teaching tool for the illiterate. On it are twenty two panels of Biblical scenes – Old Testament on the east side, the north and south sides containing scenes of Christ's life, and the west side depicting the future. What an effective way to learn Bible stories! In the graveyard of the church nearby is a dead beech tree stump, the tree blessed by a monk, but killed by the habit penitents had of embedding a coin into the tree's trunk as they prayed for cures. To remove a coin would pass the disease to the thief, so they say. Children still love to leave a coin here and say a wish, hoping to see the little grey monk who wanders as a ghost in the yard.

I stood one grey day at the cross in the field overlooking Lough Neagh and I envisioned praying devout Christians anxious to learn about God by reading the cross' story, much as people in Europe used to do by "reading" the stained glass windows. Today, I want to be as devoted to prayer and Bible study as those people were. The Ardboe High Cross inspired me to value my Bible and to take something away from it each day. I need a day to remember the fallen.

This proud Irish clan used to rule the Kingdom of Tyrone from the twelfth to the sixteenth centuries. One of the clan's seats was at Tullyhogue at a fort and a hill of the same name. The fort sits down a leafy lane off a 'B' road into Cookstown. The placid site used to ring with shouts of celebrations as the new king was inaugurated in the fort. From the towers, the new king could view not only his Tyrone, but also all six counties of modern Northern Ireland (if it was not raining!). Actually, today on a clear day, you can spot from the hill top the dome of Belfast City Hall. Instead of a visitor of the present though, I took my mind back to the past. As I listened, eyes closed, to the changing of the guard ceremony, I could see back four hundred years. I watched the heraldry and the prancing horses disappear down the lane as the entourage made its way back to the residential seat in Dungannon, where surely the ale flowed freely. I made my way back into tiny Tullyhogue village to the public house which bears four names (The Halfway House, The Tullyhogue Arms, McQueens and Murphys). Locals say the town used to have three pubs, but was reduced to one with four names in order to pay tribute to the history of them all. How three became four is beyond me and must be an Irish conundrum! It is said that Jonathan Swift wrote his Gulliver's Travels at the priory in Tullyhogue. He intended to stay just one night there, but was so taken with the smoothness of the ale at the pub (probably McQueens then) that he stayed on to finish his manuscript. Believe the Irish yarn at your peril.

Lift a glass today and toast history or hilarity or power or the creative arts.

At Malin Head is the "Wee House of Malin". "Wee" is one of those generic words, much like "nice" or "cool" which can be applied to almost any thing or circumstance or person. There's a wee spot of tea, a wee dear, a wee ways along,. It's also a wee challenge to understand the Irish. I digress. Back to the wee house. This place is actually a cave, St. Maachar's home just a short (and I mean "wee') ways from St. Machar's church. By the true definition, this church is "wee" – it's small. Legend has it that the faeries have an influence on the church. This place of worship "holds all that goes into it and the more goes into it, it holds the more." That sounds to me like Irish logic, pure irony. But, on closer examination, I see a deeper, spiritual concept which, again, the Irish are famous for handling.

First, a church is a place for worship of the soul, a place where spirits meet and depart. Viewed this way, yes, this and any other church has no limit to the number of those it can welcome. There is, as well, another perspective which we can value. Christ's body is the universal church and its number is countless millions over the ages. It holds all who go into it through faith and its love and acceptance are limitless. The more that goes into it, it holds the more. Yes, the Irish do have a grip on both the profoundly illogical and the illogically profound. Today, the church of St. Machar teaches me of God's acceptance and of my acceptability and I am profoundly grateful, in just a "wee" way.

Clearances III
(Seamus Heaney)

When all the others were away at Mass
I was all hers as we peeled potatoes.
They broke the silence, let fall one by one
Like soldiers weeping off the soldering iron.
Cold comforts set between us, things to share
Gleaming in a bucket of clean water.
And again let fall. Little pleasant splashes
From each other's work would bring us to our senses.

So while the parish priest at her bedside
Went hammer and tongs at prayers for the dying
And some were responding and some crying
I remembered her head bent over towards my head,
Her breath in mine, our fluent dipping knives-
Never closer the whole rest of our lives.

The potato is the bonding quantity of the Irish. That potato has caused both endurance and heartache in Ireland. And nothing else bonded Heaney with his dear mother – not Mass, not prayers, not grief, not death. "I was all hers" in the potato peeling process. The potatoes were stripped and then spoke. They were the essential elements of Heaney's "eucharist" with his mother: a communion which involved a union, "never closer the rest of [their] lives."

Go and look for a 'potato' today, a glue which will bond you to a loved one–a chore, a hobby, a study, a pastime, a sport or a journey. That glue will last a life time.

I visited the Planters Mansion (built from mud and rubble) in Waringstown, County Down. This plantation was not of Scottish origin as so many were in Northern Ireland when the British sent over Scots to populate the land for Britain. This town is of much Dutch background. And this plantation was not entirely agricultural for the flax it grew went to produce famed Irish linen. The owners of Planters Mansion brought to Waringstown weavers descended from those tradesmen in Flanders, Belgium. They came to work alongside the local Lagan valley weavers. Those weavers from the European mainland were Huguenots who were fleeing France's persecution of Protestants. As one can well guess, there were "interracial" marriages and so the weaving of Irish clans today in Waringstown are of mixed descent and proud of a heritage that brought together skilled artisans from other countries so as to perfect a fine trade. Today the houses in Waringstown have a distinct Dutch look. I wandered down the street where terraced cottages built for the Dutch still exist.

I felt that we have come not much further in our quest for racial unity. In fact, in some countries we frown upon immigrants building homes which reflect their heritage. I was inspired to allow multiculturalism a better chance. Our approach to acceptance of others is still a bit like mud and rubble.

Imagine being kneed or elbowed by a bony witch! Ouch! Off Steeple Road in Antrim Town is the Antrim High Tower built about 1150. It is a fine twenty eight meter specimen of a protective fort for a Celtic monastic settlement. Its conical peak pierces the sky as I wander the expansive treed grounds. Do I see a fearful monk up there spying out for Viking invaders from the slitted openings? No, my dear, it's a witch! A witch in a monastery? Ah yes; anything is possible in Ireland, you know. There is a legend that a witch was so enraged by the construction of the monks' tower that she engaged in what today would be known as a one person protest. It was not a self-immolation either. She ascended the tower and, in protest, leaped from its top. Apparently, she survived (aren't all witches invincible?), but did leave behind an impression. She landed on a large slab and dented it with her knee and elbow. Hence the witch's stone. My smile was broad as I stood at the tower's base and then bent to trace the indentation of the bone in the rock. I would not want to have that witch in opposition to me.

I was inspired to say to myself, "Don't antagonize someone today who can permanently damage you."

The Lover Mourns for the Loss of Love
(W. B. Yeats)

Pale brows, still hands and dim hair,
I had a beautiful friend
An dreamed that the old despair
Would end in love in the end:
She looked in my heart one day
And saw your image was there;
She has gone weeping away.

I would guess that this poem, on a literal interpretation, is a classic case of an ode to a jilting. The doomed lover never had a chance in the first place, just a despair that something would come of his ardour, that she would come to reciprocate his love at his strength. What irks him most is the fact that in and through him, she saw what she wanted, in another. Her weeping intrigued me. Were they tears of genuine compassion for dropping him, or were they "crocodile tears"? Maybe I am over-interpreting old W.B., but I see another level too. Had his love passed away before a consummation was possible? Is the "your image" God?

Are you experiencing a lost relationship or about to leave one and embark on another? Be inspired to be kind to that third party who is now alone.

Lough Arrow is one of Ireland's masterpieces. The country hotel at which I stayed boasted views from all rooms toward the lake about 2 kilometers away. The early morning scene, through wraith-like mists, was most impressive. I had just arrived at Reception after a morning walk to visit Ballindoon Priory on Lough Arrow's shores. I was imagining myself as a Dominican monk in 1501 meditating in that mist rising from the lake's surface. Now, that is an inspiration to holiness, a cure for materialism. Unusually, the Gothic church of the Priory has identical windows at each end. Just north-east across a forested glade, I had seen a *bullaun* stone (a stone with a cup hewn into it) or St. Dominic's Stone. I knew that it can rain at any minute in Ireland, but I had just spent a glorious 10 days of sunshine. I expected a dry cup, but the guidebook was correct. The top of the stone contained water in its cup-shaped hollow, just as had been predicted. That water was said to be a cure for warts. I was recalling all this in my decadently luxurious hotel room which included a five course dinner that evening, a pleasure to the taste- buds. I could not help but dream of the Dominicans directing a pilgrim plagued by warts to the stone. Did the faith of the friars or of the pilgrim work? I'll never know, but I do know that their lifestyle was singular and more God-oriented than mine. They had an innate belief in powers beyond them. As the Dominicans said their vespers or matins in the church, it did not matter which direction they looked. The stained glass windows, equal at either end, could remind them of their God.

Go get a cure today – a cure from society's ills. Re-establish a faith in a God who performs miracles beyond curing warts.

To an English teacher, Dublin would not be complete without a trip to the James Joyce Cultural Centre. Before dropping in there, I walked by Belvedere College, a Jesuit school which Joyce attended for five years and for which he had little love. Read *A Portrait of the Artist as a Young Man* and you'll sense sad school days. Joyce went on to become one of Ireland's great authors, best known for *Ulysses*. In the centre I stopped and read the biographies of about fifty of the characters in the novel which mirrors Homer's *Odyssey*, but is set in Dublin. All characters are real Dubliners – for example, Professor Dennis J. Maginni ran a dancing school from the same building Joyce frequented. Leopold Bloom and Molly really lived nearby at #7 Eccles Street. Bloom and *Ulysses* have become legendary and maligned (the novel was banned in Ireland until the 1960s). Some say that *Ulysses* is the greatest piece of English literature ever written, and on Bloomsday each June there is a festival when world wide visitors flock to Dublin. Since Joyce maintained that, if Dublin was ever leveled, it could be rebuilt from the pages of *Ulysses*, I doubt that any Bloomsday reveler would ever get lost.

As I ended my pilgrimage on Earl Street North before Joyce's statue, I studied his trademark hat and jacket. One man with such talent creatied such a stir. I was inspired to set out on my own odyssey.

Just outside Dublin's centre is Sandycove where James Joyce stayed for one week with one of his characters, poet Oliver St. John Gogarty, the Ulyssean Buck Mulligan. I climbed the steps to the sparsely furnished living quarters, inside what had been one of fifteen defensive Martello Towers built to withstand a Napoleonic invasion. "The pen is mightier than the sword." James Joyce conquered more hearts than did Napoleon. I could picture Gogarty and Joyce sitting with a cigar on the sunbathing deck, once a gun platform. While Joyce strummed playfully, were they discussing how to conquer the world? Now the room in the tower is a museum containing Joyce's guitar, cigar case, walking stick and his death mask. I was most taken with a deluxe edition of *Ulysses*. Illustrated by the French artist Henri Matisse; the edition is a treasure. One image shows Odysseus arriving home to Ithaca to reveal his presence to his wife, Penelope. Odysseus' voice and words convinced her of his identity more than any suitor's words could sway her.

A choice word inspires more than any weapon or force. Now, I am not saying that I advocate a Joycean lifestyle, just that his style has more influence. Speak to me convincingly and inspire me.

At 33 Synge Street, playwright and Nobel Prize winner George Bernard Shaw was born on July 26, 1856. Did he acquire J.M. Synge's spirit at birth? It was not, on the surface, an inspiring home: basic Victorian middle class. On top of that, Shaw's father was an alcoholic and his mother packed up and left the menfolk to take her daughters to live in London. George B. stayed on at Synge Street for twenty more years. The younger Shaw did not follow his father's bad model, for he writes, "I drank much tea out of brown delf [a china teapot] left to draw on the hob until it was pure tannin." Once Shaw got to England, his characters, middle class and lower, like Eliza Doolittle, came to life. I saw Eliza's ghost in Shaw's Dublin kitchen and she was sitting on one wooden chair with Professor Higgins, on the other side of the raised hearth as the elocutionist tried to raise Eliza in class, to no avail.

There's something inspiring about the "common" classes of those times. They pass on their spirit and work ethic to us.

Standing beside the great white statue of Saint Patrick at the foot of Croagh Patrick, I watched penitents about to set out on a two-hour barefoot trek up two thousand feet to hear mass. Then I looked out west over Clew Bay and knew I would rather foster the maverick in me than follow the sacrificial footsteps of the masses, and so I set out on another adventure. On Clare Island in Clew Bay is a commanding fifteenth century castle which Grace O'Malley used as a base to keep her reputation. I crossed the sea from Roonagh Quay—it took over an hour. There, I met Grace. O'Malley was a pirate Queen and an Irish nationalist in her time. Her motto was "Invincible on land and sea," and she proved it. From her stronghold on Clare Island, she controlled the whole west coast of Ireland. Although Elizabeth I received her in her court, Grace O'Malley opposed English control of Ireland right up to her death in 1603. I could well imagine this piratess haughtily and defiantly meeting British royalty on equal terms despite her rough ways and dress. I went into the little Cistercian abbey where O'Malley is buried and that's where I read her motto.

I was inspired to continue to be called a "maverick," and to encourage others to take on the name.

Is this an oxymoron? Garinish Island (Ilnacullin) became a little piece of the subtropics when a Belfast businessman engaged gardener Harold Peto to create a neo-classical landscaped retreat in 1910. The micro- climate (the Gulf Stream contributes) on the island in Bantry Bay and the peaty soil offer an ideal environment. Apart from the usual azaleas, rhodos and camellias so commonly found in the "British Isles," I found lush jungle bed flowers, Japanese bonsai and other flora native to the tropics. In addition, a Grecian Temple, a Roman folly and lily ponds all added to a Mediterranean ambience. The foil, in the typical rough and barren Irish hills and wild, pounding Atlantic breakers, further underscore Garinish's lush other-worldliness. My boat trip from Glengariff was well worth it. Not only did I get to follow cavorting seals en route, but as I sat in the sunshine by the pond in the Italianate garden, I was inspired by what can exist as a microcosm amid wider settings.

Be a light in the darkness, a ray of tropical sunshine in a rainstorm, a rainbow among the clouds. Be inspired to become an oxymoron today.

"Sonnet to Liberty"

Not that I love thy children, whose dull eyes
See nothing save their own unlovely woe,
Whose minds know nothing, nothing care to know,—
But that the roar of thy Democracies,
Thy reigns of Terror, thy great Anarchies,
Mirror my wildest passions like the sea,—
And give my rage a brother——! Liberty!
For this sake only do thy dissonant cries
Delight my discreet soul, else might all kings
By bloody knout or treacherous cannonades
Rob nations of their rights inviolate
And I remain unmoved—and yet, and yet,
These Christs that die upon the barricades,
God knows it I am with them, in some things.

(Oscar Wilde)

Millions have fought to gain or maintain freedom of speech, religion, thought or movement. God knows, we have learned to respect them, yet, like Wilde, we are never sure whether we are one hundred percent in their camp or whether the ends justify the means. I ask today to make liberty the brother of my rage.

When righteous anger and the purity of freedom are mixed, an elemental peace results.

Some say that a mote is a passage tomb. I would agree since my French linguistic background tells me that "une motte" is a mound of earth. Hence, the large or small mound or lump would indicate a grave, a passage to the underworld. Near Dunadry in Antrim is Donegore Motte. It dates back to pre-Anglo-Norman times when such types of burial mounds wee common. More recently in history, the 'motte' was used by the United Irishmen to plan the Battle of Antrim. Donegore in Gaelic could mean Fort of the Goats (why is anyone's guess) or the Bloody Fort. That meaning makes more sense to me, for annals say that those suffering from the plague were driven into the interior of the tomb and were sealed inside. The ostensible reasoning was that it would act as prevention from the spread of the disease. A sort of reverse quarantine, if you will. I imagined the cries of the dying as they protested the horrific connection with the already dead, the bodies of Celtic lords interred in the 'motte'. I envision the United Irishmen gaining inspiration from their forbears buried inside before they went out to the meadows to do battle, to go to their burial too. The scene today is more pastoral and peaceful with woods and the steeple of Saint John's Church casting a holy spell.

Is death close by today? None of the images at Donegore offered hope to me beyond the grave. I have a hope, however. I will live with Christ eternally after I die, or when He comes for me.

The brochure which I picked up in the hotel encouraged me to visit Doagh Island, since on the island was a museum and a life size diorama depicting "The Famine". The Irish have a penchant for the understatement: "The Troubles", "The Famine", "The IRA", "The UDA", "The Emigration". The Famine was one of Ireland's most chaotic disasters in which the country lost half its population from death or emigration in half a century (over 1 million to death and over 3 million to travel to the New World). This loss was a result of a mixture of the cruelty of humans and natural disaster. And the Irish euphemistically label such a calamity "The Famine"! Stoicism is what it is. We turned left at the sign to Doagh Island, but I never crossed a bridge, never saw the sea. Maybe at one point this was a true island, but not now. I arrived at a glistening whitewashed array of thatched buildings. This museum held the artifacts of families of the 1840s – evidence of a pitiful lifestyle. It hurt to see such deep degrading poverty. Then, we entered a dark tunnel, a foreboding entrance to the life sized scenes beyond: a woman and child living in a cave, a dying man begging on the road, an eviction, a clandestine mass. I stood rooted in horror at the effects of this Famine. To survive such an era must have needed a powerful will to live. The scene on Doagh Island was recast thousands of times over in those years. It is beyond imagination.

What do we call sin and evil? Do we deceive ourselves and refer to sin in "quasi-terms"? It is either sin or not, and sin is more abhorrent than the Famine was. Today I will face it and defeat it.

Ah, the true Irish ring of a classic Irish female name. Saint Brigid, second to Saint Patrick, founded a community at Kildare in 490, about the same time as Saint Patirck was doing his rounds. Historically, Brigid was both a Druid Celtic goddess (a poetess and a healer) and a Christian saint known for her kindness and love to animals. Born a Druid, she converted and was baptized as Brid. She entered a convent in her teens and founded an oratory under a large oak tree (Cill Dora – Church of the Oak – Kildare). Reputedly, she became a bishop because a senile Saint consecrated her in error. She ruled the enclave iron-fistedly. Like many Irish, she was also unorthodox. She allowed nuns and monks to live under the same roof and those who took the holy orders at Saint Brigid's Cathedral were encouraged to keep a perpetual fire burning in a pit, actually a pagan ritual. A community of nineteen nuns continued to keep the coals glowing in the pit until the 1500s. They each took turns tending the fire, and Saint Brigid herself appeared on the twentieth night over centuries to guard the flame. Saint Brigid's Day is February 1, also the pagan feast of Imbolg, a ceremony to bring on spring's fertility. What an intriguing ongoing connection between the Christian and the pagan, the conservative and the unorthodox.

Brigid inspires me to be tolerant of all worlds. "Nor was she intermittent about God's love." That's a tall order too.

I remember the TV ad by Unilever (the current company's name) which champions the ability of Lever soap to touch all two thousand of our body parts. No, I was not standing in an inadequate shower in my two star Dublin hotel to make me think of cleanliness! I was, rather, standing on Essex Quay by the Liffey River looking up at a terracotta decoration on the façade of the Sunlight Chambers. This was the central building of the Lever Brothers Company in 1900 as they began their soap manufacturing business. Ah, Sunlight and Lifebuoy soaps–they engender memories. My mother's and my wife's laborious laundry work and me as a boy trying to catch the floating bar of soap as I sat in the tub. But, back to Dublin. The wholesome bust of a young girl is central in the artwork on the façade on Essex Quay. Around her is an array of various items which to me looked like blossoms. She is wonderfully clean. She has no body odour; in fact, it was Lever Brothers who coined the distasteful cacophony of the term, "You've got BO!." William Hesketh Lever of Lincolnshire, England was a marketing master. He knew of the human penchant for cleanliness (it is next to godliness, is it not?). He had his Sunlight Soap being sold in one hundred and thirty four countries within one year after introduction to the marketplace.

To be clean, it is inspiring. Stay clean today; physically and morally. Get clean spiritually.

Now, that's an unlikely outcome in today's world. However, I can assure my astounded American friends that this defeat did occur. In Rostrevor, County Down I came across an obelisk erected to honour hometown boy, Major General Robert Ross, a hero of Wellington's campaigns and a graduate of Trinity College. He was widely decorated for his military feats. On August 24, 1814, Ross was in charge of a brigade of four thousand British soldiers which reached Washington D.C. He had had two horses shot out from under him on the road, but he succeeded to begin his assault on the White House where then President James Madison was dining calmly. When Madison heard that Ross' men were on Pennsylvania Avenue, the president fled with his dinner only partially eaten. In true Irish satirical fashion, when Ross finally entered the White House, he swaggered into the dining room, pulled himself up to the table and proceeded to polish off the abandoned dinner. I was wondering if Madison had left some Irish whiskey on the sideboard! Three weeks after, Ross, ever the strict disciplinarian, rescued an American girl, Emily Shaw who had been under the threat of rape from one of his own lieutenants. Once he had court-martialed the perpetrator, he pushed on, announcing, "I'll sup in Baltimore tonight or in Hell." He was shot en route to Baltimore by an eighteen year old militiaman. Ross' body was placed in a barrel of rum for preservation, but the ship got only as far as Halifax, Nova Scotia. It was there, in the Old Burying Grounds that I read of Ross final fate.

Our inspiration today comes from the fact that unlikely foes can defeat giants and superpowers, from a president, to a bully, to a Major General. Is there a giant or an overwhelming ghost in your life? You can cause it to flee today and you can take over its hold.

Punishment

I can feel the tug
Of the halter at the nape
Of her neck, the wind
On her naked front

It blows her nipples
To amber beads,
It shakes the frail rigging
Of her ribs

I can see her drowned
Body in the bog
The weighing stone
the floating rods and boughs

Under which at first
She was a barked sapling
That is dug up
Oak-bone, brain-firkin:

Her shaved head
Like a stubble of black corn,
Her blindfold a soiled bandage,
Her noose a ring

To store
the memories of love.

Little adulteress,
Before they punished you

You were flaxen haired,
Undernourished, and your
Tar blackface was beautiful.
My poor scapegoat,

I almost love you
But would have cast, I know,
The stones of silence.
I am the artful voyeur

Of your brain's exposed
And darkened combs,
Your muscles webbing
And all your numbered bones:

I who have stood dumb
When your betraying sisters,
Cauled in tar,
Wept by the railings,

Who would connive
In civilized outrage
Yet understand the exact
And tribal, intimate revenge.
(Seamus Heaney)

A disturbing poem. "The civilized outrage" is still lurking in the human brain. Heaney's images, whether in the Tollund Man's time or in ours during the Troubles is the ultimate in such callow behaviour, but it serves to remind us all that we can act similarly at any time – as a parent, as a teacher, as a superior, as an enemy, as an authority figure. We say, "My ways are right; yours are wrong, and thus you pay the penalty." Ah, it is wise in those circumstances to ponder that "there but for the grace of God go I." And we, the third parties who observe the punishment and pain "stood dumb". That is an indictment too. Don't allow vengeful punishment to be wreaked without considering justice.

(bonus!)

Cork will never "cork" its rebellious and bohemian spirit. It became a base for the Fenian movement in the mid 1800s. From its evolution out of the marshes of the River Lee as St. Finbarr's monastery, its penchant for the different has been evident. It has a non-British, Continental feel, and one aspect of its skyline takes the cake—it is St. Ann's Shandon, a church. Its four sides consist of two limestone walls and then two red sandstone walls. The weathervane is a "flying" salmon and its clock (until 1986) was the "four faced liar" since each of the four dials told a different time! Another kind of "rebel" is ensconced in a stone statue on St. Patrick's Street. Father Mathew founded the temperance movement in 1838. Five million Irish stayed off strong drink and the whiskey trade was cut in half. I can hardly imagine an Irishman denying himself a wee dram! My other stop in Cork was at the City Gaol where I saw how inmates were "bottled up" in harsh cells. True to Cork custom, the gaol's café offered me two menus –one the Victorian cellmates' fare or the other, the hearty prison governor's plate. All this offbeat aspect of Cork's life is presented with a satirical Irish twinkle in the eye.

We mustn't be too serious about life now, must we? If we have a cause, even to die for, we can always stop to see the lighter side of life. That inspires me.

Tomb of St Patrick - Down - Downpatrick

Turf and cottages-12 Pins Mtn Galway

Virtually everyone knows of the story of Irish heritage in eastern USA. Just attend the Saint Patrick's Day parade in New York or study the Kennedy clan. This connection is brought to life in Northern Ireland along the road to Omagh at the Ulster American Folk Park. It is a full scale outdoor museum of eighteenth and nineteenth century Irish/American relationships through the medium of the emigration of the Irish during the potato famine. Subsequently, these Irish helped develop the United States. One can see exhibitions at the Park as it was both in Ireland and in America during those trying times. The visitor leaves a deck-side scene in Ireland and emerges from the door into a street in an American port, having 'sailed' on the brig, the Union. It's a little bit of the U.S.A. in Ireland; the park even hosts an Appalachian Music Festival every September. The Folk park actually grew up around Thomas Mellon's cottage. Young Thomas emigrated at five with his family in 1813 and he became a wealthy powerful US judge. His own son, Andrew, became the richest man in America from railroads. Thomas returned to Camphill, and stated, "It is all as I had seen it." Also in the Park is the Hughes' cottage, the boyhood home of the Archbishop of New York, John Hughes. The home was rebuilt in the park, stone by stone, transported from its site close by where John was born. Hughes was the founder of the great Saint Patrick's Cathedral on Fifth Avenue.

It is honourable to be multi-cultural and it is rewarding to see people of other cultures put down roots in a new country and succeed in any walk of life. I applaud and am inspired by those men and their desire to maintain cultural ties with the homeland. Today I will support multi-culturalism and tolerance.

Andrew Jackson, the seventh president of the US in the early and mid eighteen hundreds had his roots in Ireland. His parents left Carrickfergus, County Antrim in 1765, and there gave birth to this fiery, stubborn boy who was to display that character as the hero-general in the Battle of New Orleans. There he inspired his soldiers to defeat the British in 1814/15. In the final battle, Jackson lost only seventy one men. In Carrickfergus is a centre dedicated to Jackson, the President, but the centre is only near the original cottage of the Jackson family. The actual cottage was torn down in the 1860s to make way for a railroad line. Today, only a blue plaque on a stone column marks where the Jacksons lived modestly. Another cottage has been built to depict how Jackson might have lived. As was the way of life then, the family shared the house with animals, and only a wall separated man from beast. I could imagine the stench and humidity raised, not just from the open peat fire below a daub and wattle canopy, but also from the cattle next door. I wondered if Jackson heard tales of Carrickfergus – its castle, its defences and offences and the trade from its port. He no doubt was inspired in his battle by the military history of his home town. Andrew Jackson was also known for his charismatic pluck. Despite his forces being outnumbered almost four to one, the Americans won the day in New Orleans.

Circumstances and settings may alter for us, but we need never lose our determination to succeed nor lose our interest in others. I will hold my back straight and strong today and engage others with a winning and sincere smile.

The sign was clear for a left turn off the N13. We passed a gorgeous church and began the climb to reach Griann Aileach. Soon, I realized that we had missed a second turn because we were heading down into a verdant valley. We were supposed to be ascending to the peak of this eight hundred foot hill. I backed into a three point turn and drove slowly up the single lane path to search for the correct turnoff. There it was, hidden away in a milling, jumping flock of sheep. At last we snaked up and around to the car park. The first thing I had to see was the passage between the interior and exterior triple terraced walls of the fort. There are at least four low entrances from inside the fort to reach an inky black passage cave where evidently soldiers under siege could retreat. Others say the Griann was a worship center and that the passage housed the spirit. The corridor was no more than four foot high and two foot wide. It went on around the whole seventy seven feet. This was a corridor to nowhere and claustrophobia would have been an automatic result of being cooped up here. I had to get out. Finally, outside, I came upon the remains of a holy well whose tradition states that St. Patrick baptized Eoghan (Owen) O'Neill there in 450 AD. The baptism was Owen's rite of passage to the Church, it is taught.

Are we ever sure of the way? Once we find a way, it is often dark, though sometimes the darkest ways are the most secure. We are told so many things about the correct way by religious leaders. But, there is only one way. "I am the Way, the Truth and the Life." "Come to Me," Christ said, "and I will give you rest."

The Song of the Old Mother

(W. B. Yeats)

I rise at dawn, and kneel and blow
Till the seed of the fire flicker and glow;
And then I must scrub and bake and sweep
Till stars are beginning to blink and peep;
And the young lie long and and dream in their bed
Of matching of ribbons for bosom and head,
And their day goes over in idleness,
And they sigh if the wind but lift a tress:
While I must work because I am old,
And the seed of the fire gets feeble and cold.

I interpret this as a gentle complaint about the realities of life – the generation gap. The old labour; the young relax.

I am sure that the old, as they read Yeats' poem are nodding in acquiescence. They grunt accolades about Yeats' perspective. The young, however, shake their heads in disbelief that anyone could misunderstand them so. There has to be a poem out there which takes their side and politely complains about the actions of the old people and their easy lot in life now: no exams, no school, no relationship problems etc.. It's okay to complain today, especially if you are a mother who has just slaved for Christmas. No rudeness is permitted though. And, you must hear the contrariwise complaint in return.

It sounds like a circus side show. "Step right up and see 'Skull House'."
Joyce Cary, a twentieth century author, wrote "A House of Children", a
tale of childhood memories, one of which is of a real house near Cooley on
the Inishowen Peninsula. It's a ghoulish sight to approach this small building
sitting in a stone-encrusted field with just one opening, one foot square. You
stoop low to the ground to peer in and what you see is an array of bones:
thighs and skulls. We can assume that they were once a gathering of bones
culled from caves or graves. Some one wanted to create a shrine? Maybe
some of the hundreds of thousands who died in the Great Famine rest here.
It is a haunting and unforgettable memory, and, like any other shrine (it has
been called an oratory), it evokes both pain and sympathy. But, does it call
for action?

**When I read of another "Place of the Skull", I remember
and rejoice and am grateful. So many have died in war and in
persecution and we must recall their sacrifice and loss. But, our
inspiration today is to act on others' distress. Are there steps to
take to stamp out persecution? To take a message of salvation
to the lost and dying? To comfort those in pain or in grief" Do
something about it, starting right this minute.**

I Am of Ireland
(W.B. Yeats)

'I am of Ireland,
And the Holy Land of Ireland,
And time runs on,' cried she.
'Come out of charity,
Come dance with me in Ireland.'

One man, one man alone
In that outlandish gear,
One solitary man
Of all that rambled there
Had turned his stately head.
'That is a long way off,
And time runs on,' he said,
'And the night grows rough.'

'I am of Ireland,
And the Holy Land of Ireland,
And time runs on,' cried she.
'Come out of charity
And dance with me in Ireland.'

'The fiddlers are all thumbs,
Or the fiddle-string accursed,
The drums and the kettledrums
And the trumpets all are burst,
And the trombone,' cried he,
'The trumpet and the trombone,'
And cocked a malicious eye,
'But time runs on, runs on.'

Are you an excuse-maker or a procrastinator, like the man who pled that Ireland was too far off or he who made the excuse of poor instruments and of a lack of time? But, there is no excuse; there is only time today to dance out of love – in Ireland or anywhere. I write this on St. Patrick's Day and I am not in Ireland, but I'll dance anyway and enjoy a Guinness and an Irish jig!!

I've heard that expression countless times at home when a door or window has been left open and a wintry blast is cooling down the house. It's a typical Irish phrase, for there are "gaps" all over Ireland. In some case, the word refers to an open door; in others, it is a geographic term indicating a valley or stretch between two mountains. In the Inishowen Peninsula there is Mamore (The Gap of). The view from the peak is breathtaking. Ahead lies Trawbrega Bay and on the other side one rock strewn mountain. Sheep and cottages and stone walls stand in starkness against the symmetry of the massive knolls. The mountains are the Urris Hills standing thirteen hundred feet above the seas below. One has to stop and take in the inspiring scenery. The road looks to wind on forever and end up in the ocean. There is an aura here of the endless. But, there is another darker side to the Gap of Mamore. During the times of the prohibition imposed on the Irish by the English landlords, the indomitable Irish felt a need to continue with the Irish brew, poteen. The Urris Hills were the local haven so that the *Gaeltachts* could keep the stills operating. Irish wakes and weddings are incomplete without the potent liquor. Poteen was, as well, the medicine of choice for the Irish, prescribed for sundry ills. Anyone could feel happier after a sip or two of the brew. The Prohibitionists attempted to close the gap on this Irish cultural tradition, but were unsuccessful in the Gap of Mamore.

Rules and regulations do not succeed unless they are based on God's word. And God's word is an open invitation to enjoy his grace and forgiveness freely available at any time from the Hill of Calvary. God never closes the gap. He can allow you in at any time.

When You are Old

(W. B. Yeats)

When you are old and grey and full of sleep,
And nodding by the fire, take down this book,
And slowly read, and dream of the soft look
Your eyes had once, and of their shadows deep;

How many loved your moments of glad grace,
And loved your beauty with love false or true,
But one man loved the pilgrim soul in you,
And loved the sorrows of your changing face;

And bending down beside the glowing bars,
Murmur a little sadly, how Love fled
And paced upon the mountains overhead
And hid his face amid the crowd of stars.

Yeats, in his advice to this acquaintance/friend, comments on the fate of love. Why did Love flee? At one time, this person was loved for grace, beauty, emotion, adventure, attention to duty – all laudable qualities. But, this respect was lost, vanished to unreachable places. What caused this disappearance of respect and love? The answer is found in lines 3 and 4 of stanza one. The soft look in the eyes went away, replaced by the dark glares of old age.

It is easy to lose the goodwill of others by our facial expressions. As we get older, we lose the verve for happiness; cares and bitterness crowd in. A soft smile today and a bright face from any age level, however, will work wonders in relationships. I encourage you to try it out. It's inspirational. Frown at one person and you receive the same in return, no doubt. Greet another with warmth and you'll notice the goodwill coming back from the latter. And you won't have to grow old with regrets.

No, the Vikings franchise from Minnesota has not been transferrerd to Dublin! The true Viking exploring spirit came to Dublin in 841. They settled on what is now known as "Wood Quay" in Dublin. The "wooden" part came, not from Viking building techniques, but from the timber supports used in the 1400s to reclaim land. However, in the 1070s, excavations dug up Norman and Norse villages with artifacts like pottery, swords, coins and leatherwork. Alas, "progress" took over and civic offices went up which pay only lip service to history in a modernistic Viking longboat-shaped picnic site. The arrival in 795 of those single-sailed, high-prowed longboats must have been a frightening sight for the native tribal communities in eastern Ireland and surrounding areas. The shields lining the gunwhales hid the marauders who would come ashore to pillage, particularly the monasteries at Glendalough and Kells whose round towers must have trembled at the sight of these fierce warriors. But, the Vikings were not all evil; they brought advancements to Ireland too – new agricultural techniques, coinage, art forms. As well, they founded cities which have thrived since: Dublin, Waterford and Limerick. It was not until 1014 that High King Brian Boru sent the Vikings packing at Clontarf (at the cost of his own life).

The Viking spirit has always inspired me – adventure, exploration, fearlessness, talent, knowledge. Despite their primitive and brutal ways (Dunmore cave in Kilkenny contained bones of women and children slaughtered by Vikings in 928), they had qualities to emulate and to improve the day. Ireland would not be what it is today without the Vikings. There is some good in everyone.

At Binnion Bay we found the famine wall, a relief project of the seventeenth century landlords. So that the sufferers could get subsistence living, they were offered make-work projects. The landowners, at least those who were not cruel oppressors, had indigents build walls for penning and controlling sheep. The loose stone walls run for miles up the mountains and along the roads. I paused at one spot and wondered what the Irish were thinking of as they piled and pulled stones. I wonder if they saw the significance of the wall – they were slaves in their own country. The potato blight had caused them to live outside the boundaries of their own control and within the confines of the whims of others. Near Binnion Bay, at Clonmany, I read the story of the McLaughlin brothers. Both boys set out for France to train as priests. As fate would have it, their ship was wrecked off Cornwall, England. A Protestant family sheltered the two until they parted company. Peter went on to France to take his Holy Orders, whereas Dom stayed in Cornwall to become a Protestant minister. Ironically, both would return to Clonmany and there they offered a spiritual way of life to their parishes – one a Catholic, the other a Protestant. There is no mention of whether a wall of sectarianism arose between the two brothers.

We all build walls – socially or religiously, but God through Christ has broken down the walls of partition. Let's not continue to build them.

The Irish are a resourceful bunch. They have even turned the lowly and mundane piece of turf into an art form called "turf art". Crafts people carve and polish pieces of the hardwood black peat into many forms – Celtic crosses, Claddagh rings, Tara brooches and the Black Bog Cat. Such cats roamed the bogs of Ireland hundreds of years ago (an Irish version of the Hound of the Baskervilles?). They were larger than the domestic cat and ate insects and small animals. We can presume that mice and rats were included in their diets. The farmers around Lough Neagh in Northern Ireland often sighted bog cats and were happy to do so, for whenever this black cat crossed their paths, in field or bog, good luck and wealth were certain to encounter the farmer's family in coming weeks. However, in the Midlands in Ireland, the farmers actually tried to capture the black bog cat so as to maintain the reality of their superstition. Yet, no man or woman was successful in this quest to take the cat since the cat was too cunning for the human, even the Irish mind.

Many of us have a desire to hold on to a ritual or to have a favourite piece of clothing or toy which we believe offers us a degree of stability or foundation. But, aren't such talismans or images baseless in their ability to give happiness or wealth? Like the Bog Cat, happiness is elusive unless we base it in spiritual and moral values. Go out to a field today or to a park. Don't search for the Bog Cat, but take fifteen minutes or an hour to search for contentment within.

Dear Heart, I think the young impassioned Priest
When first he takes from out the hidden shrine
His God imprisoned in the Eucharist,
And eats the bread and drinks the dreadful wine.

Feels not such wonder as I felt
When first my smitten eyes beat full on thee
And all night long before thy feet I knelt
Till thou were wearied of Idolatry.

Ah! Hadst thou liked me less and loved me more,
Through all those summer days of joy and rain,
I had not now been sorrow's heritor,
Or stood a lackey in the House of Pain.

(Quia Multum Amavi – Oscar Wilde)

It looks as if Wilde has been "stood up" by someone he desperately worshipped. He hints at one reason for his pain in stanza two, the last line. Maybe he overdid his friendship.

Our encouragement today is to foster our relationships, but not to smother them. As well, I was inspired by the image in stanza one. I recalled the enthusiasm and excitement and wonder which I brought to my first day on the job so many years ago. Can I recapture that motivation ? In my employment and in my friendships and in my church? I think I can.

In our modern times, we tend to forget that Christianity has been around for centuries. This point was driven home as I stopped in Cardonagh. The town is famed for its seventh century cross, a carved stone depicting human figures and twisting, crossing lines. It stands maybe seven feet tall under a canopy built by the town council to protect the relic. Traffic thunders by within ten feet, heedless of this most significant symbol of salvation. On either side of the cross are two short stone slabs standing erect. Most of the carvings on those stones have been worn away. Less than a kilometer away stands the Church of the Sacred Heart, the antithesis of the Cardonagh Cross. The church is high above the cross and is visible for miles around. The intricate carved marble statues around the dome are masterpieces. The church holds 1500 worshippers and was built in 1942 for a whopping 100,000 punt ($250,000 CAD). The people of Clonmany are rightly proud of their church, but when I asked directions twice earlier to find the cross, I was met with blank stares by local school children. Maybe I would have found it more easily by inquiring of adults? We sat among the flowers on the summer seat (park bench) near the cross and I shut out the din of vehicles and people. I meditated on the cross.

It has lost its significance today to many, but it really is timeless. The cross has marked countless people and its cause has interwoven cultures. It is the central cross that has eternal meaning, not other crosses borne, not trappings of churches, not religious art, not liturgy. We all must bow at the cross of Christ or bow before him as Judge.

The Old Pensioner

(W. B. Yeats)

I had a chair at every hearth,
When no one turned to see
With 'Look at that old fellow there;
And who may he be?'
And therefore do I wander on,
And the fret is on me.

The road-side trees keep murmuring –
Ah, wherefore murmur ye
As in the old days long gone by,
Green oak and poplar tree!
The well-known faces are all gone,
And the fret is on me.

"And the fret is on me." This retiree has lost his or her grip on reality. To his/her point of view, no one cares or knows. That state bothers the old person immensely. It sounds like dementia to me. To these souls there is no reason or avenue for inspiration. It is your cause today to be an inspiring force for such a pensioner. If you meet one or see one, a touch or a soft word is sufficient to inspire. The fret of dementia dissipates.

The Old Men Admiring Themselves in the Water

I heard the old, old men say,
'Everything alters,
And one by one we drop away.'
They had hands like claws, and their knees
Wee twisted like the old thorn trees
By the waters.
I heard the old, old men say,
'All that's beautiful drifts away
Like the waters.'
(W.B. Yeats)

I've seen old men like this, in Ireland, and in most countries – sitting on the benches by the ponds or rivers, or lakes. They while away the hours. Sometimes they bemoan the loss of time and innocence and beauty as they feed the geese or ducks or pigeons or sparrows. Their numbers on the benches decrease each year as one by one they meld into nature and return to the dust. Those who have passed on no longer just resemble birds and trees. They actually have become the elements of the earth and nature. Those who remain do not see the permanency of the waters and of their own aged beauty. Or, maybe they see the beauty and admire it, but fail to see how much energy still exists in their reflection in the water.

Take time out to look at your own reflection in a pond today and to see past the one-dimensional refection that slides away in the ripples. There is depth in your image because it extends into the water's depths. You are three dimensionally beautiful.

There are two towns in Donegal which provided the impetus for today's spiritual uplift. On the southwest shore of Lough Foyle are Stroove and Moville. There are two lighthouses at Stroove, an eastern one and a western one. In Gaelic they are called the "Stream of Sorrow" *(Struibh* – Stroove – Brion).* Further along in Moville one finds a small pier near Anchar Bar. In the mid 1800s, this short dock was crowded with a sad mass of humanity. Men, women and children lined up to leave Inishowen in order to survive the Famine. Tenders made a constant to and fro, packed with a hopeful but distressed cargo. These boats were taking emigrants out to ships bound for Boston. Some groups were whole families. Others were maybe just a mother and children bereft of a father already. Or, the father had promised to follow – and in many cases never did. This outflow on the tide was indeed a Stream of Sorrow and the last sight of Ireland was the two lighthouses. Many did not make it to the New World alive and were just slid overboard into the Atlantic. Others endured discrimination and persecution of a different kind when they arrived in New York. However, the outflow had positive repercussions too. The pluck of the Irish to survive despite over whelming odds produced a wealth for the USA in heritage and economic growth. We only have to name John F. Kennedy for proof.

Get on God's outflow today into the stream of Christ's consciousness and sacrificial gain. Today, swim in and float on God's water of the word and tide of joy.

In one of Belfast's alleys is "The Entries". In Cram Entry, Wolfe Tone became a leading figure in 1791 for the forces behind the creation of the United Irishmen. Tone and his men were patterning their movement after the incipient French Revolution. Tone, though Protestant, saw little good in Ireland labouring under British control, and four years later, his band took a blood pledge to die in defence of a free Ireland. On Cave Hill, next to McArt's Fort, most likely in the dead of night, these men took their vow. During the time when he and his men tried to accomplish their goals, Wolfe Tone had his heyday: in 1796, he sailed from Brest in France with the French Armada of forty three ships in support of his fight; he addressed a mass rally at Tailor's Hall in Dublin before the 1798 rebellion; dressed in a French uniform, he rubbed shoulders with Napoleon. But, ultimately, Wolfe Tone suffered defeat and loss: his French Armada never reached Ireland, turned back by bad weather; he was a drunkard; he was captured and sentenced to death, but caused his own demise by slitting his throat with his penkife.

As I stood in Merrion Row in Dublin and looked at the great statue to Wolfe Tone (Tonehenge, it is called), I came to realize what inspiration does to you. It drives you beyond reality. I would like my inspiration, though, to conclude in a more salutary way than that of Wolfe Tone. Don't build yourself a sullied monument to the past, but to the future.

Perched atop a crag at the extremity of Malin Head in Donegal is a three hundred and sixty two foot stone tower called Bamba's Head. It is a memorial to a pagan queen of Ireland, Bamba, but has been used as a signal station for shipping and trans-Atlantic communication since the nineteenth century. Lloyd's of London signal tower was situated here to report the safety of ships to protect the company's bottom line. Then, in 1902, Marconi used the tower for his first wireless commercial message which was relayed to a ship in the Atlantic (makes you value cell/smart phones, doesn't it?). One wonders what Bamba would have thought of Marconi's advancement let alone modern wireless technology. Things were simpler in pagan times and cultures. Right below the promontory is a cave called Hell's Hole which receives the pounding surf off the Atlantic and then ejects its contents again in an eruptive explosion of sound. It communicates the announcement of high tide via this gunshot-like boom all over the area. One more point about this Malin Head. History says that Druid monks assembled on the shore once per year. They ventured into the pounding surf from a cave called the "Wee House of Malin" at an inlet in order to wash away their sins.

It's just as well that God does not communicate to us in pagan rituals, or in wireless signals. Our God does not communicate his forgiveness to us via the sea. In order to keep us from eternal destruction, God's call is a gentle one through His Son, Jesus. And we can communicate with God through a single unvoiced prayer in the Son's name. Inspire yourself; pray today.

Good-night

A latch lifting, an edged den of light
Opens across the yard. Out of the low door
They stoop into the honeyed corridor,
Then walk straight through the wall of dark.

A puddle, cobble-stones, jambs and doorstep
Are set steady in a block of brightness,
Till she strides in again beyond her shadows
And cancels everything behind her.

(Seamus Heaney)

Do you have memories of telling or hearing a good night story? Many carry with them the fondness of those perfect times. My own daughter still keeps "Skittlewonder", a relic from our good night stories. Heaney's thoughts, though, are not on words, but on images. It is the silence and blackness of the seconds after the precious two words. It is a farming image, to be sure for Heaney. We see, not the bedroom, but what is beyond and outside – the yard, the puddle, the cobblestones, the doorstep. If you've ever been in an Irish farm courtyard at night, you have a clear picture of the rural and often dirty and black truth of farming. Heaney, the silent watcher, is set in one realm of blackness and the mother enters another area beyond, in light. He is left with an empty feeling, as I see it, a "cancellation". She is gone, and I am not sure if she even said "good night".

Think about saying a warm "good night" after this day ends. Don't cancel the day.

There is a river running through it. That's Sligo City and the Gavarogue River I'm talking about. The river drains a massive catchment area to the unpolluted east and north and south. Therefore, the waters of the Gavarogue are so clear that they comply with the most stringent of water purity criteria. Another intriguing feature of the Gavarogue River is its almost year round supply of salmon. The Irish are known to be avid fishers and I spotted several men almost waist deep in the river. They were decked out in Irish woolens – sweaters and caps. I admired their rustic charm. Their lines snapped back and forth as they reeled in salmon that even I could see from the bridge deck. Salmon in December? There evidently is a manuscript which tells of Saint Patrick and why the salmon are so plentiful in the Gavarogue. Saint Patrick was out for a stroll and came across two fishers. He asked them for a fish for his dinner, but was sadly informed that they could not catch salmon in the Gavarogue in winter. Paddy asked them to just try, so they did. In went the net, and out came a large salmon! Saint Patrick, so the story goes, blessed the river and told the fishermen that the Gavarogue would now yield salmon all year.

So there you have it. Is the story trying to match Patrick with Christ and one of His miracles? In any case, the river left me with an inspiration. Provision comes as a result of faith and purity results from a source close to God. The Irish don't have a lock on provision or purity. Those are accessible to all. As Jesus says, just ask. Cast your net on the other side, as Jesus told his disciples who could not find fish.

The Mask

(W. B. Yeats)

'Put off that mask of burning gold
With emerald eyes.'
'O no, my dear, you make so bold
To find if hearts be wild and wise,
And yet not cold.

'I would but find what's there to find,
Love or deceit.'
'It was the mask engaged your mind,
And after set your heart to beat,
Not what's behind.

'But lest you are my enenmy,
I must enquire.'
'O no, my dear, let all that be;
What matter, so thee is but fire
In you, in me?'

Unlike one of the partners here, not too many want to look behind the mask. Yeats' imagined conversation rarely is heard because we laud the superficial over the inner. That superficiality is the "mask [that] engages the mind" and body. Love, deceit, friendship, enmity are just facades. What's more, instant gratification is all that counts – if there is "fire in you, in me", let's indulge our desires. Today, however, is a day to make our relationships meaningful, something beyond the surface, behind or below. And, keep it up too.

There is truly such a syndrome as "small town mentality". One of the goals in the minds of young people from little villages in Ireland (and everywhere) is to disappear from the community as soon as a form of adulthood allows. The big city beckons. The other mindset is to hang around and raise a ruckus in the village because of an aimless path. One of my recent trips to Ireland impressed this latter mentality into my memory. Dungannon, County Tyrone, is a farm centre, population 45,000, seat of the great O'Neill clan. However, in the twenty first century, any night of the week is an excuse to hang about the town square, the carpark, the pub and drink and chat (*shannogh*), and then drink some more. And I am sure that the same scenario is repeated in countless other towns. Outside my bedroom window until four in the morning, I heard youths in full frolic. One loudly refused to enter the car of a designated driver. Another sang obscene songs about the Pope and the Virgin Mary. Some tossed bottles against the wall. Two men fought over a girl. All were in transit home, ironically down Church Street. The street was a veritable chicane turn on a Formula One course as car after car negotiated the hilly turn, only to return again minutes later. And this behaviour went on for three or four nights out of seven. This was the life for these young adults aged about 17-25. Many were on government subsistence, "the dole", and there was literally nothing to do.

What's your goal this week? What inspires you? The example of these rudderless and heedless young people is not a suitable lead for someone wishing to leave a positive mark on the world. Go for gold today and I don't mean the golden tinge of liquor or beer.

One winter in the 1990's, all Europe, Ireland included, suffered a severe windstorm, with gales of over a hundred miles per hour. When I arrived in beloved Ireland in March, I thought nothing of January's tempest. Making no connection to winter, we set out for some serious hiking. The first major setback came on the side of Benevenagh Mountain. The guidebook instructed us to climb the deforested side on a logging road, and then meander down through a fir forest to the foot. It was the second leg which brought defeat, for a large portion of this forest had been flattened during January's storm. The trail was unrecognizable and impassable. We had to re-climb the mountain to return by the original route. The next day, we set out for a favourite hiking haunt, Gortin Glen Forest. Alas, the park was closed. The danger of either fallen or about-to-fall trees was still too threatening. We were turned away. Twice foiled by an event which happened weeks in the past. Twice affected by a phenomenon of nature which had overreached itself.

I was inspired again to believe that it is true that "man is not an island," nor is anyone his or her own boss. The past always comes back and leaves its scars. Situations have a way of getting beyond our control. There is an inspiration in another kind of wind. If we commit our past and excesses and disasters to the Great Spirit of God the effects on our present are minimized or countered. The antidote today to the past pressing upon us is in disclosure and purging.

I am an inveterate addict of visiting homes for sale. Over the years, I have viewed hundreds and hundreds of homes, in Canada and in Ireland. One such visit stands out. I was attracted to a property named Tunnel Lodge in Dungannon, County Tyrone. The appointment to view was made. We ventured down a quarter-mile of narrow, muddy tracks to emerge into an opening in the trees. Just like the photo on the 'Net'! A picture-postcard nineteenth century secluded home—gabled windows, black and white and grey paint, towering brick chimney, wrought-iron gate and lamppost. Gorgeous, until we stepped closer and the agent took us inside. It was totally derelict, disgracefully so. Broken windows, abandoned clothes and furniture, smashed walls, even the fireplace stolen at the hands of gypsies. The back garden was a jungle, and the owner wanted $600,000 Canadian! Two years later, I discovered the situation was even graver. The home still stood, now in even sadder disrepair, and the agent had not disclosed the whole truth. The house's underpinnings had been destroyed by the trains in the railway tunnel which ran beside and under the house. The new owner was to demolish what had been a delightful and once palatial residence, and it is now no more. The developers do not even have enough money to build new homes. All that exists is a sign on a dead end road "Tunnel Lodge"!

From where does our inspiration come each morning? Does it derive from past glories? From distant idealism? From deceiving exterior trappings? From baseless foundations? Set out on today's journey with an assurance of where you reside, both materially and spiritually.

George Orwell has a singular image in his spectacular novel 1984. Winston Smith is influenced by the children's ditty, "Under the Spreading Chestnut Tree," and finally spends his futile existence in Chestnut Tree Café, deceiving himself as to the rationale for his existence. An abiding image in my mind is awaking on my first morning in Ireland decades ago to set eyes on the most massive tree I had ever seen, alone in a farmer's meadow. It was an oak tree, probably two hundred and fifty years old. Its trunk had a girth of three or four feet at least, and its canopy spread over forty feet. The rising sun was filtered through the myriad of branches and the tree seemed afire. What set this giant in starker beauty was its antithesis. To the right, across a stream, was another oak, just as large, but it had been hit by lightning at some point and was now just a skeletal, dead pillar. Just as wide and large as the other oak, but having succumbed to another, more potent force.

I'm sure we've all been inspired by one of nature's magical forces, in action or still. They are an opportunity to take a minute out and admire a power beyond ourselves. Today, look at a rose, or a hummingbird, or a mountain, or an oak tree, or a Christmas tree and marvel. Remember that this also shall pass under a higher power.

Lough Finn near Fintown in Donegal would seem to have derived its name from the great Finn (Fionn) McCool, but the Irish have playfully fooled us again. Back in Irish lore lived a great hunter, Fear Gowan who lived with his sister in the glacially plowed valley. One day on his way home with his catch, his three dogs in tow, he met a wild boar. This beast was known to the inhabitants for its fearsome predatory ramblings around the lake. Fear resolved to end its roamings then and there. Alas, the boar quickly finished off Fear's dogs and had Fear in flight. The poor man cried out for his dear sister who then set off to his aid. The echoes of his shouts in the valley bounced from side to side across the lake and the girl swam back and forth in a confused attempt to help Fear. Eventually, she came across the combatants, beast and man, both at the point of death. In exhaustion and despair, she fell beside her beloved brother and the two expired simultaneously. Ah, you say, what was her name? Finna—the lough is named in dedication of her faithfulness. What is the price to be placed upon loyalty and self-sacrifice?

Such traits are invaluable. I feel pressed this morning, this afternoon and this evening to set my sights on someone or some task to which I can give one hundred and ten percent of my attention and faithful work.

No, I'm not referring to golf here, although Ireland boasts some of the best and hardest courses and golfers in the world. I refer to artists like Picasso and Renoir. We have come upon gorgeous and peaceful scenery in Ireland, in abundance, but few can match the leaf-bowered roads and lakes near Churchill in Donegal. We were forced to meander more of those lanes than planned, since we were playfully lost in a search for Glebe House and Gallery. The home was the residence of English art collector and painter, Derek Hill (1916-2000) and, in itself, is a masterpiece. In 1952 he donated Glebe House and Gallery to the State. It is a Regency-style mansion in a deep, impressive burgundy shade. An expensive gravel courtyard would allow a sweep of carriage wheels to swing up to the door. Guests could, as I did, take a stroll along the lakeside, shaded by countless trees. The rhododendron parades would be gorgeous in May. Inside, Hill arranged his collection of art—Islamic and Japanese, Irish and Italian paintings, William Morris textiles, Picasso, Renoir, Matisse and Kokoshka originals. Derek Hill wanted his Irish home to be dedicated to international culture. He also became a mentor and teacher for fishermen artists on Tory Island.

I became aware at Glebe House that we all possess a masterful skill. I may not be a renowned painter or sculptor but I can inspire others to do their best. Find someone to inspire to be a master today.

The term "religious war" is, in reality, an oxymoron (a phrase that pits two opposite concepts against each other, yet on closer examination has some meaning). Ireland has known its share of this oxymoron, both in the South and the North. There is room for values yet to be written on the stupidity of Protestants and Catholics bashing heads. The whole history of religion and war in Ireland was encapsulated one day when I was in Belfast. I visited the Clonard Monastery on the Falls Road (a Catholic enclave). In this enclave of religious peace is a church of French Gothic style, much like Notre Dame in Paris. The Gothic arches swing up to heaven, supported by red granite columns on white marble bases. There are rich mosaics depicting Biblical times. To wander the aisles, nave and transepts and to enter the calm side chapels was a spiritual experience. Yet, even in this place of God's name, war was present. I was led down to the crypt by the friendly parish priest and learned that during WWII, the residents of the Falls Road and Shankill Road districts were sheltered there in the dark basement from air raids. I pictured the trembling families huddled there under the sheltering words of the praying priests. Were the horrors of war to come to Clonard, or would God keep them safe? I heard the rumors as well that during the worst of the Troubles, fugitive Republicans and IRA men were given sanctuary in the same crypt.

Is God a God of war or peace? Only He has the privilege of making that call.

We are free, however, to be unequivocal in our stance. Today we can choose to stand for peace. There's really no such thing as a holy war. We make either war or peace. Today, I will be a peaceful person.

The sign post does not do it justice – "Inishowen 100". That would be the tour route as I set out from Buncrana. I made straight for the far end of the Inishowen Peninsula: 'Malin Head' announced the small askew, dirty white directional marker. Once I left the town of Malin, I began to realize what was in store. The vistas became wide. The open moors were dotted with sheep and rocks and thatched cottages. Some of these latter offered B & B for hardy hikers. Back and forth over the headlands and fields the road trailed. At times, I caught glimpses of sandy strands or rocky pools far below. After leaving Malin, and in about 20 minutes, I began to wind up a torturous hill toward Bamba's Crown, the name of the last headland and of a tower built in 1805 to oversee the shipping lanes in the North Channel. The parking lot and the tower are usually deserted. The wind is, as always, at gale force tearing at hair and clothes and breath. I am now at the most northerly point in Ireland. I am at the end of the world. To step off the sheer three hundred foot cliff would be to dash my brains out on the Atlantic rocks below. Straight west is Newfoundland, nothing else but rolling boiling ocean. I hike the Cliffside trail in search of the cave which booms. At full- force incoming tide, the rollers blast into Hell's Hole Cave with such force that a cannon ball's decibel level results. The breakers crash and thunder and then I hear the voice of God. A resounding shell-burst roar.

I gaze out onto the eternal ocean and see the face of God. To stand on Malin Head is to be in the presence of God. But, the same presence, remember, is everywhere today, no matter where you are. God is in the still small voice of a friend too.

Across the river from Claddagh, Galway, famous for its wedding/companionship ring, sits Galway City. The Great Southern Hotel welcomes hordes of bus tour patrons, and so I tagged along on one of the walking tours of Galway. Naturally, this American group lingered at Kennedy Park just across the street in Eyre Square. Next, there were guffaws when the group reached the six metre high street sculpture of the "Galway Hooker" – hookers are actually Irish commercial ships which worked Galway Bay. We passed on down the High Street to Lynch's Castle, home of a wealthy merchant in Henry VIII's time. Then, we went on to Lynch's Memorial. The guide pointed out a black marble plaque commemorating a poor sixteenth century lad, son of the mayor. The boy was sentenced to hang for murder, by his own father. When the hangman refused to execute his duty, the mayor stepped in and flipped the lever to drop his son through the hole! Our final stop was at the salmon weir bridge where great shoals of salmon work their way up the Corrib River to spawn from April to July. There is a wooden statue there as a memorial to the plucky salmon.

As I separated from the tour group, I asked myself what links there were among all these sights. I found it in the salmon – pluck. The grit of little tramp ships, of men applying justice (hastily or fairly), of nature's creatures following instinct. Pluck inspires me. The Irish have pluck in spades. Put some on today.

On Saturday, December 23, 2000, I picked up a copy of The Guardian. There I saw reproduced the last part of Patrick Kavanagh's, "A Christmas Childhood." I quote some lines here:

"My father played the melodion
Outside at our gate
There were stars in the morning east
And they danced to his music
My mother made the music of milking
The light of her stable lamp was a star
And the frost of Bethlehem made it twinkle
I looked and three whinbushes rode across
The horizon—the Three Wise Kings
And I was six Christmases of age
And I had a prayer like a white rose pinned
On the Virgin Mary's blouse."

This refreshing poem inspires me that Christmas is about family, music, children, stars, imagination, worship, prayer and faith. Kavanagh, born at Inniskeen in Monaghan in 1904, was a farmer and cobbler before he moved to Dublin in 1939. When I was in Dublin, I found Kavanagh's lifelike statue sitting on a bench. I plunked down beside him and spoke to him (as some do, mistaking him for a real person). I said, "Thanks for the inspiration and the memories."

The little village of Keash on the Tour of Corran in Sligo is below Keshcorran Mountain. On this three hundred and sixty two meter summit is a large oval and a cairn, unopened. On the west face are seventeen caves dating back to early man and into the 11th century. The caves hold a special place in Irish lore. Lughaidh (Lugh- a Celtic god who has inspired a festival held each July outside the caves) McCon usurped the throne from McAirt and McAirt's wife fled from Tara, seat of royal Ireland to Connacht. On her flight, the pregnant woman gave birth to Cormac in a cave on Keshcorran. As the tired mother slept on a bed of leaves, a she-wolf stole wee Cormac. He was rescued months later as he played on all fours with his step-brother wolf-cubs. Cormac was eventually raised in civilized society and became high king himself one day. I notice a distinct resemblance to the tale of Romulus and Remus raised by a she-wolf and later to become rulers of Roman Italy. Maybe the Irish do have their roots in Mediterranean culture?

Each Christmas we are inspired to celebrate someone who became king of kings. Jesus brings us to the acceptance of our own birth and of our status in life. Whoever you are, you can be a child of the King. Royalty and quasi-royalty inspire us with their regal pomp, glitter and dignity. Walk out today as if you have a crown on your head, a head held high with dignity. You too are important.

The Truisms
(Louis MacNeice)

His father gave him a box of truisms
Shaped like a coffin, then his father died;
The truisms remained as the playbox they had been packed in
Or that other his father skulked inside.

Then he left home, left the truisms behind him
Still on the mantelpiece, met love, met war,
Sordor, disappointment, defeat, betrayal,
Till through disbeliefs he arrived at a house
He could not remember seeing before,

And he walked straight in; it was where he had come from
And something told him the way to behave.
He raised his hand and blessed his home;
The truisms flew and perched on his shoulders
And a tall tree sprouted from his father's grave.

Truism: (n) a self-evident, obvious truth

We never can forget or abandon the truisms which a father or a mother or grandparents have left in our hands. We always return to our roots and life springs again. Can you recall one truism deposited with you? I can: "Remember who you are." Those were my father's words to me as I left home at any time as I was heading out with friends. They still perch on my shoulders.

Slieve League – highest cliffs in Europe – Donegal

Wheaten Bread - an Irish Staple

Wicklow heather

Yeats' statue - Sligo town

Yeats' tomb - Sligo

Glencar Waterfall - Sligo - Yeats Inspiration

Irish Blessing

May your thoughts be as glad as the shamrocks.
May your heart be as light as a song.
May each day bring you bright happy hours,
That stay with you all year long.
For each petal on the shamrock
This brings a wish your way-
Good health, good luck, and happiness,
For today and every day.

Gaelic Prayer

Deep peace of the running waves to you.
Deep peace of the flowing air to you. Deep peace of the smiling stars to you.
Deep peace of the watching shepherds to you.
Deep peace of the Son of Peace to you.

A Year in Eire was born out of my desire to leave a legacy. Hence this set of readings came to fruition after many visits to Ireland. In a series of vignettes, some serious and others whimsical, I take the reader through Ireland and offer inspiration. There are enough and more for one per day each month. The entries were generated from weeks soaking up the culture of Ireland over a period of 45 years. They cover all areas in Eire and in Northern Ireland, from wild Donegal to the ethereal southern coast, from the tiniest villages to throbbing Dublin and Belfast. The content can be enjoyed by anyone of any background, despite the fact that Christian faith is the foundation.

Jim finds inspiration in many areas of his life: the education and tutoring of youth, literature, family, God and of course Ireland. He was born of Scottish descent, is a true Canadian, but when he married into his Northern Irish family, his focus changed. Jim teaches English in Vancouver with his wife, Esther now that his two daughters have married, both to men of Irish descent!

CPSIA information can be obtained at www.ICGtesting.com
Printed in the USA
LVOW01s0046150314

377494LV00003B/6/P